First published in 2016.

First edition.

ISBN-13: 978-1535564229

Printed by CreateSpace, an Amazon.com Company
Available from Amazon.com and CreateSpace.com

Review Panel: Susana Carvajal (lecturer in Spanish, University of Dundee), Margaret Taylor (lecturer in French, University of Dundee).

Technical editor: Andrew Hamilton

Audio Production: produced by Patricia Molina Hamilton

Voices: Andrew Hamilton, Alma Susana Gómez, Joaquín Figueroa Gallardo, Lucas Morales Moya, Marco Antonio Sepúlveda Gutiérrez, Margaret Taylor, Patricia Molina Hamilton, Rebecca Hamilton and Susana Carvajal.

Acknowledgements: I would like to thank my husband Andrew for the many hours he put into completing this book and my daughters Ana, Rebecca and Vanessa for all their support. I would also like to thank Stephanie Peer and my two colleagues Susana and Margaret for their help and hard work.

Photo acknowledgements:

Photos used with permission from: Rebecca Hamilton, Andrew Hamilton, Ana Kyle, John Kyle, Vanessa Hitchen, Brett Hitchen, María Guadalupe Molina Martínez, María Luisa Molina Martínez, Arnoldo Molina Martínez (Q.E.P.D. César Molina Martínez, José Molina Martínez, Luis Carlos Molina Martínez, Lourdes Aguilera, Gerardo Molina Martínez, Karen Molina Aguilera, Lourdes Molina Aguilera, Erik Molina Garza, José Molina Contreras (Q.E.P.D) María Luisa Molina González (Q.E.P.D.), Esteban Molina Villareal, Alma Susana Gómez, Margaret Taylor, Megan McManus. Daniel Oduwa, Robert Hamilton, Joan Hamilton, Sharon Mitchell, Faith Hamilton, Philip Hamilton, Adela Keranen and Daniel Mitchell.

Images used under license from shutterstock.com

https://www.flickr.com/photos/rod_waddington/13622377293&bvm=bv.124088155,d.d24&psig=AFQjCNE4TBF9WV81UwJ_BYNlHHt7YE_-9g&ust=1465502729396951.
http://es.aliexpress.com/store/product/A128-new-fashion-waterproof-wear-resisting-Men-s-backpack-Laptop-packs-students-bag-Trekking-rucksacks/219001_1965193885.html&psig=AFQjCNGQ9uIcGko4B6nLuhj4Eyic5oWgFA&ust=1449134856771312.
https://diversidadlinguisticadelmundo.wordpress.com/2011/02/23/mapa-mundial-de-las-lenguas-mas-importantes.
https://pixabay.com/pt/europa-geografia-mapa-colorido-23503/.
http://pixabay.com/es/langostinos-camar%C3%B3n-mariscos-239562/&h=360&w=640&tbnid=4K04P8tSH9cNFM:&zoom=1&docid=AK_4TMKMqvqRlM&hl=en&ei=bCmoU5esMseN7AbQ0IHYCQ&tbm=isch&ved=0CEcQMygiMCI&iact=rc&uact=3&dur=465&page=2&start=20&ndsp=26
http://www.pulzo.com/estilo/hasta-james-rodriguez-estuvo-en-la-cena-de-gala-en-el-palacio-real-en-honor santos/300456&psig=AFQjCNEzMeoffTEGLl3hivn58PP_h_ETig&ust=144890377081112.
http://www.rednacionalantitabaco.com/noticias-comunicados/&psig=AFQjCNGGgnfkwZQIgT4JMfYotfKdgTU4cA&ust=1448902982721677.
https://pixabay.com/es/ni%C3%B1os-ni%C3%B1o-ni%C3%B1a-dibujos-del%C3%ADneas-34124/&psig=AFQjCNGxvd6GPP6BYitxT9gt1EapET5uOA&ust=1449137966268545.
https://en.wikipedia.org/wiki/List_of_awards_and_nominations_received_by_Enrique_Iglesias&bvm=bv.109910813,d.d2s&psig=AFQjCNHRO7GwQIEo_CoiUzq7Gy1D0oL5ug&ust=1450009852191737.
http://articulo.mercadolibre.com.ve/MLV-449211731-boligrafos-plasticos-material-pop-material-de oficina_JM&psig=AFQjCNEk_92BNyPo1YIKXHBeEfD74L-l3A&ust=1449841446487987.
https://upload.wikimedia.org/wikipedia/commons/9/93/Libros_viejos.jpg
https://commons.wikimedia.org/wiki/File:Bicicleta_chacareara.jpeg&bvm=bv.109395566,d.d24&psig=AFQjCNHRILQSQBu5Xs3XpysWXylqOrZ_Cw&ust=1449841015074914.
https://commons.wikimedia.org/wiki/File:Pink_Birkin_bag.jpg&psig=AFQjCNEecEbob5S6iBEeRXE70_XBCIQpSg&ust=1449842002859190
https://www.google.co.uk/search?q=avenida&espv=2&biw=1920&bih=935&source=lnms&tbm=isch&sa=X&ved=0ahUKEwjCuO6085nOAhUqIsAKHcN4Bw0Q_AUIBygC#tbs=sur:fc&tbm=isch&q=paises+de+nueva+yugoslavia&imgrc=5ciyk6Ca2JQuVM%3A
https://www.google.co.uk/search?q=avenida&espv=2&biw=1920&bih=935&source=lnms&tbm=isch&sa=X&ved=0ahUKEwjCuO6085nOAhUqIsAKHcN4Bw0Q_AUIBygC#tbs=sur:fc&tbm=isch&q=paseo+del+prado+havana&imgrc=_DY0MvjZbOVdOM%3A
https://www.google.co.uk/search?q=africa+713336_64&espv=2&biw=1920&bih=935&source=lnms&tbm=isch&sa=X&ved=0ahUKEwi5-o6vgJrOAhWpLMAKHcQtCVYQ_AUIBygC#tbm=isch&q=africa+713336&imgrc=wSdgHoO76ePKYM%3A
https://www.google.co.uk/search?q=america&espv=2&biw=1920&bih=935&source=lnms&tbm=isch&sa=X&ved=0ahUKEwi1g-nHgJrOAhWFK8AKHXjPCnwQ_AUIBygC#tbs=sur:fc&tbm=isch&q=avinguada+de+la+reina+cristina&imgrc=Mzfjle_ICEI2BM%3A
https://www.google.co.uk/search?q=remodelacion+calle+colo&espv=2&biw=1920&bih=935&source=lnms&tbm=isch&sa=X&ved=0ahUKEwikgL6piJrOAhWLJsAKHUddB3AQ_AUICCgD#tbs=sur:fc&tbm=isch&q=calle&imgrc=4XhVhhsbxa1rSM%3A

https://www.flickr.com/photos/india_7/14324708853&psig=AFQjCNGIpv-PPM2FMU8ZgkFdQ5ICBRECyg&ust=1449841220966259.
https://commons.wikimedia.org/wiki/File:Before_Machu_Picchu.jpg&bvm=bv.110151844,d.d24&psig=AFQjCNFgfpcDeUBHw1HHeqGnLU6P1O3Zzg&ust=1451418085993994.
https://pixabay.com/es/casa-piedra-exterior-frente-20974/&bvm=bv.110151844,d.d24&psig=AFQjCNG5dWvj_l23syNT3_0ObDKjm4fkXg&ust=1452168630200993.
https://pixabay.com/es/casa-piedra-exterior-frente-20974/&bvm=bv.110151844,d.d24&psig=AFQjCNG5dWvj_l23syNT3_0ObDKjm4fkXg&ust=1452168630200993.
http://www.taringa.net/post/info/14060789/Los-Mejores-Planos-de-Casas-Gratis.html&bvm=bv.123325700,d.ZGg&psig=AFQjCNGSWsfGHG-AhP8qRR6zk8QXs4DJ7Q&ust=1464780493252724.
https://www.flickr.com/photos/antoniotajuelo/4279327971&bvm=bv.108194040,d.d2s&psig=AFQjCNGtzcdYUt_X700drA7ghVnOpsjTIQ&ust=1448733834130406.
http://edic.com/?p=1069&psig=AFQjCNFNzawVw8vhOGH65KpaPqm3y2wM7A&ust=1448735130988504
https://pixabay.com/es/arroz-plato-de-arroz-235775/&psig=AFQjCNHoF8FOOsgymgEISTjDDXwusNbtmQ&ust=1448841785421521.
https://pixabay.com/es/cintur%C3%B3n-ropa-de-hombre-hombre-952834/&psig=AFQjCNEKMOZxU0QtFWBVqfXMoq_OU8S55w&ust=1459674707329584
https://pixabay.com/es/traje-vestir-ropa-de-hombre 714357/&psig=AFQjCNG3qPU96emdjfbUJgwBcuxGBCrJKQ&ust=1459674859221948.
https://www.youtube.com/watch?v=TH5i28k6J58&bvm=bv.118443451,d.d24&psig=AFQjCNFnSV9Bukka0D3PTh9pcnueZB4Krg&ust=1459674372765756
http://www.elmundo.es/elmundosalud/2013/04/10/noticias/1365609771.html&psig=AFQjCNHO3ktyKigHB-Y8FEZZbZTNQ-ukBg&ust=1452607708944928.
https://pixabay.com/es/traje-prendas-de-vestir-elegante 158820/&bvm=bv.118443451,d.d24&psig=AFQjCNFAgZCCaw1Dlb6WQMCKIQIvqB6_zw&ust=1459680496201255.
https://pixabay.com/es/photos/zapatos%20de%20cuero/&bvm=bv.118443451,d.d24&psig=AFQjCNE68eHZXYabLxOX17ZGPZBU8XorA&ust=1459680691728360.
https://commons.wikimedia.org/wiki/File:Cine_Dore_Madrid_2008_1.jpg&psig=AFQjCNGpsZ_IXkThBIpW6gl2Xw7Bfn1wWQ&ust=1448115082453485
https://en.wikipedia.org/wiki/Teatro_Real&psig=AFQjCNESOQyp8YIMKIIwjKqWDIrZcHDTDg&ust=1448120529540202.
https://commons.wikimedia.org/wiki/File:Cine_Dore_Madrid_2008_1.jpg&psig=AFQjCNGpsZ_IXkThBIpW6gl2Xw7Bfn1wWQ&ust=1448115082453485.
https://commons.wikimedia.org/wiki/File:Madrid,_detalle_del_Cine_Dor%C3%A9,_de_la_Filmoteca_Espa%C3%B1ola.JPG&h=3672&w=4896&tbnid=bagFFnUduy2njM:&docid=sksB184dSb01PM&ei=UkBPVsmgAsmxatPxsrAM&tbm=isch&ved=0ahUKEwjJkc-5rJ_JAhXJmBoKHdO4DMYQMwgqKA4wDg.
https://vimeo.com/164400617&bvm=bv.123325700,d.ZGg&psig=AFQjCNFdpinslSVpxV85Qpswo2upWVY_sQ&ust=1464861581730141.
http://www.fulloutdoor.cl/2014/07/este-invierno-las-vacaciones-se-viven-en-mallsport/&bvm=bv.123325700,d.ZGg&psig=AFQjCNFpjsYPHemlIK6zcLzPDchsuFHftw&ust=1464860772486272.
https://pixabay.com/es/nadador-piscina-el-agua-nataci%C3%B3n-802891/&bvm=bv.115339255,d.d24&psig=AFQjCNEnT7eSbK9tDOhsdI-pyj60tCeNGQ&ust=1457191038627661.
https://an.wikipedia.org/wiki/Esqu%C3%AD&bvm=bv.115339255,d.d24&psig=AFQjCNHLGUP7ymttkzKPjdMGFFsRPWyxmw&ust=1457191152776947.
https://commons.wikimedia.org/wiki/File:MAPA_PERUANO.JPG&bvm=bv.124088155,d.d24&psig=AFQjCNFhWWzDCV7SgOx3UmNboUU8LdDsEg&ust=1465509876449770https://pt.wikipedia.org/wiki/Restaurante&bvm=bv.127178174,d.ZGg&psig=AFQjCNHfqYxRJqlNr2SwdG_ORCv7aH_0g&ust=1468655446689275
https%3A%2F%2Fpixabay.com%2Fes%2Fhombre-de-negocios-hombre-corbata-147092%2F&docid=Bi0D1UvFS_8EwM&tbnid=nNgoWVZNWw4yM%3A&w=360&h=720&bih=839&biw=1440&ved=0ahUKEwifrM6mwJTOAhXIJsAKHem7D4YQMwglKAkwCQ&iact=mrc&uact=8
https://www.google.co.uk/search?q=barcelona+la+rambla&espv=2&biw=1920&bih=935&source=lnms&tbm=isch&sa=X&ved=0ahUKEwialf72h5rOAhVMIsAKHa2KDdAQ_AUIBygC#q=barcelona+la+rambla&tbm=isch&tbs=sur:fc&imgrc=w0QaG4pKXMAO1M%3A
https://www.google.co.uk/search?q=plaza+universitat&espv=2&biw=1920&bih=935&source=lnms&tbm=isch&sa=X&ved=0ahUKEwiu89WXiJrOAhVHJsAKHbXUC1AQ_AUIBygC#imgrc=NyEcyVuZQ88yvM%3A
https://www.google.co.uk/search?q=carreteras&espv=2&biw=1920&bih=935&source=lnms&tbm=isch&sa=X&ved=0ahUKEwie-peliprOAhVDF8AKHS9TDcwQ_AUIBigB#tbs=sur:fc&tbm=isch&q=highway&imgrc=bQdbf_HR7Fkq8M%3A
https://pixabay.com/es/hombre-retrato-foto-guapo-629062/
https://en.wikipedia.org/wiki/Jarocho#/media/File:Jarocho.jpg

Contents

Descripción General del Contenido/Overview

UNIDAD UNIT **TEMAS** TOPICS	OBJETIVOS COMUNICATIVOS COMMUNICATIVE OBJECTIVES	GRAMÁTICA GRAMMAR
1 **¡HOLA!** HELLO! • **Presentaciones personales** • **Saludos y despedidas**	• **Saludar/despedirte** Saying hello and goodbye • **Dar y pedir datos personales** Asking and giving information about yourself • **Aprender el alfabeto** Learning the alphabet • **Deletrear en español** Spelling in Spanish • **Contar del 0-10** Counting from 0-10	• **Pronombres personales sujeto (singular): yo, tú** Subject pronouns (singular): I, you. • **Presente de indicativo del verbo llamarse (1ª y 2ª persona del singular)** Verb in the present tense: to be called (1st and 2nd person singular) • **Presente de indicativo del verbo ser (1ª persona singular)** Verb in the present tense: to be (1st person singular) • **Interrogativos: ¿Cómo? ¿Qué? ¿Cuál?** Interrogatives: What?
2 **NACIONALIDADES Y PROFESIONES** NATIONALITIES AND PROFESSIONS • **Países** • **Nacionalidades y profesiones/ trabajos** • **El correo electrónico** • **Tu edad**	• **Preguntar y decir la profesión** Talking about professions/jobs • **Preguntar y decir la nacionalidad** Talking about nationality • **Preguntar y decir el correo electrónico** Exchanging email addresses • **Hablar de tu edad** Talking about your age • **Contar del 0-100** Counting from 0-100	• **Adjetivos posesivos sujeto (singular): mi, tu** Possessive adjectives (singular): my, your • **Preposición de una sola palabra: de** A single word preposition: of • **Conjunción: «y/e»** Conjunction: and • **Género (masculino o femenino)** Gender (masculine or feminine) • **Presente de indicativo de los verbos: hablar, ser, tener y vivir (1ª y 2ª persona del singular)** Verbs in the present tense: to speak, to be, to have and to live (1st and 2nd person singular) • **Números: 0-100.** Numbers: 0-100 • **Interrogativos: ¿Dónde?** Interrogatives: Where?

3 **SOMOS AMIGOS** **WE ARE FRIENDS** <ul><li>Mis amigos</li><li>Los famosos</li><li>La edad</li></ul>	<ul><li>**Presentar a un/a amigo/a** Introducing a friend</li><li>**Preguntar y decir información sobre los amigos** Asking and giving information about your friends</li><li>**Hablar de los famosos** Talking about famous people</li><li>**Decir la edad** Talking about age</li></ul>	<ul><li>**Pronombres personales sujeto (singular): yo, tú (informal), usted (formal), él/ella** Subject personal pronouns (singular): I, you, he/she</li><li>**Adjetivos y pronombres demostrativos: este/a, estos/as** Demonstrative pronouns and adjectives: this/these</li><li>**Adjetivos posesivos: mi/s, tu/s, su/s** Possessive adjectives: my, your, his/her/their</li><li>**Las tres conjugaciones: ar/er/ir Presente de indicativo (1ª, 2ª, y 3ª persona singular) de los verbos: hablar, estudiar, trabajar, aprender, llamarse, leer, beber, comer, vivir, escribir, abrir, ser, hacer, tener** The three conjugations in Spanish: ar/er/ir. Present tense (1st, 2nd and 3rd person singular) of verbs: to speak, to study, to work, to be called, to learn, to read, to drink, to eat, to live, to write, to open, to be, to do/make, to have</li><li>**Interrogativos: ¿Qué? ¿Cuántos?** Interrogatives: What? How many?</li></ul>
4 **¿QUÉ QUIERE TOMAR?** **WHAT WOULD YOU LIKE TO DRINK?** <ul><li>En el bar</li><li>En el restaurante</li><li>Hablar formal</li></ul>	<ul><li>**Pedir bebidas y aperitivos** Ordering drinks and appetizers</li><li>**Pedir comida en un restaurante** Ordering in a restaurant Asking and saying what there is</li><li>**Usar el formal (usted)** Using of formal form (usted)</li></ul>	<ul><li>**Artículos indefinidos: un/una, unos/unas** Indefinite articles: a/an, some</li><li>**Adjetivos posesivos (singular/plural): mi/mis, tu/tus, su/sus** Possessive Adjectives: my, your, his/her, their</li><li>**Presente de indicativo de los verbos: querer, vivir, tener** Present tense of the verbs: to want, to live, to have</li><li>**El formal del presente de indicativo (singular) de los verbos: querer, llamarse, ser, vivir, tener** Formal of present tense (singular) of verbs: to want, to be called, to be, to live, to have</li><li>**Algunos usos de «hay»** Some uses of 'There is/there are'</li><li>**Negativos.** Negatives</li><li>**Interrogativos: ¿Qué? ¿Cuánto?** Interrogatives: What? How much?</li></ul>

5 **MI FAMILIA** MY FAMILY • **La familia** • **El estado civil** • **El árbol genealógico**	• **Pedir y dar información sobre tu familia** Asking and giving information about your family • **Aprender el vocabulario de la familia** Learning the family vocabulary • **Explicar el árbol genealógico de tu familia utilizando la gramática adecuada** Explaining your family tree using the appropriate grammar. • **Usar los plurales** Using plurals	• **Artículos determinados: el/la/los/las** Definite article: the • **Pronombres personales sujeto (singular y plural): yo, tú (informal), usted (formal), él/ella, nosotros/as, vosotros/as, ustedes (formal), ellos/ellas** Subject personal pronouns (singular and plural) I, you, he/she, we, you (plural informal), you (plural formal), they. • **Presente de indicativo de los verbos: llamarse, vivir, tener, ser/estar** Conjugation in the present tense of the verbs: to be called, to live, to have, to be • **Las formas del plural** Plurals forms • **Interrogativos: ¿Cómo? ¿Quién? ¿Cuántos/as?** Interrogatives: What? Who? How many?
6 **DESCRIPCIONES** DESCRIPTIONS • **Descripciones físicas** • **La personalidad** • **Descripciones de objetos** • **Los colores**	• **Describir el aspecto físico de las personas** • Describing people's physical appearance • **Describir el carácter** Describing character • **Describir objetos** Describing objects • **Aprender los colores** Learning about the colours • **Hablar en plural** Talking in plural form	• **Adjetivos calificativos: bonito/a, inteligente…** Qualifying adjectives: pretty, intelligent… • **Concordancia del adjetivo con el sustantivo en género y número: El/la chico/a es muy alto/a** Agreement of the adjective with the noun in gender and number: The boy/girl is very tall • **Presente de indicativo (1ª, 2ª, y 3ª persona singular) de los verbos: ser, tener y llevar** Present tense (1st, 2nd and 3rd person singular) of verbs: to be, to have, to take • **Los plurales** Plural form • **Cuantificadores: muy y bastante** Quantifiers: very and quite • **Comparativos: más…que/menos…que/tan…como** Comparatives: more…than/less…than/as…as • **Superlativos: Madrid es la ciudad más grande de España** Superlatives: Madrid is the biggest city of Spain • **Interrogativos: ¿Cómo?** Interrogatives: What

7		
¿DÓNDE ESTÁ? WHERE IS IT? • **Lugares de interés** • **Geografía de lugares** • **Más números**	• **Describir lugares** Describing a location • **Preguntar y responder:** **¿De dónde eres?** **¿Dónde está?** Asking and answer: Where do you come from? Where is it? • **Hablar de la situación geográfica de una población** Talking about the geographical situation of a location • **Hablar del número de habitantes de una población** Talking about the number of inhabitants of a city or town/village • **Contar desde 100…** Counting from 100…	• **Contraste entre los verbos irregulares:** **ser y estar** The contrast between: ser (to be)/estar (to be in a place) • **Diferencia entre: está en el/está al** Differentiation between: It is in/It is to the • **Preposiciones: cerca y lejos** Prepositions: near and far • **Los números a partir del 100** Numbers from 100 • **Interrogativos: ¿Dónde? ¿Cuál? ¿Qué? ¿Cuántos/as?** Interrogatives: Where? Which? What? How many?
8 **MI CIUDAD/ MI PUEBLO** MY HOME TOWN • **La vida en mi ciudad/pueblo** • **Dónde está exactamente** • **Mi ciudad es más pequeña que tu ciudad**	• **Describir cómo es tu ciudad/pueblo** Describing what your hometown is like • **Expresar ubicación** Indicating location • **Decir qué hay en tu ciudad/pueblo** Saying what there is in your hometown • **Saber usar los comparativos y los superlativos** Using the comparative and superlative	• **Adjetivos calificativos: grande, bonito/a, feo/a…** Qualifying adjective: large/big, nice/pretty, ugly… • **Adjetivos posesivos: mi/mis, tu/tus, su/sus…** Possessive adjectives: my, your, his/her/their… • **Preposiciones indicando un lugar específico** Prepositions indicating the exact location • **Algunos usos del verbo 'hay' con el vocabulario de lugares** Some uses of 'There is/there are' with location vocabulary • **Preposiciones: de/a+ artículo determinado** Prepositions: from/to+ definite article • **Adverbios de cantidad: muy, mucho/a, muchos/as** Adverbs of quantity: very, a lot of/many

9 **HOGAR DULCE HOGAR** HOME SWEET HOME • **El hogar** • **Los muebles de tu casa** • **¿Cuál es tu dirección?**	• **Hablar de tu casa/piso** Talking about your house/flat • **Explicar dónde está y cómo llegar a tu casa/piso** Explain where is it and how to get there • **Aprender el vocabulario de la casa** Learning home vocabulary • **Preguntar y decir «qué hay»** Asking and saying 'what is/are there' • **Usar los números ordinales** Using ordinal numbers • **Usar interrogativos y exclamativos** Using interrogatives and exclamations	• **Hay + artículo determinado + sustantivo** There is/are + definite article + noun • **Artículo determinado + sustantivo + está(n)** Definite article + noun + to be (in a place) • **Verbos irregulares en el presente: ir y hacer** Irregular verbs in present tense. To go and to do/to make. • **Presente de indicativo de verbos con irregularidad vocálica (e →ie): pensar, querer y preferir** Present tense verbs with vowel irregularity: to think, to want and to prefer • **Números ordinales: primero, segundo, tercero…** Ordinal numbers: first, second, third… • **Interrogativos y exclamativos: ¿Qué? ¡Hola!** Interrogatives and exclamations: What? Hello!
10 **¿CUÁNTO CUESTA?** HOW MUCH IS IT? • **Vamos de compras** • **En el mercado** • **En el centro comercial** • **El dinero**	• **Hacer la compra** Doing the food shopping • **Ir de compras** Going shopping for clothing • **Aprender el uso de pesos y medidas** Using weights and measures • **Hablar de precios** Expressing prices • **Aprender el uso de los colores como adjetivos** Learning the colours as adjectives	• **Artículos determinados: el/la/los/las** Definite articles: the • **Artículos indefinidos: un/una, unos/unas** Indefinite articles: a/an and some • **Adjetivos cuantitativos: ¿Cuánto/a? ¿Cuántos/as?** Adjective of quantity: How much? How many? • **Pronombres demostrativos: este/a, ese/a, aquel/aquella…** Demonstrative pronouns: this, these… • **Colores como adjetivos:** Colours as adjectives • **Adverbios de lugar: aquí/allí** Adverbs of place: here/there • **Presente de indicativo de los verbos: llevar y preferir.** Present tense of the verbs: to wear/to take and prefer • **Caro/barato.** Expensive/cheap • **Contraste de los verbos: ser/estar (de compras)** The contrast between: ser/estar (shopping)

11 **LA RUTINA DIARIA** THE DAILY ROUTINE • **El reloj** • **La rutina diaria** • **El calendario**	• **Preguntar y decir la hora** Asking and saying the time • **Hablar de tu rutina diaria** Talking about your daily routine • **Aprender los días de la semana y los meses del año** Learning the days of the week and months of the year • **Usar el calendario** Using the calendar • **Invitar, aceptar/rechazar invitaciones** Inviting, accepting/declining invitations • **Preguntar y responder ¿Por qué?/porque** Asking and saying: Why?/because	• **La hora: Es la una, son las dos, son las tres y media…** Time: It's one, It's two, It's half past three… • **Preposición a + artículo (el/la)** The preposition a + article (the) • **Presente de indicativo de algunos verbos regulares e irregulares** Some regular and irregular verbs in present tense. • **Presente de indicativo de los verbos reflexivos: levantarse, ducharse y acostarse…** The reflexive verbs in the present tense: to get (oneself) up, to shower (oneself), and to go to bed… • **Verbos irregulares con cambio vocálico** Irregular radical changing verbs • **Tengo que + verbo en infinitivo (ar/er/ir)** I have to + verb in infinitive
12 **GUSTOS Y PASATIEMPOS** LIKES/DISLIKES AND HOBBIES • **Los gustos** • **El tiempo libre/ pasatiempos** • **Me gusta mi ciudad/pueblo**	• **Expresar y preguntar sobre qué te gusta/qué no te gusta** Talking about likes/dislikes • **Hablar del tiempo libre/pasatiempos** Talking about leisure activities/hobbies • **Usar: también/tampoco** Using: too/also and neither/nor • **Opinar de lo que te gusta o no te gusta de tu ciudad/pueblo** Talking about your hometown likes/dislikes	• **Verbos: gustar/encantar** Verbs: (to like/to please)/to love it • **Verbos en plural de presente de indicativo: estudiamos, trabajamos, vivimos y salimos.** Present tense of the verbs in plural: we study, we work, we live and we go out • **«A» personal.** The personal 'a' • **Pronombres de objeto indirecto: me/te/le/nos/os/les** • **Pronombres preposicionales: a mí, a ti, a él/ella/usted…** • **Adverbios: también y tampoco** Adverbs: too/also and neither/nor • **Cuantificadores: mucho, bastante…** Quantifiers: a lot/very much, quite…

INTRODUCTION

AMIGOS 1 is a simple, clear and complete book for all beginner students who want to learn Spanish and at the same time enjoy the learning experience. This book is focused on secondary, college/university and adult students. The book seeks to teach the 5 basic skills (reading, writing, listening, speaking and grammar) to learn a foreign language, using a simple but concentrated methodology where the instructions are to be in Spanish and English. In terms of the **Common European Framework of Reference**, it delivers level A1 and has some content from level A2.

The book is divided into 14 units. Units 1 – 12 provide approximately 3 hours of class material. Each unit is subdivided into topics to develop the reading, writing, listening, speaking, grammar and vocabulary skills. Unit 13 is the grammar content and Unit 14 is the Spanish/English vocabulary content of the complete book, catering for British and American English.

Each unit contains audio content to re-enforce the listening skills, dialogue to re-enforce communication skills, exercises to re-enforce grammar and written skills, reading content to re-enforce reading skills and introduce the student to Spanish-speaking cultures.

The exercise answers, the audio files and the transcriptions of these can be found free at
https://discoverlearningspanish.wordpress.com/

1 ¡HOLA!

1 ¡Hola!

2. Buenos días.

3. Buenas tardes.

4. Buenas noches.

5 ¿Qué tal?

6. Adiós.

7. Hasta mañana.

8. Hasta luego.

TEMAS TOPICS	**OBJETIVOS COMUNICATIVOS** COMMUNICATIVE OBJECTIVES	**GRAMÁTICA** GRAMMAR
Presentaciones personales. **Saludos y despedidas.**	**Saludar/despedirte.** Saying hello and goodbye. **Dar y pedir datos personales.** Asking and giving information about yourself. **Aprender el alfabeto.** Learning the alphabet. **Deletrear español.** Spelling in Spanish. **Contar del 0-10.** Counting from 0-10.	**Pronombres personales sujeto (singular): yo, tú.** Subject pronouns (singular): I, you. **Presente de indicativo del verbo llamarse (1ª y 2ª persona del singular).** Verb in the present tense: to be called (1st and 2nd person singular). **Presente de indicativo del verbo ser (1ª persona singular).** Verb in the present tense: to be (1st person singular). **Interrogativos: ¿Cómo? ¿Qué? ¿Cuál?** Interrogatives: What?

1. SALUDOS Y DESPEDIDAS. GREETINGS.

Audio 1

1a. Escucha, lee y repite. Listen, read and repeat.

¡Hola!   Buenos días   Buenas tardes   Buenas noches
¿Qué tal?   Adiós   Hasta mañana   Hasta luego

1b. Empareja las expresiones del español con el inglés.
Match the Spanish expressions with the English ones.

1. ¡Hola!	a) Goodbye
2. Buenos días	b) Good afternoon
3. Buenas tardes	c) How are you? /How're you doing?
4. Buenas noches	d) Good night/Good evening
5. ¿Qué tal?	e) See you later
6. Adiós	f) See you tomorrow
7. Hasta mañana	g) Good morning
8. Hasta luego	h) Hi! /Hello!

1c. Escribe la expresión correspondiente en cada imagen.
Write the correct expression under the pictures below.

1   2.   3.   4.

5.   6.   7.   8.

Audio 2

1d. Vas a escuchar algunos saludos y despedidas en diferente orden. Escríbelos en los siguientes espacios vacíos. You'll hear some greetings in a different order. Write them below.

1. _____
2. _____
3. _____
4. _____

1e. Saluda a tu compañero/a y a otros estudiantes, utilizando varias expresiones.
Practise greeting your partner and other students, using a variety of expressions.

2. PRESENTACIÓN PERSONAL. INTRODUCING YOURSELF.

¡Hola! Buenos días. Me llamo Rosa ¿Y tú? ¿Cómo te llamas?

¡Hola! ¿Qué tal? Me llamo

Audio 3

2a. Escucha, lee y repite. Listen, read and repeat.

- Me llam**o**   - My name is…
- Te llam**as**   - Your name is…
- ¿Cómo te llam**as**?   - What's your name?
- ¿Y tú?   - And you?

Audio 4

2b. Escucha y lee. Listen and read.

Patricia	**¡Hola! Buenos días, me llamo <u>Patricia</u>. ¿Y tú? ¿Cómo te llamas?**
Susana	¡Hola! ¿Qué tal? Me llamo <u>Susana.</u>
Patricia	**Adiós.**
Susana	Hasta luego.

13

2c. En parejas completa las frases y practica el diálogo con tu compañero/a.
In pairs complete the sentences and practise the dialogue with your partner.

A. ¡Hola! Buenos días, me llamo [   ]
    ¿Y tú? ¿Cómo te llamas?

B. ¡Hola! ¿Qué tal? Me llamo [   ]

A. Adiós.

B. Hasta luego.

2d. Cambia de roles y practica el diálogo con tu compañero/a.
Swap roles and practise the dialogue with your partner.

GRAMÁTICA

The verb llamar on its own means "*to call*", but when you add **se** it means "*to be called*" so it's used for names.

llamarse	to be called
(yo) me llamo	I am called/my name is
(tú) te llamas	you are called/your name is

3. EL ALFABETO. THE ALPHABET.

3a. Escucha, lee y repite. Listen, read and repeat.

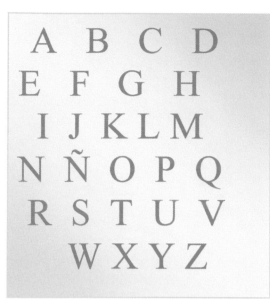

Símbolo Symbol	Nombre Name	Ejemplo Example
A	A	Argentina
B	be	Bolivia
C	ce	Colombia Ceuta
D	de	Dinamarca
E	e	Europa
F	efe	Francia
G	ge	Guatemala Gibraltar
H	hache	Honduras
I	i	Italia
J	jota	Jamaica
K	ca	Kuwait
L	ele	Lima
M	eme	México
N	ene	Nicaragua
Ñ	eñe	España
O	o	Oviedo
P	pe	Perú
Q	cu	Quito
R	ere	Reino Unido
S	ese	Sevilla
T	te	Toledo
U	u	Uruguay
V	uve	Venezuela
W	uve doble	Washington
X	equis	Luxemburgo
Y	i- griega	Yucatán
Z	zeta	Zaragoza

Note: For more information about the alphabet, see Gramática at the end of the unit and Unit 13 (Gramática).

¡DESCUBRE!

- **b** and **v**: have the same sound (**b**) e.g: *beber, vivir*
- **c**: before **e** and **i** the sound is soft (**th/s***) e.g: *cine*
  before **a, o,** and **u** the sound is hard (**k**) e.g: *casa*
- **g**: before **a, o, u** the sound is soft e.g: *Guatemala*
  before **e** and **i** the sound is hard e.g: *gerente*
- **j**: this sound is harsh, like jam e.g: *jamón*
- **ll**
  ¹ in standard Spanish, this sounds like the '**ll**' in '*million*'
  ² in Latin-America: it sounds like the '**j**' in '*jeans*' e.g. *me llamo*
- **h**: this letter is silent e.g: *hola, hora*
- **ñ**: this letter has a nasal sound, as in '*senior*'

*Note, the 'th' sound is used in Spain, and the 's' sound is used in Latinamerica and the Canary Islands.

Audio 6

3b. Escucha, lee y repite.
Listen, read and repeat.
Las vocales
A, E, I, O, U

A	**Á**frica
E	**E**dimburgo
I	**I**ndia
O	**O**slo
U	**U**niverso

Audio 7

3c. Escucha y marca los nombres que oyes.
Listen and mark the names that you hear.

1. López	3. Gonzalo	5. Molino
Lourdes	González	Molina
2. Ramos	4. Martínez	6. Fernando
Rosa	Miranda	Fernández

4. NOMBRE Y APELLIDO. NAME AND SURNAME.

Audio 8

4a. Escucha y lee. Listen and read.

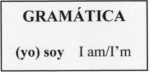

Me llamo Sonia.

Soy Carlos.

Carlos	**¡Hola! Buenas noches.** **¿Cómo te llamas?**
Sonia	¿Qué tal? Me llamo Sonia.
Carlos	**¿Y de apellido?**
Sonia	López García.
Carlos	**¿Cómo se escriben?**
Sonia	L Ó P E Z - G A R C Í A. ¿Y tú? ¿Cómo se escribe tu nombre completo?
Carlos	**Carlos es mi nombre: C A R L O S.** **Ramos Infante son mis apellidos: R A M O S - I N F A N T E.**
Sonia	Adiós.
Carlos	**Hasta luego.**

GRAMÁTICA

(yo) soy   I am/I'm

4b. Rellena los espacios vacíos con tu información personal y después practica con tu compañero/a. Fill in the blanks with your own personal details, then practise the conversation with your partner.

Estudiante A	**¡Hola! Buenas tardes, ¿Cómo te llamas?**
Estudiante B	
Estudiante A	**¿Y de apellido?**
Estudiante B	
Estudiante A	**¿Cómo se escribe tu nombre y tu apellido?**
Estudiante B	[ ] es mi nombre.
	[ ] es mi apellido.
Estudiante A	**Adiós.**
Estudiante B	Hasta luego.

¡DESCUBRE!

In Spain and Latin-America, everyone has two surnames (**apellidos**): their father's and their mother's.

5. NÚMEROS (0-10). NUMBERS (0-10).

Audio 9

5a. Escucha y repite. Listen and repeat.

0	cero
1	uno
2	dos
3	tres
4	cuatro
5	cinco
6	seis
7	siete
8	ocho
9	nueve
10	diez

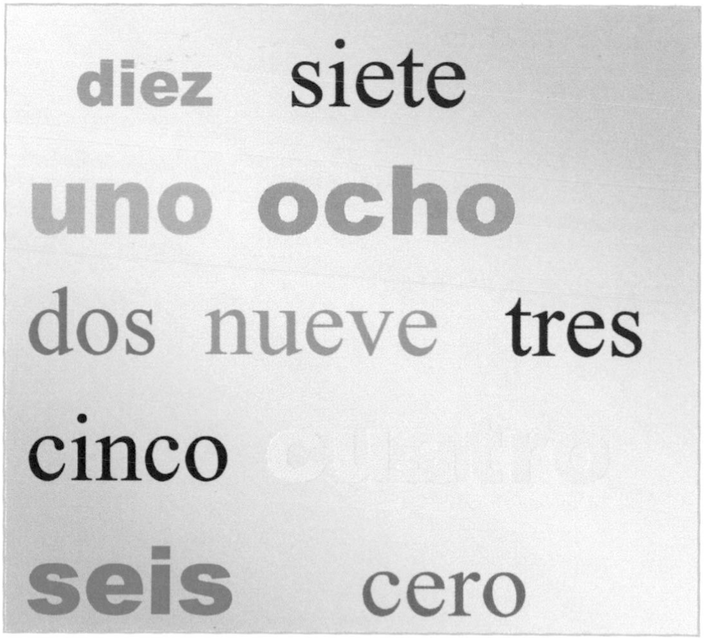

diez siete

uno ocho

dos nueve tres

cinco cuatro

seis cero

5b. Completa las palabras con las letras correctas. Complete the words with the appropriate letters.

1. c__ n__o
2. c__ r__
3. s__ e__ e
4. c__ a__ r__
5. u__o

6. d__ e__
7. o__ h__
8. d__ s
9. t__ e__
10. n__ e__ e

5c. Utilizando los dedos de las manos, practica con tu compañero/a. ¿Qué número es?
'How many fingers?' Test your partner on numbers 0-10.

cero   uno   tres

GRAMÁTICA	
¿Qué número es?	What number is this?
¿Cuál es tu número de teléfono?	What's your phone number?

5d. ¿Cuál es tu número de teléfono? [   ]

6. CONVERSACIÓN. CONVERSATION.

6a. Rellena los espacios vacíos con tu información personal.
Fill in the blanks with your own personal details.

Estudiante A	**¡Hola! Buenas tardes. ¿Cómo te llamas?**
Estudiante B	[ ]
Estudiante A	**¿Y de apellido?**
Estudiante B	[ ]
Estudiante A	**¿Cómo se escribe tu nombre completo?**
Estudiante B	[ ]
Estudiante A	**¿Cuál es tu número de teléfono?**
Estudiante B	[ ]
Estudiante A	**Adiós.**
Estudiante B	[ ]

6b. Contesta a las siguientes preguntas y después practica con tu compañero/a.
Answer the following questions then practise the dialogues with your partner.

- ¿Cómo te llamas?
- ¿Cómo se escribe tu nombre?
- ¿Cómo se escribe tu apellido?
- ¿Cuál es tu número de teléfono?

6c. Responde a las siguientes preguntas y practica con tus compañeros/as.
Answer the following questions and practise the dialogues with your partner.

	Compañero/a 1	Compañero/a 2	Compañero/a 3
¿Cómo te llamas?			
¿Cómo se escribe?			
¿Cuál es tu número de teléfono?			

7. LECTURA Y COMPRENSIÓN. READING COMPREHENSION.

7a. Lee los siguientes textos. Read the following texts.

¡Hola! Me llamo Rosa García López. **Soy** española de Madrid. Rosa es mi nombre, García López son mis apellidos. Mi número de teléfono es: cero, siete, cuatro, ocho, nueve, seis, dos, cuatro, cinco.

¡Hola! Me llamo Luis González Martínez. **Soy** peruano de Lima. Luis es mi nombre, González Martínez son mis apellidos.

¿Qué tal? Me llamo Jack Stewart. **Soy** escocés de Glasgow. Jack es mi nombre, Stewart es mi apellido.

¿Qué tal? Me llamo Alison Wilson. **Soy** inglesa de Londres. Mi número de teléfono es: cero, siete, tres, cuatro, dos, nueve, seis, cinco, cuatro.

7b. Marca verdadero o falso enfrente de cada texto. Tick true or false.

		V	F
1.	Me llamo Alison Wilson. Soy francesa. Mi número de teléfono es: cero, seis, tres, cuatro, dos, nueve, seis, cinco, cuatro.		
2.	Soy Luis González Moreno y soy colombiano.		
3.	Me llamo Jack Stewart. Soy irlandés.		
4.	Soy Alison Wilson. Soy inglesa de Londres.		
5.	Me llamo Rosa García López. Mi número de teléfono es: cero, siete, cuatro, ocho, nueve, seis, dos, cuatro, cinco.		
6.	Soy Rosa García López. Soy española de Barcelona.		

8. VAMOS A ESCRIBIR. LET'S WRITE.

Lee el siguiente texto y escribe uno similar con tus datos personales.
Read the following text and write a similar one containing your own corresponding details.

¡Hola! Me llamo Robert Mitchell. Robert es mi nombre «ere– o – be – e– ere – te» Mitchell es mi apellido «eme– i – te– ce – hache – e– ele– ele». Mi número de teléfono es: cero, siete, cuatro, ocho, nueve, uno, cinco, seis.

GRAMÁTICA

(yo) soy	I am/I'm
de	from
mi	my

GRAMÁTICA

- **Adjetivo posesivo «mi».** Possessive adjective "my"

- **El alfabeto (guía para la pronunciación en español).**
  There are five vowels in Spanish: **a, e, i, o, u**, and they have one sound each. All the other letters are called consonants.

  - **b** and **v**: have the same sound (**b**) e.g: **b**e**b**er, **v**ino, **B**arcelona, **V**alencia.
  - **c**: -before **e** and **i** the sound is soft (**th/s**) e.g.: **c**ine, **c**ien, **c**emento, **c**inco.
    -before **a**, **o**, and **u** the sound is hard (**k**) e.g.: **c**asa, ban**c**o, **C**uba, cin**c**o.
  - *****ch**: it sounds like the "ch" in the English word church e.g.: **ch**ico, **ch**ile, **ch**ocolate, o**ch**o.
  - **g**: -before **a, o, u** the sound is soft e.g.: **G**lasgow, **g**ato, a**g**ua, **G**uatemala.
    -before **e** and **i** the sound is hard e.g.: **g**ente, **g**erente, **g**iro, **g**imnasio.
  - **j**: this sound is harsh, like the '**ch**'at the end of the Scottish 'lo**ch**'e.g.: **j**amón, **j**inete, **j**ueves, **j**ulio.
  - *****ll**: [1] in standard Spanish, this sounds like the '**ll**' in 'million' e.g. me **ll**amo, **ll**ave, pae**ll**a, ape**ll**ido.
    [2] in Latin-America: it sounds like the '**j**' in 'jeans' e.g.
  - **h**: this letter is silent e.g: **h**ola, **h**ora, **h**ijo, **h**ermano.
  - **ñ**: this letter has a nasal sound, as in 'se**ni**or' e.g.: a**ñ**o, ni**ñ**o, ni**ñ**era, cu**ñ**ado/a.
  - **r**: this sound is always pronounced and slightly rolled e.g.: pe**r**o, pe**r**a, po**r**, pa**r**a.
  - *****rr**: this sound is stronger in the middle of a word and when word begins with "r" e.g.: pe**rr**o, **R**oma.
  - **w**: is only found in imported words e.g.: **w**hisky, **W**ashington.
  - **z**: the sound is soft (**th/s**) e.g.: **z**apato, **z**ona.

> **¡DESCUBRE!**
> *Although these are no longer
> Spanish letters, their sound still exist.

- **Pronombres personales sujeto (singular).** Subject pronouns (singular).
  *Note: Subject pronouns are normally omitted in Spanish (I, You…).

1ª persona	yo	I
2ª persona	tú	you

- **Preposición «de».** Preposition "from"

- **Verbo «llamarse» (Presente de indicativo [1ª /2ª persona del singular])**
  The verb 'to be called' (Present tense [1st/2nd person singular])

(yo) me llamo	I'm called/My name is.
(tú) te llamas	You're called/Your name is.

- **Verbo «ser» (Presente de indicativo [1ª persona del singular])**
  The verb 'to be' (Present tense [1st person singular])

(yo) soy	I am/I'm

EJERCICIOS

1. Escribe la palabra correspondiente en el espacio vacío.
Write the appropriate words in the blanks.

a) _____ días.

b) _____ noches.

c) ¿_____ te llamas?

d) Yo _____ _____ (llamarse) Carlos.

e) Tú _____ _____ (llamarse) Margarita.

f) ¿Cómo se escribe tu _____ completo?

g) Molina Martínez son mis _____.

h) ¿Qué _____ es?

2. Escribe el nombre de la letra enfrente de cada símbolo.
Write the name of each letter.
Ejemplo: x = equis

1. a	**8.** q
2. m	**9.** h
3. c	**10.** s
4. n	**11.** j
5. d	**12.** v
6. p	**13.** l
7. e	**14.** z

3. Escribe en letra el número. Write the numbers in words.
Ejemplo: 3 = tres.

a. 8	**f.** 7
b. 5	**g.** 4
c. 0	**h.** 6
d. 9	**i.** 1
e. 2	**j.** 10

4. Completa el siguiente diálogo con las palabras correctas.
Complete the dialogue with the correct words.

Estudiante A	¡Hola! (1) _____ noches, ¿Cómo (2) _____ llamas?
Estudiante B	¡Hola! ¿Qué (3) _____? (4) _____ llamo Mario. ¿Y (5) _____?
Estudiante A	Me (6) _____ Angela Bartoli. ¿(7) _____ se escribe tu (8) _____ completo?
Estudiante B	Mario es mi nombre y López Ramos son mis (9) _____.
Estudiante A	**Adiós.**
Estudiante B	(10) _____ luego.

VOCABULARIO

1. SALUDOS Y DESPEDIDAS	**1. GREETINGS.**
Adiós	*Goodbye*
Buenos días	*Good morning!*
Buenas noches	*Good night/Good evening*
Buenas tardes	*Good afternoon*
Hasta luego	*See you later*
Hasta mañana	*See you tomorrow*
¡Hola!	*Hi! /Hello!*
¿Qué tal?	*How are you? /How're you doing?*

2. PRESENTACIÓN PERSONAL	**2. INTRODUCING YOURSELF**
Me llamo…	*My name is…*
Te llamas	*Your name is…*
¿Cómo te llamas?	*What's your name? (informal)*
¿Y tú?	*And you?*

3. EL ALFABETO	**3. THE ALPHABET.**
¿Cómo se escribe?	*How do you spell it?*

4. NOMBRE Y APELLIDO	**4. NAME AND SURNAME**
apellido (m)	*surname*
de	*from*
mi	*my*
mis	*my*
nombre (m)	*name*
son	*they are*

5. NÚMEROS.	**5. NUMBERS.**
¿Cuál es tu número de teléfono?	*What's your telephone number?*
¿Qué número es?	*What number is this/ (is it)?*

VERBOS	**VERBS**
llamarse	*to be called*
ser	*to be*

LECTURA Y COMPRENSIÓN	**READING COMPREHENSION**
escocés/escocesa	*Scottish*
Escocia (f)	*Scotland*
falso	*false*
Inglaterra (f)	*England*
inglés/inglesa	*English*
verdadero	*true*

2 NACIONALIDADES Y PROFESIONES

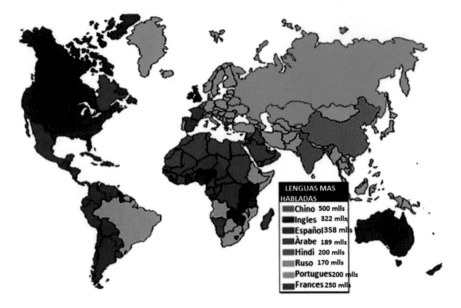

TEMAS TOPICS	OBJETIVOS COMUNICATIVOS COMMUNICATIVE OBJECTIVES	GRAMÁTICA GRAMMAR
Países. **Nacionalidades y profesiones/trabajos.** **El correo electrónico.** **Tu edad.**	**Preguntar y decir la profesión.** Talking about jobs/professions. **Preguntar y decir la nacionalidad.** Talking about nationality. **Preguntar y decir el correo electrónico.** Exchanging email addresses. **Hablar de tu edad.** Talking about your age. **Contar del 0-100.** Counting from 0-100.	**Adjetivos posesivos: mi, tu.** Possessive adjectives: 'my, your'. **Preposición: «de».** Preposition: 'of'. **Conjunción: «y/e».** Conjunction: 'and'. **Género.** Gender. **Presente de indicativo de los verbos: hablar, ser, tener y vivir.** Present tense of the verbs: 'to speak', 'to be', 'to have and 'to live'. **Números: 0-100.** Numbers: 0-100. **Interrogativos: ¿Dónde?** Interrogatives: Where?

1. NACIONALIDADES. NATIONALITIES.

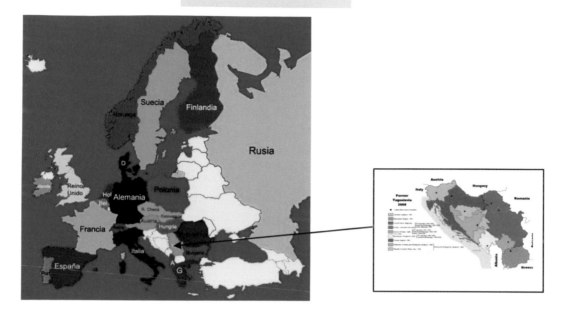

MAPA DE EUROPA

Audio 10

1a. Escucha y repite los nombres de los países y nacionalidades que se mencionan.
Listen and repeat the names of the countries and nationalities.

PAÍSES	NACIONALIDADES	
	masculino	femenino
Escocia	escocés	escocesa
Inglaterra	inglés	inglesa
Irlanda	irlandés	irlandesa
Gales	galés	galesa
Reino Unido/ Gran Bretaña	británico	británica
Alemania	alemán	alemana
Francia	francés	francesa
Polonia	polaco	polaca
Italia	italiano	italiana
Rusia	ruso	rusa
Letonia	letón	letona
Lituania	lituano	lituana
Rumanía	rumano	rumana

GRAMÁTICA

masculino	femenino
- o	- a
polaco	polaca
ruso	rusa
consonante	consonante + a
irlandés	irlandesa
francés	francesa

masculino y femenino
-e
estadounidense

1b. Escribe en el recuadro de abajo el género femenino enfrente de cada masculino.
Write the feminine equivalent of each masculine adjective in the table below.

Masculino	Femenino	Masculino	Femenino
1. escocés		11. árabe	
2. alemán		12. lituano	
3. italiano		13. noruego	
4. irlandés		14. inglés	
5. polaco		15. suizo	
6. canadiense		16. holandés	
7. japonés		17. búlgaro	
8. chino		18. brasileño	
9. estadounidense		19. francés	
10. ruso		20. finlandés	

1c. Escribe en español las nacionalidades de toda la clase.
Write down the nationality of everyone in the class.
Ejemplo: español/española

> **¡DESCUBRE!**
> Nationalities always start with
> **lower case** letters in Spanish.

1d. Completa con: «me llamo», «te llamas», «soy» o «eres» en presente.
Fill in the blanks with: 'me llamo', 'te llamas', 'soy' or 'eres' in the present tense.

1. Yo _____ _____ Juan y _____ canadiense.
2. Tú _____ _____ Lourdes y _____ francesa.
3. Yo _____ polaco de Varsovia.
4. Tú _____ inglés de Manchester.
5. Yo _____ española de Barcelona.
6. Tú _____ de Italia, _____ italiano de Roma.

1e. Escribe las terminaciones de género correctas. Write correct gender endings.

1. Ella es Hanna, es ingles_____.
2. Él es David, es estadunidens____.
3. Ella es Alison, es escoces____.
4. Él es Carlos, es brasileñ_____.
5. Ella es Christina, es canadiens_____.
6. Ella es María, es español_____.
7. Él es Amadeus, es polac_____.
8. Él es Muhammad, es árab_____.

1f. Contesta a las siguientes preguntas y practica con tus compañeros de toda la clase.
Practise asking and answering the following questions with your fellow-students.

- ¿Cómo te llamas?
- ¿Cuál es tu nacionalidad?
- ¿De dónde eres?

> ¡Hola! Me llamo Demetrio Petra.
> Soy griego de Atenas.

2. PROFESIONES. PROFESSIONS.

música

barista y
camarero

veterinario

artista

policía

cantante

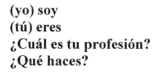
Audio 11

2a. Escucha, lee y repite. Listen, read and repeat.

(yo) soy
(tú) eres
¿Cuál es tu profesión?
¿Qué haces?

Audio 12

GRAMÁTICA
ser.........to be
(yo) soy.........I'm/I am
(tú) eres.........you're/you are

2b. Escucha y traduce al inglés o a tu idioma las siguientes profesiones.
Listen and translate the following professions into English or into your native language.

Profesiones en español	Traducción al inglés o tu idioma natal
1. arquitecto/a	
2. escritor/escritora	
3. cantante	
4. camarero/a	
5. vendedor/vendedora	
6. trabajador/ trabajadora social	
7. científico/a	
8. investigador/investigadora	
9. ingeniero/a	
10. periodista	
11. estudiante	
12. deportista	
13. profesor/profesora	
14. contable	

GRAMÁTICA		
Masculino	**Femenino**	**Masculino y femenino**
- o	- a	-e
veterinario	veterinaria	estudiante
consonante	**consonante + a**	-ista
profesor	profesora	periodista

27

2c. Relaciona las siguientes columnas: nombres, nacionalidades y profesiones.
Match the following columns: names, nationalities and professions.

NOMBRE	NACIONALIDAD	PROFESIÓN
Ludwig van Beethoven	argentina	escritor
Gabriel García Márquez	polaca	**pintor**
Marie Curie	escocés	actriz
Nelson Mandela	**español**	músico y compositor
Pablo Picasso	estadounidense	futbolista
Pelé	surafricano	poeta
Robert Burns	alemán	política
Marilyn Monroe	colombiano	político
Eva Perón	brasileño	científica

2d Escribe el femenino enfrente de cada profesión. Write the feminine version of each profession.

Masculino	Femenino
1. secretari**o**	
2. pinto**r**	
3. cantant**e**	
4. arquitect**o**	
5. estudiant**e**	
6. dent**ista**	
7. trabajado**r** social	
8. peluquer**o**	
9. programado**r**	
10. vendedo**r**	
11. electr**ista**	
12. enfermer**o**	

> **¡DESCUBRE!**
>
> Nationalities and professions always start with **lower case** letters in Spanish.

2e. Practica con tu compañero/a. Practise with your partner.

¡Hola! / ¿Qué tal? Buenos días/Buenas tardes/Buenas noches.
¿Cómo te llamas?
¿De dónde eres?
¿Cuál es tu profesión? / ¿Qué haces?
Adiós/Hasta luego.

Audio 13

2f. Escucha y lee. Listen and read.

Antonio	**¡Hola! Buenas tardes. Me llamo Antonio Pedraza ¿Y tú? ¿Cómo te llamas?**
Rosa	¿Qué tal? Me llamo Rosa Cantú.
Antonio	**Soy peruano de Lima. ¿Y tú? ¿De dónde eres?**
Rosa	Soy colombiana de Bogotá. ¿Cuál es tu profesión?
Antonio	**Soy pintor. ¿Y tú? ¿Qué haces?**
Rosa	Soy secretaria en un hotel.
Antonio	**Adiós.**
Rosa	Hasta luego.

3. ¿DE DÓNDE ERES? WHERE ARE YOU FROM?

3a. Escucha, lee y repite. Listen, read and repeat.

(yo) soy	I'm/I am
(tú) eres	You're/you are
¿De dónde eres?	Where do you come from?
¿Eres australiano?	Are you Australian?
¿Dónde vives?	Where do you live?
¿Cuál es tu profesión?	What's your profession?
¿Qué idiomas hablas?	What languages do you speak?

Audio 15

3b. Escucha y lee. Listen and read.

> ¡Hola! Me llamo Isabel Martínez González. Soy mexicana de Guadalajara pero vivo en Madrid. Soy cantante y actriz. Hablo español e inglés.

> ¿Qué tal? Me llamo David Smith. Soy escocés de Edimburgo pero vivo en Londres. Soy ingeniero. Hablo inglés y español.

1. ¿Cómo te llamas?	- Me llamo <u>Isabel Marín González</u>.
2. ¿Cuál es tu nacionalidad?	- Soy <u>mexicana</u>.
3. ¿De dónde eres?	- Soy de <u>Guadalajara</u>.
4. ¿Cuál es tu profesión?	- Soy <u>cantante y actriz</u>.
5. ¿Qué idiomas hablas?	- Hablo <u>español **e** inglés</u>.
6. ¿Dónde vives?	- Vivo en <u>Madrid</u>.

a) ¿Eres <u>irlandés</u>?	- No, no soy <u>irlandés</u>, soy <u>escocés</u>.
b) ¿Te llamas <u>John</u>?	- No, no me llamo <u>John</u>, me llamo <u>David</u>.
c) ¿Eres <u>ingeniero</u>?	- Sí, soy <u>ingeniero.</u>
d) ¿Hablas <u>francés</u>?	- No, no hablo francés. Hablo <u>español **e** inglés.</u>
e) ¿Vives en <u>Londres</u>?	- Sí, vivo en <u>Londres</u>.

GRAMÁTICA

habl**ar**	to speak	viv**ir**	to live
(yo) habl**o**	I speak	**(yo)** viv**o**	I live
(tú) habl**as**	you speak	**(tú)** viv**es**	you live

y/e - and : y changes to e before i and hi (e.g. español e inglés)

3c. Escribe un texto similar a los ejemplos del ejercicio 3b y practica con tu compañero/a tus respuestas. Following the example in exercise 3b, write a similar paragraph and practise the conversation with your partner.

---

4. NÚMEROS DEL 0-100. NUMBERS FROM 0-100.

Audio 16

4a. Escucha, lee y repite. Listen, read and repeat.

0	cero		
1	uno*	21	veintiuno*
2	dos	22	veintidós
3	tres	23	veintitrés
4	cuatro	24	veinticuatro
5	cinco	25	veinticinco
6	seis	26	veintiséis
7	siete	27	veintisiete
8	ocho	28	veintiocho
9	nueve	29	veintinueve
10	diez	30	treinta
11	once	31	treinta y uno*
12	doce	32	treinta y dos
13	trece	40	cuarenta
14	catorce	41	cuarenta y uno*
15	quince	50	cincuenta
16	dieciséis	60	sesenta
17	diecisiete	70	setenta
18	dieciocho	80	ochenta
19	diecinueve	90	noventa
20	veinte	100	cien

¡DESCUBRE!

Spanish telephone numbers are usually grouped **in pairs:**

074 - 60 - 08 -57 - 86

GRAMÁTICA

- **uno** changes to **un** before masculine nouns: **un** hermano/**un** libro
- **uno** changes to **una** before feminine nouns: **una** mujer, **una** hermana/hija
- '**y**' is only used between tens and units: cuarenta y uno, noventa y nueve

4b. Practica con tu compañero/a. Practise with your partner.

A **¿Cuál es tu número de teléfono?**
B Mi móvil es 079-43-57-89-21 / Mi teléfono de casa es 46-25-82.

Audio 17

4c. Escucha y marca los números que oyes. Listen and mark the numbers that you hear.

5	16	25	38	47	53	35	82	15	35	0
62	72	89	98	100	67	99	18	73	63	50

4d. Practica con otros estudiantes. Practise with other students.

¿Cómo te llamas?	¿Cómo se escribe?	¿Cuál es tu número de teléfono?
Alberto López Ramos	A L B E R T O – L Ó P E Z – R A M O S	073-32-73-46-96

5. CORREO ELECTRÓNICO. EMAIL.

Audio 18

5a. Escucha, lee y repite. Listen, read and repeat.

@ arroba
. punto
/ barra
- guión
_ guión bajo

5b. Escucha a tu profesor/a, lee y repite. Listen to your teacher, read and repeat.

Mi correo electrónico es: umo@mex.com
U - M - O - ARROBA - M - E - X - PUNTO - C O M

Mi número de teléfono es: **074- 32-53-36-98.**
cero- setenta y cuatro - treinta y dos - cincuenta y tres - treinta y seis
noventa y ocho.

5c. Practica los siguientes diálogos con tu compañero/a.
Practise the following dialogues with your partner.

A ¿Cuál es tu correo electrónico?
B Mi correo electrónico es:

<table>
<tr><td></td></tr>
</table>

GRAMÁTICA
mi……..my
tu……..your

A ¿Cuál es tu número de teléfono?
B Mi número de teléfono es:

<table>
<tr><td></td></tr>
</table>

5d. Practica con otros estudiantes. Practise with other students.

¿Cómo te llamas? ¿Cómo se escribe?	¿Cuál es tu correo electrónico?	¿Cuál es tu número de teléfono?
Fernando Garza Ramos	f.ga54za@ntle.co	074-32-53-36-98

Audio 19

5e. Escucha la conversación y después marca Verdadero o Falso enfrente de cada texto.
Listen the conversation and then tick true or false.

Mike	**¡Hola! Me llamo <u>Mike Douglas.</u> ¿Y tú? ¿Cómo te llamas?**
Lucía	¿Qué tal? Me llamo <u>Lucía Ramos López.</u>
Mike	**Soy <u>canadiense</u> de <u>Toronto.</u> ¿Y tú? ¿De dónde eres?**
Lucía	Soy <u>venezolana</u> de <u>Caracas.</u>
Mike	**¿Cuál es tu profesión?**
Lucía	Soy <u>estudiante de psicología y camarera en un bar.</u> ¿Y tú? ¿Qué haces?
Mike	**Soy <u>estudiante de medicina.</u>**
Mike	**Hablo <u>inglés, italiano y español.</u> ¿Y tú? ¿Qué idiomas hablas?**
Lucía	Hablo <u>español e inglés.</u>
Mike	**¿Cuántos años tienes?**
Lucía	Tengo <u>22</u> años. ¿Y tú? ¿Cuántos años tienes?
Mike	**Tengo <u>25</u> años. ¿Tienes email?**
Lucía	Sí tengo. Mi correo electrónico es: <u>lurl@lim.com</u> ¿Y tú? ¿Cuál es tu correo electrónico?
Mike	**Mi email es: <u>mike@can.com</u> ¿Cuál es tu número de teléfono?**
Lucía	Mi número móvil es: <u>074-32-53-36-98</u>. ¿Y tú? ¿Cuál es tu número móvil?
Mike	**Mi número es: <u>076-65-84-38-22.</u>**
Lucía	Adiós.
Mike	¡Hasta luego!

	V	F
1. Me llamo Mike. Soy estudiante de psicología y camarero en un bar.		
2. Soy Lucía. Mi número móvil es: cero, setenta y cuatro, treinta y dos, cincuenta y tres, treinta y seis, noventa y ocho.		
3. Me llamo Lucía. Tengo 25 años.		
4. Soy Mike. Mi email es: eme, a, ca, e, arroba, ce, a, ene, a, punto, ce, o, eme		

5f. Practica con tu compañero/a la conversación del ejercicio 5e. Tienes que cambiar la información subrayada por tus datos personales. Practise the conversation from exercise 5e with your partner and replace the underlined information with your own details.

GRÁMATICA	
tener	to have
(yo) tengo	I have
(tú) tienes	you have

¡DESCUBRE!	
tener	to have
tengo (X) años	I'm (X) years old.
tienes (X) años	You're (X) years old.

Audio 20

5g Escucha y repite. Listen and repeat.

Canto: **La Bamba**
www.youtube.com/watch?v=jSKJQ18ZoIA

5h Escucha el canto una vez más y escribe en los espacios vacíos la palabra que falta.
Listen to the song again and fill in the blanks with the missing words.

La Bamba

Para _____ la bamba
Para _____ la bamba
Se necesita _____ poca _____ gracia
_____ poca _____ gracia pa' _____, pa' _____.
Y, arriba y arriba
Ay, arriba y arriba, por _____ seré
por _____ seré
por _____ seré

Yo _____ _____ marinero
Yo _____ _____ marinero, _____ capitán
_____ capitán
_____ capitán

Bamba, bamba, bamba, bamba, bamba, bamba, bam

Para _____ la bamba
Para _____ la bamba
Se necesita _____ poca _____ gracia
___poca _____gracia pa' _____ pa'__

Ay arriba, y arriba

R-r-r-r-r

¡ÓRALE!

Para _____ la bamba
Para _____ la bamba
Se necesita _____ poca _____ gracia
_____ poca _____ gracia pa' _____ pa'____
Ay arriba y arriba
Ay arriba y arriba, por _____ _____
Por ti seré
Por ti seré

Bamba, bamba, bamba, bamba, bamba, bamba, bamba

¡DESCUBRE!	
bailar	to dance
se necesita una poca de gracia	you need a Little grace
pa' mí, pa'ti (para mí, para ti)	for me, for you
ay arriba y arriba	Ay, up and up
yo no soy marinero	I'm not a sailor
soy capitán	I'm a captain
por ti seré	for you, I will be
¡ÓRALE!	Come on!

6. LECTURA Y COMPRENSIÓN. READING COMPREHENSION.

6a. Lee los siguientes textos. Read the following texts.

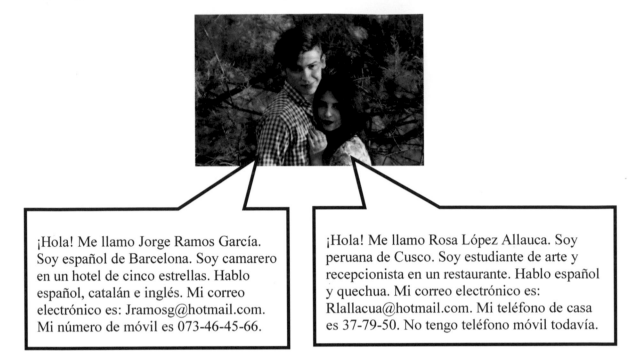

¡Hola! Me llamo Jorge Ramos García. Soy español de Barcelona. Soy camarero en un hotel de cinco estrellas. Hablo español, catalán e inglés. Mi correo electrónico es: Jramosg@hotmail.com. Mi número de móvil es 073-46-45-66.

¡Hola! Me llamo Rosa López Allauca. Soy peruana de Cusco. Soy estudiante de arte y recepcionista en un restaurante. Hablo español y quechua. Mi correo electrónico es: Rlallacua@hotmail.com. Mi teléfono de casa es 37-79-50. No tengo teléfono móvil todavía.

6b. Marca Verdadero o Falso enfrente de cada texto. Tick true or false.

	V	F
1. Jorge es español de Madrid.		
2. Rosa habla español y francés.		
3. Jorge habla español, inglés y catalán.		
4. Él número de teléfono de Jorge es: cero, setenta y tres, cuarenta y siete, cuarenta y cinco, sesenta y seis.		
5. Rosa es de Cusco Perú.		
6. Jorge es camarero en una cafetería.		
7. El correo electrónico de Jorge es: Jranag@ hotmail.co		
8. Rosa no tiene teléfono móvil.		
9. Rosa es cantante en un restaurante.		
10. El número de teléfono de Rosa es: tres, seis, siete, nueve, cinco, cero.		

7. VAMOS A ESCRIBIR. LET'S WRITE.

Escribe un mensaje a tu amigo/a español/a en Facebook. Tienes que incluir lo siguiente.
Write a message for your Spanish penfriend on Facebook. Include the following details:

- Nombre y apellido
- Nacionalidad y profesión
- Edad e idiomas que hablas
- Número de teléfono y correo electrónico

GRAMÁTICA

- **Adjetivos posesivos sujeto (singular).** Possessive adjectives (singular).

mi	Mi número de teléfono es...	my	My phone number is...
tu	¿Cuál es tu número de teléfono?	your	What's your phone number?

- **Conjunción: «y».** The conjunction 'and'.

y/e - and
y changes to **e** before **i** and **hi**

⎱ **inglés y español** - English and Spanish
⎰ **español e inglés** - Spanish and English

- **Género (masculino o femenino).** Gender (masculine or feminine).

Spanish **nouns** are classified as either **masculine** or **feminine**. Nouns that end in 'o' are **usually** masculine and those which end in 'a' are **usually** feminine. When a masculine noun ends in a consonant, the letter 'a' is added to make it feminine. Nouns which end in 'e' and 'ista' don't change.

Masculino	secretario	pintor	estudiante	dentista
Femenino	secretaria	pintora	estudiante	dentista

- **Números.** Numbers.
  - **uno** changes to **un** before masculine nouns: **un** hombre, **un** hermano/hijo.
  - **uno** changes to **una** before feminine nouns: **una** mujer, **una** hermana/hija.
  - 'y' is only used between tens and units: treinta **y** dos, noventa **y** ocho, cincuenta **y** tres.

- **Verbos: llamarse, hablar, vivir, tener y ser (Presente de indicativo [1ª y 2ª persona del singular]).** Verbs: to be called, to speak, to live, to have and to be (Present tense [1st and 2nd person singular]).

	llamarse to be called	**hablar** to speak	**vivir** to live	**tener** to have	**ser** to be
(yo) I	**me llamo** I am called/My name is	**hablo** I speak	**vivo** I live	**tengo** I have	**soy** I am
(tú) you	**te llamas** you are called/Your name is	**hablas** you speak	**vives** you live	**tienes** you have	**eres** you are

- **Preposición de una sola palabra: «de».** The preposition 'from'.

Soy de Colombia	I'm **from** Colombia

- **Preguntas.** Questions.

¿De dónde eres?	Where do you come from?
¿Eres español?	Are you Spanish?
¿Cuál es tu profesión? / ¿Qué haces?	What's your profession? /What do you do?
¿Cuál es tu número de teléfono?	What's your phone number?
¿Cuál es tu correo electrónico?	What's your email address?
¿Qué idiomas hablas?	What languages do you speak?
¿Cuántos años tienes?	How old are you?

EJERCICIOS

1. Escribe el género femenino enfrente de cada masculino.
Write the feminine equivalent of these masculine adjectives.

a) pintor	
b) griego	
c) camarero	
d) noruego	
e) cantante	
f) bombero	
g) dentista	
h) escritor	

2. Completa los adjetivos de nacionalidad en masculino o femenino.
Complete with the appropriate masculine or feminine nationality adjective.

País	Masculino	Femenino
a) Escocia	escocés	
b) Alemania	alemán	
c) Italia	italiano	
d) Irlanda	irlandés	
e) Polonia	polaco	
f) Canadá		canadiense
g) Japón	japonés	
h) China	chino	
i) Estados Unidos		estadounidense
j) Grecia	griego	

3. Empareja las expresiones del español con el inglés.
Match the Spanish expressions with the English ones.

a) ¿De dónde eres?	1.	What do you do?
b) ¿Hablas español?	2.	What languages do you speak?
c) ¿Cuál es tu nacionalidad?	3.	Are you Scottish?
d) ¿Cuál es tu profesión?	4.	Do you speak Spanish?
e) ¿Eres escocés?	5.	What's your nationality?
f) ¿Qué idiomas hablas?	6.	Where do you come from?
g) ¿Cuál es tu número de teléfono?	7.	What's your profession? /What's your job?
h) ¿Qué haces?	8.	What's your phone number?

4. Escribe una pregunta adecuada para cada palabra del recuadro.
Write a question for each of the words in the box below.

Qué   Cuál   Cómo   Dónde

a) _____
b) _____
c) _____
d) _____

5. Escribe con letras el número. Write the numbers in words.
Ejemplo: 33 = treinta y tres.

a) 18	f) 74
b) 25	g) 43
c) 100	h) 61
d) 99	i) 11
e) 82	j) 60

6. Escoge la palabra correcta para completar las oraciones.
Complete the sentences with the correct words.

1. Yo me _____ Julián Ramos.
a) llamas
b) llamo
c) llame
d) llama

2. Tú_____ español.
a) soe
b) es
c) soy
d) eres

3. Yo_____de Barcelona.
a) son
b) es
c) soy
d) sos

4. Tú _____ inglés y español.
a) hablas
b) hablo
c) hablamos
d) hablan

5. ¿_____es tu nacionalidad?
a) Coma
b) Cuál
c) Cual
d) Cómo

6. Yo _____en Madrid.
a) vivie
b) vivo
c) viven
d) viva

7. Relaciona la pregunta con la respuesta. Match the questions with the answers.

¿Qué estudias?	Inglés y español.
¿Qué haces?	Psicología e idiomas.
¿Qué idiomas hablas?	Soy español.
¿Cuál es tu nacionalidad?	Soy veterinario.

VOCABULARIO.

1. NACIONALIDADES
Alemania (f)	*Germany*
alemán/alemana	*German*
Arabia (f)	*Arabia*
árabe (m/f)	*Arab*
británico/a	*British*
Canadá (m)	*Canada*
canadiense (m/f)	*Canadian*
Estados Unidos (mpl)	*United States*
estadounidense (m/f)	*American*
Finlandia (f)	*Finland*
finlandés/finlandesa	*Finnish*
Francia (f)	*France*
francés/francesa	*French*
Gales (f)	*Wales*
galés/galesa	*Welsh*
Grecia (f)	*Greece*
griego/a	*Greek*
Irlanda (f)	*Ireland*
irlandés/irlandesa	*Irish*
Italia	*Italy*
italiano/a	*Italian*
Letonia/Latvia (f)	*Latvia*
letón/letona	*Latvian*
Lituania (f)	*Lithuania*
lituano/a	*Lithuanian*
Noruega (f)	*Norway*
noruego/a	*Norwegian*
país (m)	*country*
Polonia (f)	*Poland*
polaco/a	*Polish*
Reino Unido (m)	*United Kingdom*
Rumanía (f)	*Romania*
rumano/a	*Romanian*
Rusia (f)	*Russia*
ruso/a	*Russian*
Suecia (f)	*Sweden*
sueco/a	*Swedish*
Suiza (f)	*Switzerland*
suizo/a	*Swiss*
¿Cuál es tu nacionalidad?	*What's your nationality?*
¿De dónde eres?	*Where do you come from?*

2. PROFESIONES
actor/actriz	*actor/actress*
arquitecto/a	*architect*
ama de casa	*housewife*
bombero/a	*fire-fighter*
camarero/a	*waiter/waitress*
cantante (m/f)	*singer*
cartero/a	*postman/postwoman*
científico/a	*scientist*
cocinero/a	*cook*
contable	*accountant*
dentista (m/f)	*dentist*
doctor/doctora	*doctor*
electricista (m/f)	*electrician*
enfermero/a	*nurse*
escritor/escritora	*writer*
estudiante (m/f)	*student*
ingeniero/a	*engineer*
investigador/a	*researcher*
peluquero/a	*hairdresser*
pero	*but*
pintor/pintora	*painter*
profesor/profesora	*teacher*
recepcionista (m/f)	*receptionist*
trabajador/a social	*social worker*
¿Cuál es tu profesión?	*What's your profession?*
¿Qué haces?	*What do you do?*
¿Qué idiomas hablas?	*What languages do you speak?*

3. ¿DE DÓNDE ERES?
3. WHERE DO YOU COME FROM?
No, no soy	*No, I'm not*
Sí, soy	*Yes, I am*
¿Dónde vives?	*Where do you live?*
¿Eres escocés?	*Are you Scottish?*

4. NÚMEROS
4. NUMBERS
¿Cuál es tu correo electrónico?	*What's your email?*

5. CORREO ELECTRÓNICO
5. EMAIL
arroba (f)	*at*
punto (m)	*dot*
barra (f)	*forward slash*
guión (m)	*dash*
guión bajo (m)	*underscore*

VERBOS
VERBS
hablar	*to speak*
tener	*to have*
vivir	*to live*

3 SOMOS AMIGOS

TEMAS TOPICS	OBJETIVOS COMUNICATIVOS COMMUNICATIVE OBJECTIVES	GRAMÁTICA/GRAMMAR
Mis amigos. Los famosos. Tu edad y la edad de los demás.	**Presentar a un/a amigo/a.** Introducing a friend. **Preguntar y decir información sobre los amigos.** Asking and giving information about your friends. **Hablar de los famosos.** Talking about famous people. **Decir la edad.** Talking about age.	**Pronombres personales sujeto (singular): yo, tú (informal), usted (formal), él/ella.** Subject personal pronouns (singular): I, you, he/she. **Adjetivos y pronombres demostrativos: este/a, estos/as.** Demonstrative pronouns and adjectives: this/these. **Adjetivos posesivos: mi/s, tu/s, su/s.** Possessive adjectives. my, your, his/her/their. **Las tres conjugaciones: ar/er/ir** **Presente de indicativo (1ª, 2ª, y 3ª persona singular) de los verbos: hablar, estudiar, trabajar, aprender, llamarse, leer, beber, comer, vivir, escribir, abrir, ser, hacer, tener.** The three conjugations in Spanish: ar/er/ir. Present tense (1st, 2nd and 3rd person singular) of verbs: to speak, to study, to work, to be called, to learn, to read, to drink, to eat, to live, to write, to open, to be, to do/make, to have. **Interrogativos: ¿Qué? ¿Cuántos?** Interrogatives: What? How many?

1. ¿QUIÉN ES? WHO IS HE/SHE?

1a. **Escucha y lee la siguiente información sobre estas cuatro personas y subraya los verbos.**
Listen and read the following information about these four people and underline the verbs.

Se llama María Ramos Ruiz. Es periodista.
Es colombiana de Bogotá pero vive en Sevilla.
Habla español y aprende inglés. Tiene 25 años.

Se llama Marcello Pedercini. Es estudiante
de relaciones públicas. Es italiano de Roma.
Vive en Roma. Habla italiano y aprende
español. Tiene 21 años.

Se llama María Martínez González. Es
psicóloga, es española de Madrid pero vive en
París. Habla español y francés. Aprende inglés.
Tiene 50 años.

Se llama John Kyle. Es mánager de varias
cafeterías. Es irlandés pero vive en Londres.
Habla inglés y aprende español. Tiene 30
años.

GRAMÁTICA

- **¿Cómo se llama?**
  What's his/her name? /What's he/she called?
- **¿De dónde es?**
  Where is he/she from?

- **¿Cuál es su profesión?**
  What is his/her profession?
- **¿Dónde vive?**
  Where does he/she live?
- **¿Qué idioma(s) aprende?**
  What language(s) is he/she learning?
- **¿Qué idioma(s) habla?**
  What language(s) does he/she speak?
- **¿Cuántos años tiene?**
  How old is he/she?

- **Se llama**
  His/her name is/He/she is called.
- **Es (colombiano/a). Es de Bogotá.**
  He/she is (Colombian).
  He/she is from Bogotá.
- **Es...**
  He/she is
- **Vive en**
  He/she lives in
- **Aprende**
  He/she is learning
- **Habla**
  He/she speaks
- **Tiene... años**
  He/she is…years old.

- ¿Cómo se llama **la** señorita de la foto A?
- ¿Cómo se llama **el** chico de la foto B?
- ¿Cómo se llama **la** señora de la foto C?
- ¿Cómo se llama **el** señor de la foto D?

¡DESCUBRE!	
Señor/Sr.	Mr
Señora/Sra.	Mrs
Señorita/Srta.	Miss
chico/a	boy/girl

1b. Vamos a hablar. Escoge una foto de la página anterior (A/B/C/D) y practica con tu compañero/a las preguntas del recuadro de abajo. Después continúa con el resto de las fotografías.
Let's talk. Choose a photo from the previous page (A/B/C/D) and practise the questions and answer below with your partner. Do the same for the rest of the photographs.

FOTO_____

o ¿Cómo se llama?	Se llama………………………………
o ¿Dónde vive?	Vive en……………………………………
o ¿De dónde es?	Es de…………………………………
o ¿Es español/española?	No es……………………Es……………
o ¿Cuál es su profesión?	Es……………………………………
o ¿Qué idioma habla?	Habla……………………………………
o ¿Qué idioma aprende?	Aprende…………………………………
o ¿Cuántos años tiene?	Tiene………… años.

1c. Ejercicio comunicativo. Escribe tu nombre en un papel y colócalo enfrente de ti donde tu compañero/a pueda verlo. En grupos de tres o cuatro estudiantes, presenta a tus compañeros.
Speaking exercise. Write your name on a piece of paper and put it on the table where your partner can see it. In groups of three or four, introduce your partners to the others.

¡Este es mi amigo! / ¡Esta es mi amiga!

Me llamo_____(nombre)
Se llama
Soy _____(nacionalidad)
Es
Soy _____(profesión)
Es
Vivo en_____(ciudad/pueblo)
Vive en
Tengo_____años
Tiene

GRAMÁTICA

	ser	to be
(yo)	soy	I am
(tú)	eres	you are
(él/ella)	es	he/she is

1d. Escribe un párrafo similar a los de sección 1a sobre un amigo y otro sobre una amiga.
Write similar paragraphs to the section 1a about a male and female friend.

Este es mi amigo.

Esta es mi amiga.

GRAMÁTICA

	Masculino	**Femenino**
Singular	est<u>e</u> (this)	est<u>a</u> (this)
Plural	est<u>os</u> (these)	est<u>as</u> (these)

2. CONOCIENDO A LOS FAMOSOS. GETTING TO KNOW CELEBRITIES.

2a. Lee cada texto y cambia a la 3ª persona del singular la información de los famosos.
Read the following texts about famous people and change the verbs to the 3rd person singular.

1

2

Me llamo Rafael Nadal Parera. **Soy** español de Mallorca. **Vivo** en Mallorca. **Soy** tenista. **Hablo** español, francés e inglés. **Tengo** 30 años.

Me llamo Andrew Murray. **Soy** escocés de Dunblane pero **vivo** en Londres. **Soy** tenista. **Hablo** inglés. **Tengo** 30 años.

3

4

Me llamo Penélope Cruz Santos. **Soy** española de Madrid. **Soy** actriz. **Vivo** en Los Ángeles, Estados Unidos y en Madrid. **Hablo** español e inglés. **Tengo** 45 años.

Me llamo Ángela Merkel. **Soy** alemana de Hamburgo pero **vivo** en Berlín. **Soy** política. **Hablo** alemán, inglés y latín. **Tengo** 60 años.

2b. Lee cada texto una vez más, contesta a las siguientes preguntas y practica con tu compañero/a.
Read each text over again and practise answering the following questions with your partner.
Foto _____

- ¿Cómo se llama?
- ¿Cuál es su profesión? / ¿Qué hace?
- ¿De dónde es?

- ¿Dónde vive?
- ¿Cuántos años tiene?
- ¿Qué idioma(s) habla?

2c. Completa la forma de estos verbos. Complete the table with the appropriate verb forms.

	llamarse	hablar	aprender	vivir	tener	ser
yo						
tú						
él/ella						

3. MIS AMIGOS/AS. MY FRIENDS.

3a. Relaciona la pregunta con la respuesta adecuada.
Match the question with the correct English translations.

1. **¿De dónde es?**
2. **¿Cuál es su profesión?**
3. **¿Qué hace?**
4. **¿Dónde vive?**
5. **¿Qué idiomas habla?**
6. **¿Qué idiomas aprende?**

a) What's his/her profession?
b) What languages is he/she learning?
c) Where does he/she come from?
d) What languages does he/she speak?
e) What does he/she do?
f) Where does he/she live?

GRAMÁTICA

	llamarse	hablar	aprender	vivir	tener	ser
yo	me llamo	hablo	aprendo	vivo	tengo	soy
tú	te llamas	hablas	aprendes	vives	tienes	eres
él/ella	se llama	habla	aprende	vive	tiene	es

Audio 22

3b. Escucha y lee. Listen and read.

GRAMÁTICA		
	trabajar	to work
(yo)	**trabaj**o	I work
(tú)	**trabaj**as	you work
(él/ella)	**trabaj**a	he/she works

Esta es mi amiga Maggie.
Esta es mi amiga Susana.

Patricia	**¡Hola Maggie! ¿Cómo estás?**
Maggie	Estoy bien, gracias.
Patricia	**Mira Maggie esta es mi amiga Susana, es española de Madrid. Aprende inglés aquí en Escocia. Hola Susana, esta es mi amiga Maggie, es escocesa, habla francés e inglés y es estudiante de música.**
Maggie	Hola Susana, mucho gusto. ¿Dónde vives? y ¿Qué haces?
Susana	Encantada, vivo aquí en Dundee. Soy pintora y estudiante de arte ¿Y tú?
Maggie	Yo no vivo aquí, vivo cerca de Perth. Soy profesora de francés y estudiante de música ¿Y tú Patricia? ¿Dónde vives?
Patricia	**Vivo en Edimburgo pero trabajo en Dundee. ¿Y tú Susana? ¿Dónde trabajas?**
Susana	Trabajo en Glasgow. ¿Y tú Maggie? ¿Dónde trabajas?
Maggie	Trabajo en Dundee. ¡Hasta luego!
Patricia	**Adiós.**
Susana	Hasta pronto.

3c. Lee una vez más la conversación anterior y contesta en español las siguientes preguntas.
Read the previous conversation again and answer the following questions in Spanish.

1. ¿De dónde es Susana?
2. ¿De dónde es Maggie?
3. ¿Qué idiomas habla Maggie?
4. ¿Qué idioma aprende Susana?
5. ¿Dónde vive Maggie?

6. ¿Dónde vive Susana?
7. ¿Dónde trabaja Maggie?
8. ¿Dónde trabaja Susana?
9. ¿Cuál es la profesión de Maggie?
10. ¿Qué hace Susana?

¡DESCUBRE!

aquí	here	**pero**	but
cerca	near	**Mucho gusto**	Pleased to meet you
mira	look	**Encantado/a**	Nice to meet you

4. ¿CUÁNTOS AÑOS TIENES? HOW OLD ARE YOU?

 Audio 23

4a. Escucha y repite. Listen and repeat.

A ¿Cuántos años **tienes**?　　　　A ¿Cuántos años **tiene** Carlos.
B **Tengo** 20 años　　　　　　　B Carlos **tiene** 35 años.

Audio 24

4b. Escucha y escribe la edad correcta.
　　Listen and fill in the correct age.

1. Juan tiene_____ años.
2. Mi amiga tiene _____ años.
3. Yo tengo _____ años.
4. Mi padre tiene _____ años.
5. El amigo de Ricardo tiene _____ años.

¡DESCUBRE!

Tener......to have

tengo X años.	I am X years old.
tienes X años.	you are X years old.
tiene X años.	he/she is X years old.

GRAMÁTICA

	tener	to have
(yo)	**tengo**	I have
(tú)	**tienes**	you have
(él/ella)	**tiene**	he/she has

4c. Completa los espacios vacíos con los siguientes verbos: trabajar, vivir, ser, llamarse y tener.
Fill in the blanks with the correct verb: trabajar, vivir, ser, llamarse and tener.

a) Ella _____ _____ **(1. llamarse)** María. _____ **(2. ser)** profesora y
_____ **(3. trabajar)** en un colegio. _____ **(4. tener)** veinticinco años.

b) Luis _____ **(1. ser)** español. _____ **(2. ser)** doctor y _____ **(3. vivir)** en Madrid.
_____ **(4. tener)** cuarenta años.

c) Yo _____ _____ **(1. llamarse)** Carlos y _____ **(2. vivir)** en Barcelona.
_____ **(3. ser)** profesor y _____ **(4. trabajar)** en una universidad en
Barcelona. _____ **(5. tener)** cincuenta años.

d) Tú _____ **(1. ser)** pintor. _____ **(2. ser)** de Sevilla pero _____ **(3. vivir)** en
Madrid y _____ **(4. trabajar)** en una galería de arte.

4d. Contesta a las siguientes preguntas y después practica con tus compañeros/as de la clase.
Practise answering the following questions with your fellow students.

- ¿Cómo te llamas?
- ¿Dónde vives?
- ¿De dónde eres?
- ¿Cuál es tu profesión?
- ¿Dónde trabajas?
- ¿Cuántos años tienes?

Audio 25

4e. Escucha el siguiente diálogo y contesta a las preguntas. Listen and answer the questions.

1. ¿Cómo se llama? ………
2. ¿Dónde vive? …………..
3. ¿De dónde es?…………… .
4. ¿Es español? ……………
5. ¿Cuál es su profesión? …
6. ¿Qué idioma habla? ……
7. ¿Qué idioma aprende? …
8. ¿Cuántos años tiene? ….

GRAMÁTICA		
	estudi**ar**	to study
(yo)	estudi**o**	I study
(tú)	estudi**as**	you study
(él/ella)	estudi**a**	he/she studies

4f. Lee los siguientes textos y contesta a las preguntas.
Read the following texts and answer the questions below.

¡Hola! Me llamo César Maldonado. Soy español de Barcelona y vivo en Barcelona. Soy abogado, tengo 65 años y estudio francés. Este es mi amigo, se llama Raúl y es contable. Tiene 55 años, es de Sevilla pero vive en Barcelona.

¡Hola! Me llamo Rosa Villareal, soy venezolana de Caracas y vivo en Caracas. Soy secretaria en una compañía de exportaciones, estudio inglés y tengo 38 años. Esta es mi amiga, se llama Laura y es trabajadora social. Tiene 35 años, es argentina de Buenos Aires pero vive en Caracas Venezuela.

1. ¿De dónde es César y cuál es su profesión?
2. ¿Cuál es la profesión de Rosa y cuántos años tiene?
3. ¿Cuál es la profesión de Raúl y dónde vive?
4. ¿Cuántos años tiene César y dónde vive?
5. ¿Cuántos años tiene Raúl y de dónde es?
6. ¿Cuál es la profesión de Laura y dónde vive?
7. ¿De dónde es Rosa y dónde vive?
8. ¿De dónde es Laura y cuántos años tiene?
9. ¿Qué estudia César?
10. ¿Qué estudia Rosa?

5. LECTURA Y COMPRENSIÓN. READING COMPREHENSION.

5a. Lee los siguientes textos y subraya los verbos. Read the following texts and underline the verbs.

¡**Hola!** Me llamo **José María Contreras Ríos.** Soy argentino de Buenos Aires, pero vivo en París. Soy estudiante. Estudio medicina. Hablo español y aprendo francés. Trabajo en una tienda de ropa para caballeros. Soy empleado. Tengo 24 años.

¡**Hola!** Me llamo **Cristina García Moreno.** Soy española de Barcelona, pero vivo en París. Soy estudiante de psicología. Hablo español e inglés y aprendo francés. También trabajo, soy camarera en un restaurante. Tengo veintitrés años.

5b. Completa los espacios vacíos con el verbo correcto. Fill in the blanks with the correct verb.

José	¡**Hola!** (yo) _____ _____ **(1. llamarse)** José Contreras Ríos. **¿Y tú?** **¿Cómo** _____ _____ **(2. llamarse)?**
Cristina	¡Hola! _____ _____ (3. llamarse) Cristina García Moreno. _____ (4. ser) española de Barcelona. ¿Y tú? ¿De dónde eres?
José	**Yo _____ (5. ser) argentino de Buenos Aires. ¿Dónde vives?**
Cristina	_____ (6. vivir) en París. ¿Y tú? ¿Dónde _____ (7. vivir)?
José	**Yo también _____ (8. vivir) en París. ¿Cuál es tu profesión? ¿Trabajas o estudias?**
Cristina	Yo _____ (9. trabajar) y _____ (10. estudiar). _____ (11. ser) estudiante de psicología y _____ (12. ser) camarera en un restaurante. ¿Y tú? ¿Qué haces?
José	**Yo también _____ (13. trabajar) y estudio. _____ (14. ser) empleado en una tienda de ropa para caballeros y _____ (15. estudiar) medicina. ¿Cuántos años tienes Cristina?**
Cristina	_____ (16. tener) veintitrés años. ¿Y tú? ¿Cuántos años_____ (17. tener)?
José	**Yo _____ (18. tener) veinticinco años.**
Cristina	Adiós.
José	**Hasta luego.**

6. VAMOS A ESCRIBIR. LET'S WRITE.

6a. Escribe un texto sobre tu amigo/a. Tienes que incluir lo siguiente.
   Write a paragraph about your friend. Include the following details:

- Nombre y apellido
- Nacionalidad y profesión
- Estudios

- Edad
- Número de teléfono y correo electrónico
- Idiomas que habla

6b. Busca información en la web y escribe un párrafo similar sobre un personaje famoso.
   Find information on the web and write a paragraph about a famous person.

GRAMÁTICA

- **Adjetivos y pronombres demostrativos.** Demonstrative pronouns and adjectives.

	Masculino	Femenino
Singular	est**e** (this)	est**a** (this)
Plural	est**os** (these)	est**as** (these)

- **Adjetivos posesivos.** Possessive adjectives.

Singular	Plural
mi (my)	**mis** (my)
tu (your)	**tus** (your)
su (his/her/their)	**sus** (his/her/their)

- **Pronombres personales.** Personal pronouns.

yo	I
tú (informal)	you
usted (formal)	you
él/ella	he/she

- **Verbos terminados en** ar. Conjugation of -ar verbs.

Pronombres	**hablar**	to speak
yo	**hablo**	I speak
tú (informal) usted (formal)	**hablas** **habla**	you speak
él/ella	**habla**	he/she speaks

More -ar verbs: trabaj**ar**, estudi**ar**, cant**ar**, cen**ar**, escuch**ar**, tom**ar**.

- **Verbos terminados en** er. Conjugation of -er verbs.

Pronombres	**aprender**	to learn
yo	**aprendo**	I learn
tú (informal) usted (formal)	**aprendes** **aprende**	you learn
él/ella	**aprende**	he/she learns

More er verbs: le**er**, beb**er**, com**er**, entend**er**, corr**er**, comprend**er**.

- **Verbos terminados en** ir. Conjugation of -ir verbs.

Pronombres	**vivir**	to live
yo	**vivo**	I live
tú (informal) usted (formal)	**vives** **vive**	you live
él/ella	**vive**	he/she lives

More **ir** verbs: escrib**ir**, abr**ir**, sub**ir**, asist**ir**.

- **Verbos irregulares.** Conjugation of irregular verbs.

Pronombres	ser	to be
yo	soy	I am
tú (informal) usted (formal)	eres es	you are
él/ella	es	he/she is

Pronombres	tener	to have
yo	tengo	I have
tú (informal) usted (formal)	tienes tiene	you have
él/ella	tiene	he/she has

Pronombres	hacer	to do/make
yo	hago	I do/make
tú (informal) usted (formal)	haces hace	you do/make
él/ella	hace	he/she does/makes

- **Verbos reflexivos.** Reflexive verbs.

Pronombres	llamarse	to be called
yo	me llamo	I am called/My name is
tú (informal) usted (formal)	te llamas se llama	you are called/your name is
él/ella	se llama	he/she is called/his/her name is

More reflexive verbs: levantarse, ducharse…

EJERCICIOS

1. **Escribe el verbo correcto (soy, eres o es) en cada frase.**
    Complete the sentences with the correct verb form (I am, you are or he/she is).

    1. Yo_____ estudiante.
    2. Manuel_____ español.
    3. Tú _____ camarera.
    4. Ella _____ estudiante.
    5. Usted_____ ingeniero.
    6. Él_____ escocés.
    7. María_____ inglesa.

2. Une las frases de español con el inglés correspondiente. Match the Spanish with the English.

Español	English
1. Eres	a) My name is
2. Te llamas	b) I am learning
3. Vivo	c) He/she is learning
4. Aprendo	d) I live
5. Me llamo	e) His/her name is
6. Vive	f) He/she lives
7. Hablo	g) You are
8. Vives	h) You live
9. Aprende	i) Your name is
10. Se llama	j) I speak
11. Soy	k) He/she is
12. Es	l) I am

3. Completa los verbos que faltan. Complete the sentences with the appropriate verbs.

A. ¡Hola! Yo ____ _____ (llamarse) Javier García Santos, _____ (ser) español
    de Barcelona pero _____ (vivir) en Madrid. _____ (ser) profesor.
    _____ (hablar) español y _____ (aprender) inglés. _____
    (tener) 30 años.

B. Ella _____ (ser) Marisol Torres, _____ (ser) secretaria, _____
    (ser) de Sevilla España pero _____ (vivir) en París. _____ (hablar) español
    y _____ (aprender) francés. _____ (tener) 49 años.

C. Mi amigo _____ _____ (llamarse) Julián Garza Lozano, _____ (ser)
    argentino de Buenos Aires pero_____ (vivir) en Londres. _____
    (ser) dentista. _____ (hablar) español y _____ (aprender) inglés.
    _____ (tener) 25 años.

4a. Lee las siguientes presentaciones y subraya los verbos.
Read the following introductions and underline the verbs.

- Yo me llamo Ramón Ríos. Soy español de Barcelona pero vivo en Londres.
  Soy profesor en una universidad. Hablo inglés y aprendo alemán. Tengo 38 años.
- Él se llama Gustavo Sandoval. Es ecuatoriano de Quito pero vive en Lima. Es estudiante
  de ingeniería y cartero. Habla español. Aprende inglés. Tiene 20 años.
- Se llama Paola Pedercini. Es italiana de Roma pero vive en Madrid. Es arquitecta.
  Habla inglés e italiano. Aprende español. Tiene 30 años.

4b. Escribe párrafos similares; uno sobre tu persona, otro sobre un amigo y otro sobre una amiga. Write similar paragraphs about yourself, a male friend and a female friend.

5. Escribe la forma del verbo que falta en los espacios vacíos. Fill in the blanks with the correct verb forms.

Pronombres	llamarse
yo	
tú	te llamas
usted	
él/ella	

Pronombres	trabajar	estudiar	hablar
yo		estudio	
tú	trabajas		
usted			
él/ella			habla

Pronombres	beber	comer	aprender
yo			aprendo
tú			
usted		come	
él/ella	bebe		

Pronombres	escribir	asistir	abrir
yo		asisto	
tú	escribes		
usted			abre
él/ella			

Pronombres	ser	tener	hacer
yo	soy		
tú			haces
usted			
él/ella		tiene	

VOCABULARIO

1. ¿QUIÉN ES?	1. WHO IS HE/SHE?
idioma (m)	language
periodista (m/f)	journalist
relaciones publicas	public relations
¿Cómo se llama?	What's his/her name?
¿Cuál es su profesión?	What's his/her profession?
¿Cuántos años tienes?	How old are you?
¿De dónde es?	Where does he/she come from?
¿Dónde vive?	Where does he/she live?
¿Es español/española?	Are you Spanish?
¿Qué hace?	What does he/she do?
¿Qué idioma habla?	What languages does he/she speak?
¿Qué idioma aprende?	What languages is he/she learning?

2. CONOCIENDO A LOS FAMOSOS	2. GETTING TO KNOW CELEBRITIES
actor/actriz	actor
Este/a es mi amigo/a	This is my friend
político/a	politician
tenista (m/f)	tennis player

3. MIS AMIGOS/AS	3. MY FRIENDS
amigo/a (m/f)	friend
aquí	here
cerca	near
Encantado/a	Pleased to meet you
este/a (m/f)	this
estoy bien	I'm fine
estudiante de arte	art student
estudiante de música	music student
gracias	thank you
mira	look
Mucho gusto	Nice to meet you
pero	but
trabajo	I work
vivo	I live

¿Cómo estás?	How are you?
¿Dónde vives?	Where do you live?
¿Dónde trabajas?	Where do you work

4 ¿CUÁNTOS AÑOS TIENES?	4. HOW OLD ARE YOU?
abogado/a	lawyer
contable (m/f)	accountant
compañía de exportaciones	export company
Tengo X años	I am X years old

VERBOS	VERBS
aprender	to learn
estar	to be
estudiar	to study
trabajar	to work
vivir	to live

4 ¿QUÉ QUIERES TOMAR?

TEMAS TOPICS	OBJETIVOS COMUNICATIVOS COMMUNICATIVE OBJECTIVES	GRAMÁTICA GRAMMAR
En el bar. **En el restaurante.** **Hablar formal.**	**Pedir bebidas y aperitivos.** Ordering drinks and appetizers. **Pedir comida en un restaurante.** Ordering in a restaurant. **Preguntar y decir qué hay.** Asking and saying what there is. **Usar el formal [singular] (usted).** Use of formal form [singular] (usted).	**Artículos indefinidos: un/una, unos/unas.** Indefinite articles: a/an, some. **Adjetivos posesivos: mi/mis, tu/tus, su/sus.** Possessive Adjectives: my, your, his/her, their. **Presente de indicativo de los verbos: querer, vivir, tener.** Present tense of the verbs: to want, to live, to have. **El formal del presente de indicativo (singular) de los verbos: querer, llamarse, ser, vivir, tener.** Formal of present tense (singular) of verbs: to want, to be called, to be, to live, to have. **El verbo «hay».** Verb: 'There is/there are'. **Negativos.** Negatives. **Interrogativos: ¿Qué? ¿Cuánto?** Interrogatives: What? How much?

1. ¿QUÉ QUIERE TOMAR? WHAT WOULD YOU LIKE TO EAT/DRINK?

Audio 26

1a. Escucha, lee y repite. Listen, read and repeat.

Quiero un café.	I'd like/I want a coffee.
Quiero una cerveza.	I'd like/I want a beer.
¿Qué hay?	What is there?
¿Qué quieres? / ¿Qué quiere (usted)?	What do you want/What would you like?

Audio 27

1b. Escucha y lee la siguiente conversación. Listen and read the next conversation.

un café negro	**una cerveza**	**tapas/aperitivos**	**un café latte**

Camarera	**¿Qué quiere tomar?**
María	Quiero una cerveza, por favor.
Camarera	**¿Grande o pequeña?**
María	Pequeña, por favor.
Camarera	**¿Algo más?**
María	¿Hay tapas?
Camarera	**Sí. Hay tortilla de patata, jamón, queso, patatas fritas, calamares, olivas…**
María	Pues… tortilla de patata y queso.
Camarera	**¿Algo más?**
María	No, nada más. ¿Cuánto es?
Camarera	**Son diez con cincuenta euros.**

¡DESCUBRE!

por favor	please
pues	well
grande	big
pequeño/a	small
tomar	to drink/to order
un/una	a/an

1c. Lee el diálogo una vez más y contesta a las preguntas.
Read the dialogue again and answer the questions.

1. **¿Qué pide María?** What does Maria order?
2. **¿Qué tipo de tapas hay?**
   What kind of appetizers are there?
3. **¿Cuánto es?** How much is it?

GRAMÁTICA

Hay	There is/There are
¿Hay?	Is there? /Are there?
¿Qué hay?	What is there?
¿Cuánto es?	How much is it?
¿Algo más?	Anything else?
Nada más	Nothing else.

En grupos de dos, practica la conversación anterior (1b).
In groups of two, practise the above conversation at (1b) above.

1d. Escucha y lee. Listen, and read.

EL MENÚ

BEBIDAS

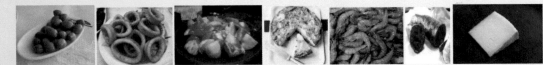

un chocolate	2,20€	*una coca cola	1,30€
un café	1,90€	una infusión de fresa o manzanilla	1,50€
*un café con leche	1,95€	una cerveza	2,90€
un expreso	2,00€	una piña colada	3,00€
un café latte	2,10€	una copa de vino blanco o tinto	3,50€
un capuchino	2,10€	*una gaseosa	95 cts
un refresco	95 cts		
un té	2,00€		
un zumo de manzana/naranja	99 cts		
un tequila	3,00€		
un whisky	3,10€		
*un agua mineral	1,25€		

con/sin:
- azúcar
- gas
- hielos

TAPAS

*Olivas	3,55€	*Calamares	3,60€
*Jamón Serrano	4,20€	*Salchichas	3,70€
*Queso Manchego	4,50€	*Pan con ajo	1,90€
*Patatas fritas	3,00€	*Patatas bravas	3,50€
Tortilla de patatas	3,25€	Empanadilla	2,50€
Sándwich de pollo o de queso o de jamón.	5,45€	*Nachos	3,10€
Bocadillo de pollo o de atún	5,35€	Ensalada	2,70€
*Chorizo Ibérico	3,70€	*Gambas	4,50€

ración de…portion of

1e. Practica los siguientes diálogos utilizando los diferentes precios del menú.
Practise the following dialogues using the different prices from the previous menu.

A. ¿Cuánto cuesta un café?	A. ¿Cuánto cuesta una ración de nachos?
B. (Cuesta) 1,95€	B. (Cuesta) 3,10€

1f. Escribe un/una/unos/unas. Write 'un', 'una', 'unos' or 'unas'.

1. _____ té
2. _____ limonada
3. _____ patatas fritas
4. _____ gaseosa
5. _____ zumo de naranja

6. _____ olivas
7. _____ bocadillo de pollo
8. _____ chocolate caliente
9. _____ cerveza
10. _____ nachos

GRAMÁTICA

	M	F	
Singular	un	una	a/(an)
Plural	unos	unas	some

GRAMÁTICA

	querer	to want
(yo)	**quiero**	I want
(tú)	**quieres**	you want
(usted)	**quiere**	you want

1g. Sí gracias/No gracias. Yes, thank you/No, thank you.

¿Quieres un café?

Sí quiero, gracias.

¿Quieres un café?

No gracias. Quiero una copa de vino blanco.

Practica con tu compañero/a los siguientes diálogos utilizando el vocabulario de diferentes bebidas y aperitivos/tapas. Practise the following dialogue with your partner, referring to a variety of drinks and tapas from the menu.

A. ¿Quieres un/una_____?	A. ¿Quieres un/una_____?
B. Sí quiero, gracias.	B. No, gracias. Quiero un/una_____

1h. Practica con tu compañero/a los siguientes diálogos utilizando el vocabulario de arriba de las diferentes bebidas y tapas. Practise the following dialogue with your partner, referring to a variety of drinks and tapas, as above.

¡Camarero! ¿Hay olivas?

¡Camarero! ¿Hay tortilla de patatas?

Sí hay olivas.

No, no hay tortilla de patatas.

59

Audio 29

2. EN EL RESTAURANTE. AT THE RESTAURANT.

RESTAURANTE EL TORO

MENÚ DEL DÍA

Primer plato
Sopa de ajo
Ensalada mixta
Gazpacho

Segundo plato
Paella
Pollo asado
Chuletas de cordero
Merluza asada
Pescado (bacalao) frito
Bistec con patatas
Arroz con vegetales

Postres
Helados
Flan
Fruta del día
Arroz con leche

2a. Escucha y lee. Listen and read.

Camarera	Buenos días. ¿Qué quieren comer los señores?
Cliente 1	**El menú del día, por favor.**
Camarera	¿Qué quiere de primer plato?
Cliente 1	**Quiero ensalada mixta.**
Cliente 2	**Para mí… una sopa de ajo.**
Camarera	Muy bien. ¿Y de segundo?
Cliente 2	**Yo quiero paella.**
Camarera	¿Y para usted señora?
Cliente 1	**Para mí pollo asado.**
Camarera	¿Qué quieren beber?
Cliente 1	**Quiero un vino.**
Camarera	¿Blanco o tinto señora?
Cliente 1	**Tinto, un rioja por favor.**
Cliente 2	**Para mí agua con gas.**
Camarera	¿Y de postre?
Cliente 1	**Yo quiero un helado de fresa.**
Cliente 2	**Yo quiero fruta del día.**
Camarera	¿Quieren café los señores?
Cliente 1	**Si un café con leche.**
Cliente 2	**Para mí un expreso.**
Camarera	¿Algo más?
Cliente 1	**No gracias.**
Cliente 2	**La cuenta por favor.**
Camarera	Son 67,60 euros.

2b. Marca falso o verdadero enfrente de cada oración.
Indicate whether the following statements are true or false.

	F	V
1. Cliente uno quiere de primero gazpacho.		
2. Cliente dos quiere de segundo paella.		
3. Cliente uno quiere de postre helado de fresa.		
4. Cliente dos no quiere café.		

2c. En grupo de tres, practica la conversación anterior (2a).
In groups of three, practise the conversation above (2a).

BEBIDAS

Zumos de frutas
Coca-Cola
Cerveza
Vino de la casa
  (blanco y tinto)
Café
Café con leche
Capuchino
Café latte
Agua con gas

3. INFORMAL O FORMAL. INFORMAL OR FORMAL.

3a. Escribe debajo de cada foto si el saludo es formal o informal.
Write under each picture if the greeting is formal or informal.

| A. ¡Hola! ¿Cómo **te llamas**? | A. Buenas tardes. ¿Cómo **se llama (usted)**? |
| B. ¿Qué tal? **Me llamo** Carolina. | B. Buenas tardes. **Me llamo** Lorenzo Ramos. |

Audio 30

3b. Escucha las siguientes conversaciones y rellena el cuadro de abajo.
Listen to the following conversations and fill in the following table.

	Conversación 1	Conversación 2
Formal/Informal		
Nombre		
Nacionalidad		
Lugar de residencia actual		
Edad		
Profesión		
Lugar de trabajo		

¡DESCUBRE!

In Spanish, the **informal** register is used when speaking with friends and family.

The **formal** register is used to communicate with older people or in-laws and in formal situations, such as work, visits to the doctor, etc. It is used more in Latin America than in Spain.

3c. Lee las siguientes conversaciones y practica con tu compañero/a.
Read the following dialogues and practise with your partner.

Informal	Formal
A ¡Hola! ¿Cómo **te llamas**?	A Buenas tardes. ¿Cómo **se llama (usted)**?
B ¿Qué tal? **Me llamo** Carlos.	B ¡Mucho gusto! **Me llamo** Mike Stuart.
A ¿De dónde **eres**?	A ¿De dónde **es (usted)**?
B **Soy** de España/**soy** español de Madrid.	B **Soy** de Escocia/**soy** escocés de Glasgow.
A ¿Dónde **vives**?	A ¿Dónde **vive (usted)**?
B **Vivo** en Barcelona.	B **Vivo** en Edimburgo.
A ¿Cuántos años **tienes**?	A ¿Cuántos años **tiene (usted)**?
B **Tengo** 30 años.	B **Tengo** 55 años.

3d. Contesta a las siguientes preguntas y practica con tu compañero/a.
Answer the following questions and practise the conversations with your partner.

Informal	Formal
A. ¡Hola! ¿Cómo **te** llamas?	A. Buenas noches. ¿Cómo **se** llama (**usted**)?
B. ¿Qué tal? Me llamo _____	B. ¡Mucho gusto! Me llamo _____
A. ¿De dónde **eres**?	A. ¿De dónde **es** (**usted**)?
B. Soy de_____	B. Soy de_____
A. ¿Cuál es **tu** nacionalidad?	A. ¿Cuál es **su** nacionalidad?
B. Soy_____	B. Soy_____
A. ¿Dónde vives?	A. ¿Dónde **vive** (**usted**)**?**
B. Vivo en_____	B. Vivo en_____
A. ¿Cuántos años tienes?	A. ¿Cuántos años tiene (**usted**)?
B. Tengo_____ años.	B. Tengo_____ años.

3e. Completa los espacios vacíos con el verbo correcto.
Fill in the blanks with the appropriate verb forms.

1. Yo _____ (vivir) en Australia.
2. Tú _____ (ser) de Australia.
3. Usted _____ (vivir) en España.
4. Cristina _____ (querer) un café con leche y sin azúcar.
5. Mi amigo _____ (ser) polaco pero _____ (vivir) en Madrid.
6. Usted _____ (ser) italiano pero _____ (vivir) en París.
7. Laura _____ (tener) dieciocho años pero su amiga _____ (tener) diecinueve años.
8. Yo _____ (hablar) inglés pero usted _____ (hablar) español.

3f. Escribe en los espacios vacíos el adjetivo posesivo adecuado.
Fill in the blanks with the correct possessive adjective.

a. Este es _____ (*my*) amigo _____ (*his*) mujer se llama Carolina. Tienen una hija que se llama Carmen y _____ (*her*) novio se llama Juan.

b. ¿Qué tal? Jacinto, _____ (*my*) amiga se llama Raquel. ¿Cómo se llama _____ (*your informal*) amiga?

c. _____ (*my*) casa es _____ (*your formal*) casa pero _____ (*my*) dinero no es _____ (*your formal*) dinero.

d. María tiene veintiún años, _____ (*her*) amigo tiene veintidós años. ¿Cuántos años tienes tú?

e. _____ (*my*) hijo y _____ (*his*) mujer tienen un perro. _____ (*their*) perro se llama Tito.

f. _____ (*my*) número de teléfono es 077-89-56-60-38. ¿Cuál es _____ (*your informal*) número de teléfono?

GRAMÁTICA

¿Qué tal?	How are you? (informal)
¡Mucho gusto!	Pleased to meet you (formal).

mi	my
tu	your (*informal*)
su	your (*formal*)/his/her/their

3g. Cambia las siguientes frases al formal. Change the following sentences to the formal form.

1. Tú eres español de Madrid pero vives en Barcelona.
2. Eres estudiante de medicina y trabajas en un hospital.
3. Tengo treinta años. ¿Cuántos años tienes tú?
4. Nosotros siempre vamos de vacaciones a la playa. ¿Vosotros a dónde vais de vacaciones?
5. Toda mi familia vive en España. ¿Dónde vive tu familia?

4. LECTURA Y COMPRENSIÓN. READING COMPREHENSION.

4a. Lee los siguientes textos. Read the following texts.

LA COMIDA

En España

La cocina española es una de las más variadas del mundo. Los vinos españoles son unos de los más famosos del mundo; especialmente los vinos tintos como el rioja. Los platos más típicos son:

- -En el norte los platos de **pescado** y **mariscos** son los más populares.

- -En Asturias el plato típico es **la fabada.**
- -En Castilla **el cocido** y **los callos.**

- -En Andalucía **el gazpacho** (sopa fría de vegetales) es un buen plato para cuando hace mucho calor.

- -En Madrid y casi todo el país, **la paella** y **la tortilla** española son platos muy populares.

En Latinoamérica/Hispanoamérica

En países de Latinoamérica/Hispanoamérica la gastronomía es muy variada dependiendo de cada país. El maíz, los frijoles/las judías, el arroz y el tomate, la papa/patata y el tomate son unos de los alimentos principales de Latinoamérica.

- -En Guatemala y Venezuela, **los tamales** son muy populares.

- -En Cuba y Colombia, **el ajiaco** (verduras, pollo, pimienta y alcaparras) es un plato muy popular.

- -En Perú, **el cebiche** (pescado cocido en jugo de limón verde).

- -En México, **las enchiladas** y **los tacos** son muy famosos mundialmente. **El mole** (pollo en salsa de chocolate sin azúcar y con chile y especies).

- -En Argentina, **el asado/la barbacoa.**
- -En Chile, **las empanadas de carne**.

4b. Marca verdadero o falso enfrente de cada texto.
Indicate whether the following statements are true or false.

		V	F
1.	En Castilla el gazpacho (sopa fría de vegetales) es un buen plato para cuando hace mucho calor.		
2.	La paella y la tortilla española son platos muy populares en Perú.		
3.	En México el ajiaco es muy popular.		
4.	En el norte de España los platos de pescado y mariscos son los más populares.		
5.	En Argentina el plato típico es la fabada.		
6.	Las enchiladas y los tacos son platos típicos de México.		
7.	El maíz, los frijoles/las judías, el arroz y el tomate, la papa/patata y el tomate son unos de los alimentos principales de España.		
8.	En Guatemala y Venezuela los tamales son muy populares.		

5. VAMOS A ESCRIBIR. LET'S WRITE.

5a. Ve a la web y encuentra recetas de comida de algún país donde se habla español y elige algunos platos. Después ordénalos en la siguiente tabla.
Go to a website where you find recipes from a Spanish speaking country and select some dishes. Then arrange them in the following table.

De primero	De segundo	Postres

5b. ¿Cuáles son los platos más tradicionales de tu país?
What are the most traditional dishes of your country?

GRAMÁTICA

- **Artículos indefinidos.** Indefinite articles.

	Masculino	Femenino	
Singular	un	una	a/(an)
Plural	unos	unas	some

- **Pronombre «mí».** Pronoun "me".

- **Adjetivos posesivos.** Possesive adjectives.

Singular	Plural	
mi	mis	my
tu	tus	your (informal)
su	sus	your (formal)/his/her/their

- **Preposiciones: para, con, sin.** Prepositions: to/for, with, without.

- **El formal del presente de indicativo (singular) de los verbos: llamarse y ser.**
  Formal of present tense (singular) of verbs: to want, to be called, and to be.

	llamarse	to be called	ser	to be
yo	me llamo	I'm called	soy	I am
tú	te llamas	you're called	eres	you are
usted (formal)	se llama	you're called	es	you are
él/ella		he/she is called		is

- **Presente de indicativo de los verbos: vivir, tener y querer.**
  Present tense of the verbs: to live, to have and to want.

	vivir	to live	tener	to have	querer	to want
yo	vivo	I live	tengo	I have	quiero	I want
tú	vives	you live	tienes	you have	quieres	you want
usted (formal)	vive	you live (singular formal)	tiene	you have (singular formal)	quiere	you want (singular formal)
él/ella	vive	he/she lives	tiene	he/she has	quiere	he/she wants
nosotros/as	vivimos	we live	tenemos	we have	queremos	we want
vosotros/as	vivís	you live (plural informal)	tenéis	you have (plural informal)	queréis	you want (plural informal)
ustedes (formal)	viven	you live (plural formal)	tienen	you have (plural formal)	quieren	you want (plural formal)
ellos/ellas	viven	they live	tienen	they have	quieren	they want

- **Verbo haber.** To have/to be.

Hay	There is/are
¿Hay...?	Is/are there...?
¿Qué hay?	What is/are there?

EJERCICIOS

1. Escribe el artículo indeterminado correspondiente: un, una, unos o unas.
Write the corresponding indefinite articles: 'un', 'una', 'unos' or 'unas'.

1. _Un_ vino
2. _una_ cervezas
3. _un_ té
4. _una_ coca cola
5. _un_ zumo
6. _un_ whisky
7. _unos_ bocadillos
8. _unas_ tapas

2. Escribe «hay» o «quiero» en los espacios vacíos. Write: 'hay' or 'quiero' in the blanks.

1. No _hay_ bocadillos de jamón en el bar.
2. En el restaurante _hay_ platos muy deliciosos.
3. De primero yo _hay_ una ensalada.
4. ¿Qué tipo de tapas _quiero_ ?
5. Yo no _hay_ un chocolate, _hay_ un café con leche.

3. Mira el recuadro y escribe la palabra correspondiente en el espacio vacío.
Look at the box and fill in the blanks with the appropriate words.

son	hay	quieren	una	mí	hay	quiero	mí	cuánto	es	más	quiero

Camarero	**¿Qué (1) _quieren_ tomar los señores?**
Cliente 1	Yo (2) _quiero_ (3) _una_ cerveza por favor.
Camarero	**¿Algo (4) _mas_ ?**
Cliente 2	Para (5) _mí_ un café con leche. ¿(6) _quiero_ tapas?
Camarero	**Sí, sí (7) _quiero_ tortilla de patata, jamón, queso, patatas fritas, calamares y olivas.**
Cliente 2	Bueno. Yo (8) _hay_ tortilla de patata y queso.
Cliente 1	Para (9) _mí_ patatas fritas y olivas.
Camarero	**¿Algo más?**
Cliente 2	No, nada más. ¿(10) _Cuánto_ (11) _es_ ?
Camarero	**(12) _Son_ quince euros.**

4. Completa las siguientes oraciones con la forma correcta del verbo «querer».
Complete the next sentences with the correct form of the verb to want.

¿Qué _quiene_ tomar la señora?
Yo _quiero_ un café con leche por favor.
¿Qué _quiene_ tomar ella?
¿Tú qué _quieres_ tomar?
Nosotros _queremos_ tomar vino tinto.
¿Vosotros qué _queréis_ tomar?

5. Escribe en los espacios vacíos el verbo correcto. Fill in the blanks with the appropriate verb.

1. Usted ____vive____ (vivir) en Polonia.
2. Usted ____Es____ (ser) de Polonia.
3. Tú ____vives____ (vivir) en Inglaterra.
4. Mario ____quiero____ (querer) una cerveza fría.
5. Mi amiga __es__ (ser) brasileña pero __vive__ (vivir) en Madrid.
6. Usted __es__ (ser) escocés pero __vive__ (vivir) en Londres.
7. Lorenzo __Tiene__ (tener) 30 años pero su amigo __tienes__ (tener) 29.
8. Yo __Aprendo__ (aprender) inglés pero usted __aprendes__ (aprender) español.

6. Rellena los espacios vacíos con «mi» o «mí». Fill in the blanks with 'my' or 'me'.

1. Este es __mi__ amigo.
2. Para __mí__ un café con leche.
3. __Mi__ amiga se llama Marta.
4. Esta es __mi__ casa.
5. Para __mí__ un zumo de naranja.

7. Empareja las expresiones del español con el inglés.
   Match the words or sentences in Spanish with the English.

Español	English
1. por favor	a) there is/are 5
2. ¿Algo más?	b) crisps/chips 9
3. nada más	c) nothing else 3
4. bueno	d) Anything else? 2
5. hay	e) please 1
6. tortilla de patata	f) a/an 7
7. un/una	g) for me 8
8. para mí	h) well 4
9. patatas fritas	i) Spanish omelette 6

8. Rellena los espacios vacíos con el adjetivo posesivo correspondiente: mi, tu, o su.
   Fill in the blanks with the correct possessive adjective: **mi** (my)/**tu** (your informal)/**su** (your formal) or **su** (his/her/their).

1. ¡Hola! Soy Luis este es__mi__ amigo Juan, __su__ padre se llama Roberto y __su__ madre se llama María.
2. ¿Qué tal, Rosa? ¿Cómo se llama __tu__ perro?
3. Buenas tardes señorita García, este es __su__ escritorio.
4. ¡Hola Pedro! ¿Cuál es __tu__ teléfono móvil?
5. Buenos días señor. ¿Cuál es __su__ nombre por favor?
6. Mario y su mujer tienen un gato, __su__ gato se llama Toto.

VOCABULARIO

1. ¿QUÉ QUIERE TOMAR?	1. WHAT WOULD YOU LIKE TO EAT/DRINK?
bueno	well/good
camarero/a	waiter
cliente (m/f)	customer
gracias	thank you
grande	big
hay	there is/are
nada más	nothing else
para mí	for me
pequeña	small
por favor	please
pues…	well
tomar	to drink/to have
un/una	a/an
¿Algo más?	Anything else?
¿Cuánto es?	How much is it?
¿Hay…?	Is/Are there…?
¿Qué hay?	What is there?

Bebidas	Drinks
agua mineral (m) (con/sin gas)	mineral water (with/without gas)
azúcar (m)	sugar
café (m)	coffee
café con leche (m)	coffee with milk
café capuchino (m)	cappuccino
café latte (m)	coffee latte
café solo (m)	black coffee
cerveza (f)	beer
chocolate (m)	chocolate
copa de vino (f)	glass of wine
expreso (m)	espresso
fresa (f)	strawberry
gaseosa (f)	fizzy drink
hielo (m)	ice
infusión de limón (f)	lemon tea
manzana (f)	apple
manzanilla (f)	chamomile
naranja (f)	orange
refresco (m)	fizzy drink
té (m)	tea
tequila (m)	tequila
whisky (m)	whiskey(UK)/whisky(US)
zumo (m)	juice

TAPAS.	SNACKS/APPETIZERS.
atún	tuna
bocadillo	sandwich
calamares	squid
chorizo	chorizo sausage
empanadilla	pasty(UK)/empanada(US)
ensalada	salad
gambas	prawns
jamón	ham
nachos	nachos
olivas	olives
pan con ajo	bread with garlic
patatas bravas	potatoes with hot sauce
patatas fritas	chips
queso	cheese
ración de	portion of
salchichas	sausages
tortilla de patata	Spanish omelette

2. EN EL RESTAURANTE.	2. AT THE RESTAURANT.
arroz (m)	rice
arroz con leche (m)	rice pudding
bacalao (m)	cod
chuletas de cordero (fpl)	lamb chops
ensalada mixta (f)	mixed salad
flan (m)	flan
fruta del tiempo/día (f)	seasonal fruit
gazpacho (m)	gazpacho (cold soup)
helado (m)	ice cream
merluza asada (f)	grilled hake
paella (f)	paella
pescado frito (m)	fried fish
pollo asado (m)	roast chicken
postre (m)	dessert
primer plato (m)	first course
segundo plato (m)	second course
sopa de ajo (f)	garlic soup
verduras (fpl)	vegetables

3. INFORMAL O FORMAL.	3. INFORMAL OR FORMAL.
¡Mucho gusto!	Pleased to meet you (formal)
¿Qué tal?	How are you (informal)

5 MI FAMILIA

TEMAS TOPICS	OBJETIVOS COMUNICATIVOS COMMUNICATIVE OBJECTIVES	GRAMÁTICA GRAMMAR
La familia. El estado civil. El árbol genealógico.	**Pedir y dar información sobre tu familia.** Asking and giving information about your family. **Aprender el vocabulario de la familia.** Learning family vocabulary. **Explicar el árbol genealógico de tu familia utilizando la gramática adecuada.** Describing your family tree using the appropriate grammar. **El uso de los plurales.** Using plurals.	**Artículos determinados: el/la/los/las.** Definite article: the. **Pronombres personales sujeto: yo, tú (informal), usted (formal), él/ella, nosotros/as, vosotros/as, ustedes (formal), ellos/ellas.** Subject personal pronouns: I, you, he/she, we, you (plural informal), you (plural formal), they. **Presente de indicativo de los verbos: llamarse, vivir, tener, ser/estar (3ª persona del singular).** Conjugation in the present tense of the verbs: to be called, to live, to have, to be (3rd person singular). **Las formas del plural.** Plurals forms. **Interrogativos. ¿Cómo? ¿Quién? ¿Cuántos/as?** Interrogatives: What? Who? How many?

1. LA FAMILIA. THE FAMILY.

Audio 31

1a. Escucha, lee y repite. Listen, read and repeat.

Masculino	Femenino	Plural
padre	madre	padres
hermano	hermana	hermanos
hijo	hija	hijos
marido (esposo)	mujer (esposa)	matrimonio
abuelo	abuela	abuelos
nieto	nieta	nietos
tío	tía	tíos
sobrino	sobrina	sobrinos
primo	prima	primos
novio	novia	novios
amigo	amiga	amigos
soltero	soltera	solteros
casado	casada	casados

1b. Practica con tu compañero/a. Practise with your partner.

Estudiante A. ¿Cómo se llama tu **padre**?
Estudiante B. Mi **padre** se llama **Juan**.

Estudiante A. **¿Cómo se llama tu** [   ]
Estudiante B. **Mi** [   ] **se llama** [   ]

Practica con tu compañero/a. Practise with your partner.

- ¿Cómo se llama tu [   ]
- ¿Cuántos años tiene?
- ¿Dónde vive?
- ¿Cuál es su profesión?

1c. Practica con tu compañero/a. Practise with your partner.

- ¿Tienes **hermanos/hijos…**?
- ¿Cómo se llaman?
- ¿Dónde viven?
- ¿Cuántos años tienen?
- ¿Cuál es su profesión? / ¿Qué hacen?

¡DESCUBRE!	
soy hijo/a único/a	I'm an only child
mayor	older
menor	younger
no tengo	I do not have
está muerto/a	he/she is dead

Audio 32

1c. Escucha y escribe en los espacios vacíos la palabra adecuada.
Listen and fill in the blanks with the right word.

Esta es mi familia. Mi (1) _____ se llama Luis.
Tengo tres (2) _____ un (3) _____ y
dos (4) _____. Mi (5) _____ (6)
_____ se llama Marisa. Mi segunda (7) _____ se
llama Cristina y mi (8) _____ (9) _____ se
llama Rita. Mi (10) _____ tiene tres años y se llama
Daniel.

Audio 33

MÁS VOCABULARIO

amigo/amiga: friend
suegro: father-in-law
suegra: mother-in-law
cuñado: brother-in-law
cuñada: sister-in-law
yerno: son-in-law
nuera: daughter-in-law
pareja: partner

medio hermano: half-brother
media hermana: half-sister
padrastro: stepfather
madrastra: stepmother
hermanastro: stepbrother
hermanastra: stepsister
gato/a: cat
perro/a: dog

1d. Empareja las expresiones del español con el inglés.
Match the Spanish expressions with the English ones.

1. **hermano**   a) grandmother
2. **hija**   b) sister
3. **abuelo**   c) husband
4. **sobrino**   d) uncle
5. **padre**   e) wife
6. **nieta**   f) mother
7. **novia**   g) son
8. **marido/esposo**   h) brother
9. **tío**   i) girlfriend

10. **madre**   j) nephew
11. **sobrina**   k) granddaughter
12. **tía**   l) boyfriend
13. **mujer**   m) grandfather
14. **hijo**   n) daughter
15. **abuela**   ñ) father
16. **nieto**   o) aunt
17. **hermana**   p) grandson
18. **novio**   q) niece

GRAMÁTICA

	Singular	Plural
yo I	**mi** ...my	**mis**...my
tú ....you singular informal	**tu**....your (singular informal)	**tus**....your (plural informal)
usted ....you singular formal	**su**....your (singular formal)	**sus**....your (plural formal)
él/ella ...he/she	**su**....his/her/their	**sus**....his/her/their

1e. Escribe en los espacios vacíos el adjetivo posesivo correspondiente.
Fill in the blanks with the appropriate possessive adjective.

1. Este es _____ (*my*) hijo, _____ (*his*) novia se llama María.
2. Mario y Luis son _____ (*their*) primos.
3. _____ (*my*) tío Javier es piloto y _____ (*his*) mujer es dentista.
4. _____ (*your informal*) tía tiene 55 años y _____ (*her*) marido tiene 50 años.
5. ¿Tiene usted _____ (*your formal*) carnet de identidad señora?
6. _____ (*my*) hermano se llama Luis. ¿Cómo se llama _____ (*your informal*) hermano?
7. _____ (*my*) hijo está casado, _____ (*his*) mujer se llama Jacinta y _____ (*his*) hija se llama Laura.
8. Juana y Alberto no están casados pero tienen dos hijos. _____ (*their*) hijos se llaman Ricardo y Luis.
9. ¿Tiene usted _____ (*your formal*) pasaporte señor González?
10. _____ (*my*) sobrinos viven en Barcelona. ¿Dónde viven _____ (*your plural informal*) sobrinos?

Audio 34

2. MI FAMILIA. MY FAMILY.

2a. Escucha, lee y subraya los verbos en el texto de abajo.
Listen, read and underline the verbs in the text below.

¡Hola! <u>Soy</u> **Isabel**. Mi familia es muy grande. Tengo siete hermanos: cinco hermanos y dos hermanas. Mis padres son José y María. Mi padre es abogado jubilado y tiene noventa años, mi madre es ama de casa y pintora. Ella tiene ochenta y siete años. Estoy casada. Mi marido se llama Roberto, tiene cincuenta y cinco años y es ingeniero. Tenemos tres hijas y dos nietos. Mis hijas se llaman: Alma, Rita y Verónica. Mi hija mayor está casada, su marido se llama Luis y es gerente de una compañía. Ellos tienen dos hijos, su hija que se llama Paz y su hijo que se llama David. Mi hija menor está casada también, su marido se llama Bruno y es administrador en una academia. Mi segunda hija Rita está soltera y es investigadora.

Esta soy yo

Esta soy yo

2b. Mi árbol genealógico. My family tree.

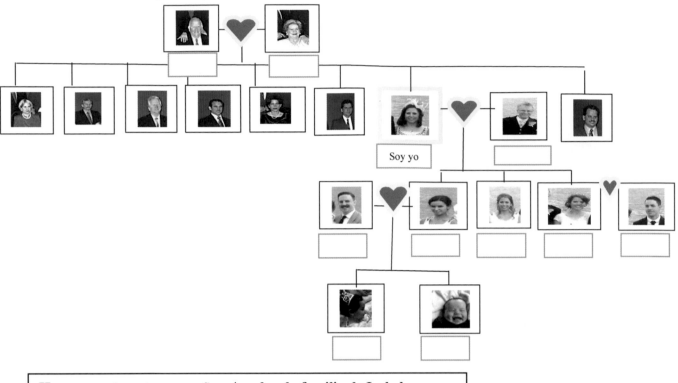

Soy yo

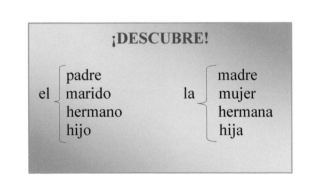

Haz preguntas a tu compañero/a sobre la familia de Isabel:

- nombre
- nacionalidad
- profesión
- estado civil
- edad

Ejemplo:

¿Cómo se llama el marido de Isabel?
¿Cómo se llaman los padres de Isabel?
¿Cómo se llama la hija mayor de Isabel?
¿Cómo se llaman los nietos de Isabel?

GRAMÁTICA

está/es casado/a	he/she is married
está/es soltero/a	he/she is single
el padre de David	David's father
son	they are
tienen	they have

¡DESCUBRE!

el	padre marido hermano hijo	la	madre mujer hermana hija

2c. Dibuja tu árbol genealógico. Draw your family tree.

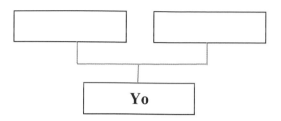

2d. Comparte con tus compañeros/as de clase tu árbol de la familia. Debes de incluir para cada miembro de la familia lo siguiente: nombre, profesión, edad y estado civil.
Share with your classmates your family tree. You must include the following for each family member: name, profession, age and marital status.

Ejemplo:
Mi hermano se llama Jacinto, es estudiante de filosofía. Tiene veinte años y está soltero.

3. LOS FAMILIARES. THE RELATIVES.

3a. Escribe el nombre del familiar correspondiente.
Write the name of the corresponding relative.

1. El hijo de mi mujer es mi ___hijo___
2. La madre de mi hijo es mi ___mujer___
3. El abuelo de mi hijo es mi ___padre.___
4. La hermana de mi hijo es mi ___hija___
5. La madre de mi madre es mi ___abuela___
6. El hijo de mi madre es mi ___hermano___

> **GRAMÁTICA**
>
> **el/la/los/las**…the

3b. Traduce al inglés las siguientes frases. Translate the following phrases into English.

1. El padre de Juan se llama Pedro. ....
2. La madre de María se llama Carolina. ....
3. Los nietos se llaman Raquel y Jaime. ....
4. La sobrina de Carlos se llama Lola. ....
5. El hijo de Antonio se llama Vicente. ....

3c. Cambia las siguientes frases de singular al plural.
Change the following sentences from singular to plural.

1. El hermano es doctor. ....
2. Mi padre vive en Madrid. ....
3. La abuela es española. ....
4. Tu amigo es estudiante. ....
5. Su nieto tiene 10 años. ....

GRAMÁTICA

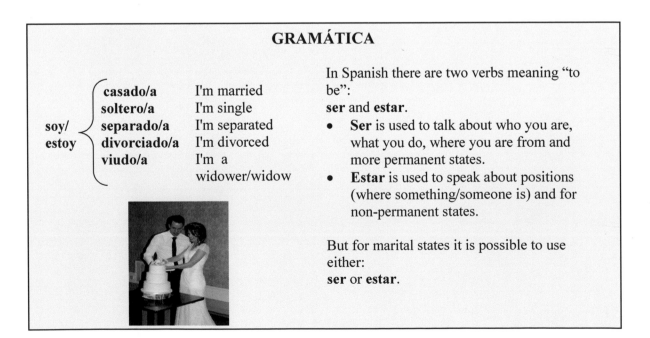

soy/ estoy	casado/a	I'm married
	soltero/a	I'm single
	separado/a	I'm separated
	divorciado/a	I'm divorced
	viudo/a	I'm a widower/widow

In Spanish there are two verbs meaning "to be":
ser and **estar**.
- **Ser** is used to talk about who you are, what you do, where you are from and more permanent states.
- **Estar** is used to speak about positions (where something/someone is) and for non-permanent states.

But for marital states it is possible to use either:
ser or **estar**.

3d. Escribe el verbo correcto (soy, eres, es, estoy, estás o está).
Fill in the blanks with the correct form of 'to be'.

1. (Yo) _____ Pedro. _____ arquitecto y _____ casado.
2. (Tú) _____ Rosa. _____ música y _____ soltera.
3. (Él) _____ Javier. _____ electricista y _____ divorciado.
4. (Ella) _____ Raquel. _____ profesora jubilada y _____ viuda.

3e. Escribe el adjetivo posesivo correspondiente.
Write the corresponding possessive adjectives.

1. _____ (*my*) marido se llama Javier.
2. Soy casada y _____ (*my*) hijos se llaman Leo y Luna.
3. Mónica es mi hermana está casada y _____ (*her*) hija se llama Antonella.
4. Eduardo, Mónica y Salma son _____ (*my*) hermanos.
5. Mi padre tiene otra hija con su nueva pareja. _____ (*his*) hija se llama Salma.

3f. Muestra una foto o dibujo de tu familia a tu compañero/a. Explica: nombre, nacionalidad, profesión y edad de cada uno de tus familiares.
Show a picture or drawing of your family to your partner. Explain: name, nationality, profession and age of your relatives.

4. LECTURA Y COMPRENSIÓN. READING COMPREHENSION.

4a. Lee el siguiente texto sobre Penélope Cruz y dibuja su árbol genealógico.
Read the following text about Penélope Cruz and draw her family tree.

Me llamo Penélope Cruz Sánchez. Soy española pero vivo en España y Estados Unidos. Soy actriz. Estoy casada. Mi marido se llama Javier Bardem también es español y es actor. Tenemos dos hijos: mi hijo mayor se llama Leo Bardem Cruz y mi hija se llama Luna Bardem Cruz. Mis padres se llaman Eduardo Cruz y Encarna Sánchez, ellos están divorciados. Tengo 3 hermanos en total y yo soy la mayor de todos. Dos hermanos de parte de mis padres; un hermano y una hermana que se llaman Eduardo y Mónica y una media hermana de parte de mi padre y su pareja Carmen que se llama Salma. Mónica mi hermana menor es madre soltera y tiene una hija que se llama Antonella, mi sobrina.

4b. Lee el siguiente texto sobre Plácido Domingo y cambia la gramática a la 3ª persona del singular.
Read the following text about Plácido Domingo and change the verbs to the 3rd person singular.

Me llamo Plácido Domingo Embil. Soy español de Madrid pero vivo en México desde muy niño. Soy cantante de ópera, compositor, productor y director de orquesta. Tengo ochenta y tres años. Estoy casado. Mi mujer se llama Marta Ornelas, tiene 79 años y es mexicana de Veracruz. Es cantante de ópera y ama de casa. Tengo tres hijos y tres nietos. Mis hijos son mexicanos. Mis hermanos son españoles y viven en España. Mis padres están muertos.

4c. Lee el siguiente texto y contesta a las preguntas en español.
Read the next text and answer the questions.

ESTA ES MI AMIGA SHONA

Esta es mi amiga Shona. Es escocesa de Glasgow. Es dentista. Tiene 40 años. Está casada y tiene tres hijas. Su marido se llama Alan. Es inglés y tiene 46 años. También es dentista. Sus hijas se llaman Clare, Alison y Helen. Shona vive en un pueblo pequeño en las afueras de Londres. Habla inglés y español. Trabaja en una universidad como profesora y también trabaja en un barco clínica como dentista voluntaria para «Amazon Hope» en Perú. Viaja dos veces al año a Perú y trabaja en un barco clínica que navega por el Río Amazonas visitando todos los pueblitos cerca del río ya que la carretera no llega a estos pueblos. Junto con su marido ha fundado una caridad que se llama Esperanza la cual ayuda al pueblo de Iquitos que está en la selva de Perú.

1. ¿Cuál es su nacionalidad?
2. ¿Está casada o soltera?
3. ¿Cuál es su profesión? ¿Dónde trabaja?
4. ¿Cuántas hijas tiene y cómo se llaman?
5. ¿Qué idiomas habla?
6. ¿Cómo se llama su marido y cuál es su nacionalidad?
7. ¿Cuál es la profesión de su marido?
8. ¿Cómo se llama el pueblo dónde trabaja en Perú?
9. ¿Cómo se llama la caridad que han fundado?
10. ¿Cuántos años tienen Shona y su marido?

> **¡DESCUBRE!**
>
> **Han fundado.** They have founded.

5. VAMOS A ESCRIBIR. LET'S WRITE.

5a. Escribe un texto sobre tu persona y sobre tu familia. Incluye: nombre, nacionalidad, profesión, edad, estado civil y lugar de residencia de cada uno de tus familiares.
Write a paragraph about yourself and your family. Include: name, nationality, profession, age and the place of residence of each of your relatives.

5b. Busca en la web un personaje famoso y escribe sobre él/ella y su familia. Tienes que incluir: nombre, nacionalidad, profesión, edad, estado civil y lugar de residencia y familia. Look on the web for a famous person and write about him/her and his/her family. You have to include: name, nationality, profession, age, marital status and place of residence and family.

GRAMÁTICA

- **Artículos determinados**. Definite articles.

	Singular	Plural	
Masculino	el	los	the
Femenino	la	las	the

- **Los plurales.** The plural forms.
  El hermano **es** alto.
  Los hermanos **son** alto**s**.
  La hermana **es** bonita.
  Las hermanas **son** bonita**s.**

- **Interrogativos.** Interrogatives.
  ¿Cómo? (What?) **¿Quién?** (Who?) / **¿Cuántos/as?** (How many?)

- **Pronombres personales sujeto.** Subject pronouns.

Pronombres personales sujeto	Subject pronouns
Singular	Singular
yo	I
tú	you (singular informal)
usted	you (singular formal)
él	he
ella	she

Pronombres personales sujeto	Subject pronouns
Plural	Plural
nosotros/nosotras	we
vosotros/vosotras	you (plural informal)
ustedes	you (plural formal)
ellos	they
ellas	they

- **Adjetivos posesivos.** Possessive Adjectives.

Pronombres personales sujeto	Singular	Plural
yo	**mi** (my)	**mis** (my)
tú	**tu** (yours informal)	**tus** (yours informal)
usted	***su** (yours formal)	**sus** (yours formal)
él	***su** (his)	**sus** (his)
ella	***su** (her)	**sus** (her)

> ***Su** can mean your formal, his, her, or their. The exact meaning is usually clear from the context

- **Concordancia del adjetivo con el sustantivo en género y número.** Agreement of the adjective with the noun in gender and number.
  Ejemplo: Mi hijo/a es muy alto/a. My son/daughter is very tall.

- **Presente de indicativo del verbo vivir.** Present tense of verb to live.

	vivir	to live
yo	**vivo**	I live
tú (informal)	**vives**	you live
usted (formal)	**vive**	you live
él/ella	**vive**	he/she lives
nosotros/as	**vivimos**	we live
vosotros/as (informal)	**vivís**	you live
ustedes (formal)	**viven**	you live
ellos/ellas	**viven**	they live

- **Llamarse.** To be called.

	llamarse	to be called
yo	**me** llamo	I am called/My name is
tú (informal)	**te** llamas	You are called/Your name is
usted (formal)	**se** llama	You are called/Your name is
él/ella	**se** llama	He/she is called/His/her name is
nosotros/as	**nos llam**amos	We are called/Our name is
vosotros/as (informal)	**os llam**áis	You are called/Your name is
ustedes (formal)	**se llam**an	They are called/Your name is
ellos/ellas	**se llam**an	They are called/Their name is

- **Presente de indicativo del verbo irregular tener.** Present tense of the irregular Spanish verb to have.

	tener	to have
yo	tengo	I have
tú (informal)	tienes	you have
usted (formal)	tiene	you have
él/ella	tiene	he/she has
nosotros/as	tenemos	we have
vosotros/as (informal)	tenéis	you have
ustedes (formal)	tienen	you have
ellos/ellas	tienen	they have

- **Ser/estar.** To be.

  In Spanish there are two verbs meaning "to be": **ser** and **estar**.

  - **Ser** is used to talk about who you are, what you do, where you are from and more permanent states.
  - **Estar** is used to speak about positions (where something/someone is) and for non-permanent states.

But for marital states it is possible to use either: **ser** or **estar**.

soy/ estoy
- **casado/a** — I'm married
- **soltero/a** — I'm single
- **separado/a** — I'm separated
- **divorciado/a** — I'm divorced
- **viudo/a** — I'm a widower/widow

  o **Ser** is used to talk about who you are, what you do, where you are from and more.

	ser	estar	to be
yo	**soy**	**estoy**	I am
tú (informal)	**eres**	**estás**	you are
usted (formal)	**es**	**está**	you are
él/ella	**es**	**está**	he/she is
nosotros/as	**somos**	**estamos**	we are
vosotros/as (informal)	**sois**	**estáis**	you are
ustedes (formal)	**son**	**están**	you are
ellos/ellas	**son**	**están**	they are

EJERCICIOS

1. Escribe el pronombre personal sujeto correspondiente. Write the corresponding subject pronoun.

a) _____ son el señor González y la señora Ríos.
b) _____ es escocesa.
c) _____ son estudiantes de arte.
d) _____ somos ingleses.
e) _____ soy psicólogo.
f) _____ sois los amigos de Juan.
g) _____ es profesor.

2. Escribe el artículo determinado correspondiente: el, la, los y las.
Write the corresponding definite article in Spanish (the).

1. _____ hermano
2. _____ padres
3. _____ sobrina
4. _____ prima
5. _____ nietas

6. _____ tío
7. _____ abuelo
8. _____ hijos
9. _____ madre
10. _____ novios

3. Escribe el adjetivo posesivo correspondiente. Write the corresponding possessive adjective.

a) Esta es_____ (1. *my*) amiga, _____ (2. *her*) novio se llama Mario. Mario tiene dos hermanos. _____ (3. *his*) hermanos son estudiantes.
b) _____ (1. *my*) primo Jorge es pintor y _____(2. *his*) pareja es profesora.
c) _____ (1. *our*) vecina tiene 80 años y _____ (2. *her*) marido tiene 79 años.
d) ¿Tiene usted _____ (*your formal*) pasaporte señor López?
e) Estos son _____ (1. *my*) primos, _____ (2. *their*) amigos se llaman José y Lupe.
f) _____ (1. *your informal*) tía tiene dos hijas._____ (2. *their*) nombres son Marisol y Laura.
g) Señora Ramos ¿Cuántos años tiene _____ (*your formal*) hija?
h) Todos _____ (*my*) amigos tienen novia exepto yo.
i) _____ (*my*) abuelos se llaman Sara y Carlos.

4. Escribe el verbo correspondiente en el espacio vacío.
Write the corresponding verb in empty space.

	llamarse	vivir	tener	ser	estar
yo	me llamo	vivo	tengo		
tú (informal)			tienes	eres	
usted (formal)	se llama	vive			está
él/ella					
nosotros/as	nos llamamos	vivimos	tenemos	somos	
vosotros/as (informal)					estáis
ustedes (formal)	se llaman	viven		son	
ellos/ellas			tienen		están

5a. Lee el siguiente texto sobre la vida de Mario y marca verdadero o falso enfrente de cada frase. Read the following text about Mario's life. Tick true or false.

Soy Mario. Soy español de Sevilla, pero vivo en Italia. Mi familia es muy grande. Tengo cuatro hermanos: dos hermanos y dos hermanas. Mis padres son españoles y viven en Sevilla. Mi padre se llama Luis y es doctor jubilado, mi madre se llama María y es ama de casa. Mi hermana mayor, tiene cincuenta y cinco años y es doctora. Mi hermano menor, tiene cuarenta y ocho años y es contable. Toda mi familia vive en España excepto yo. Vivo en Florencia Italia. Estoy casado. Mi mujer se llama Margarita, tiene cincuenta y cuatro años y es profesora de primaria. Tenemos tres hijos y dos nietos. Mis hijos se llaman Antonio, Raquel y Vicente. Mi hijo mayor está casado y tiene dos hijos. Su mujer se llama Juana y sus hijos se llaman Pablo y Ricardo. Mi hijo menor está casado, su mujer es colombiana y se llama Rosa. No tienen hijos todavía. Mi segunda hija se llama Raquel y está soltera. Vive en Madrid y es estudiante de medicina.

		V	F
1.	Soy Mario, soy español de Sevilla pero vivo en Madrid.		
2.	Mi familia es muy grande. Tengo ocho hermanos: dos hermanos y seis hermanas.		
3.	Mi hermana mayor tiene cincuenta y cinco años y es doctora.		
4.	Vivo en Florencia. Mi mujer se llama Margarita y tiene cincuenta y cuatro años.		
5.	Tenemos tres nietos y dos hijos.		
6.	Mi mujer se llama Margarita, tiene cincuenta y cuatro años y es profesora de primaria.		
7.	Mi hijo mayor está divorciado y tiene dos hijos.		
8.	Mi hijo menor está casado, su mujer es argentina y se llama Rosa.		
9.	Mi segunda hija se llama Raquel, es soltera y vive en Barcelona.		
10.	Raquel es estudiante de medicina.		

5b. Dibuja el árbol genealógico de Mario. Draw Mario's family tree.

5c. Trae una foto de la familia para la próxima clase.
Bring a photo of your family for the next class.

VOCABULARIO

1. MI FAMILIA — *1 MY FAMILY*

abuela	*grandmother*	perro/a	*dog*
abuelo	*grandfather*	primo/a	*cousin*
abuelos	*grandparents*	primos	*male cousins/male and female cousins*
amigo/a	*friend*		
amigos	*male friends/male and female friends*	sobrina	*niece*
		sobrino	*nephew*
casado/a	*married man/woman*	sobrinos	*nephews/nephews and nieces*
casados	*married men/married*		
cuñada	*sister-in-law*	soltero/a	*single man/woman*
cuñado	*brother-in-law*	solteros	*single men/single men and women*
esposa	*wife*		
esposo	*husband*	suegra	*mother-in-law*
gato/a	*cat*	suegro	*father-in-law*
hermana	*sister*	suegros	*parents-in-law*
hermanastra	*stepsister*	tía	*aunt*
hermanastro	*stepbrother*	tío	*uncle*
hermano	*brother*	tíos	*uncles/uncles and aunts*
hermanos	*brothers/siblings*		
hija	*daughter*	yerno	*son-in-law*
hijo	*son*		
hijos	*sons/children*		
madrastra	*stepmother*	**2. El ÁRBOL GENEALÓGICO**	**2. FAMILY TREE**
madre	*mother*		
marido	*husband*		
matrimonio	*married couple*	árbol (m)	*tree*
mayor	*older*	casado/a	*married*
media hermana	*half-sister*	divorciado/a	*divorced*
medio hermano	*half-brother*	estado civil (m)	*marital status*
menor	*younger*	familia (f)	*family*
muerto/a	*dead*	gerente (m/f)	*manager*
mujer	*wife/woman*	mayor	*older*
nieta	*granddaughter*	menor	*younger*
nieto	*grandson*	separado/a	*separated*
nietos	*male grandchildren/grandchildren*	viudo/a	*widower/widow*
novia	*girlfriend*	¿Cuántos hermanos tienes?	*How many brothers/siblings do you have?*
novio	*boyfriend*		
novios	*boyfriends/boyfriends and girlfriends*	¿Cuántos hijos tienes?	*How many sons/children do you have?*
nuera	*daughter-in-law*		
padrastro	*stepfather*		
padre	*father*		
padres	*parents*		
pareja	*partner*		

6 DESCRIPCIONES

TEMAS TOPICS	OBJETIVOS COMUNICATIVOS COMMUNICATIVE OBJECTIVES	GRAMÁTICA GRAMMAR
Descripciones físicas. **La personalidad.** **Descripciones de objetos.** **Los colores.**	**Describir el aspecto físico de las personas.** Describing people's physical appearance. **Describir el carácter.** Describing character. **Describir objetos.** Describing objects. **Aprender los colores.** Learning about colours. **Hablar en plural.** Talking in plural form.	**Adjetivos calificativos: bonito/a, inteligente…** Qualifying adjectives: pretty, intelligent… **Concordancia del adjetivo con el sustantivo en género y número: El chico/a es muy alto/a.** Agreement of the adjective with the noun in gender and number: The boy/girl is very tall. **Presente de indicativo (1ª, 2ª, y 3ª persona singular) de los verbos: ser, tener y llevar.** Present tense (1st, 2nd and 3rd person singular) of verbs: to be, to have, to wear. **Los plurales.** Plural form. **Cuantificadores: muy y bastante.** Quantifiers: very and quite. **Comparativos** Comparatives. **Superlativos.** Superlatives. **Interrogativos: ¿Cómo?** Interrogatives: What?

1. ¿CÓMO ERES? WHAT DO YOU LOOK LIKE?

CITA A CIEGAS. BLIND DATE.

Escucha la siguiente conversación y contesta a las preguntas junto con toda la clase.
Listen to the following conversation and answers the questions together with all the class.

María	**Rin, rin, rin.**
Pablo	Dígame.
María	**¿Está Pablo?**
Pablo	Sí soy yo. ¿Quién es?
María	**Soy María, la chica que quieres conocer.**
Pablo	Sí, sí quiero conocerte. ¿Cómo eres?
María	**Soy morena, alta y delgada. Tengo el pelo largo, moreno y liso. Tengo los ojos marrones y llevo gafas. Soy simpática y trabajadora. Tengo 25 años. ¿Y tú? ¿Cómo eres?**
Pablo	Pues, yo soy bajo y rubio. No soy gordo ni delgado. Tengo el pelo corto, rubio y rizado. Tengo los ojos verdes. No llevo gafas pero llevo bigote. Soy simpático y organizado. Tengo 26 años. ¿Dónde quedamos?
María	**En el Bar Pepe.**
Pablo	Vale. ¿Qué día? y ¿A qué hora quedamos?
María	**Este sábado a las nueve de la noche.**
Pablo	Estupendo, quedamos en el Bar Pepe este sábado a las nueve de la noche.
María	**Hasta el sábado.**
Pablo	Adiós.

> 1. ¿Cómo es María?
> 2. ¿Cómo es Pablo?

1a. Escucha y repite los siguientes adjetivos sobre descripciones físicas.
Listen and repeat the following adjectives about physical descriptions.

Descripciones físicas.

moreno/a	dark
muy moreno/a	very dark
negro/a	black
blanco/a	white
rubio/a	blond
pelirrojo/a	ginger
guapo/a	handsome/pretty
bonito/a	pretty
feo/a	ugly
alto/a	tall
bajo/a	short/small
gordo/a	fat
delgado/a	thin
joven	young
adulto/a	adult
viejo/a	old
mayor	old

Descripciones de personalidad.

simpático/a _____	**antipático/a**
trabajador(a) _____	**perezoso/a**
organizado/a _____	**desorganizado/a**
optimista _____	**pesimista**
inteligente _____	**tonto/a**
independiente ____	**dependiente**

¡DESCUBRE!

muy	very
un poco	a bit/little
No soy <u>gordo/a</u> ni	I'm not fat nor
<u>delgado/a</u>	thin

85

¿Y tú? ¿Cómo eres?
And you? What do you look like?

¡Hola! Me llamo Enrique Iglesias. Soy cantante. Soy español de Madrid pero vivo en Florida. Soy muy alto, guapo, moreno y joven. Soy simpático, optimista, trabajador e inteligente. Estoy soltero. Tengo cuarenta y un años.

1b. Contesta a las preguntas y practica con tu compañero/a.
Answer the questions and practise with your partner.

- o ¿Cómo te llamas?
- o ¿De dónde eres?
- o ¿Cuál es tu profesión? / ¿Qué haces?
- o ¿Estás casado/a o soltero/a?
- o ¿Tienes familia?
- o ¿Cómo eres? (What do you look like?)

1c. Lee el siguiente texto sobre Shakira y su pareja y subraya los verbos.
Read the following text about Shakira and her partner and underline the verbs.

¡Hola! Soy Shakira, soy cantante, escritora y bailarina. Soy colombiana de Barranquilla. Soy baja, rubia, guapa y organizada. Soy muy trabajadora y simpática. Tengo 39 años. Estoy soltera pero tengo pareja. Tengo dos hijos.

Este es Gerardo, es mi pareja. Es futbolista. Es español de Barcelona. Es alto, moreno y guapo. Es simpático, optimista y un poco desorganizado. Tiene 30 años.

1d. Lee los siguientes textos y contesta a las preguntas.
Read the following texts and answer the questions.

Esta es mi amiga Margarita, es argentina de Buenos Aires. Es estudiante de docencia. Tiene 24 años. Es guapa, baja, morena, simpática y trabajadora. Está soltera.

Este es mi amigo Carlos. Es español de Sevilla. Es estudiante de medicina. Tiene 25 años. Es muy alto, moreno y delgado. Es inteligente y optimista. Está soltero.

	Carlos	Margarita
¿De dónde es?		
¿Cuál es su profesión?		
¿Cuántos años tiene?		
¿Está soltero/a o casado/a?		
¿Cómo es? (What does he/she look like?)		

1e. Escribe un texto similar donde hablas sobre ti mismo/a, otro sobre un amigo y otro sobre una amiga. Después compártelos con tus compañeros/as. Write a paragraph about yourself, about a male friend and about a female friend and then share them with your classmates.

2. TENGO. I HAVE.

Audio 37

2a. Escucha y repite. Listen and repeat.

Tengo el pelo

Color	Textura	
negro/moreno	liso	Straight
castaño brown	rizado	curly
rubio	ondulado	wavy
pelirrojo	largo	Long
blanco/canoso	corto	Short

Tengo el pelo **castaño** y mi gato tiene el pelo **negro.**

Tengo los ojos …

- verdes
- negros
- marrones o cafés
- azules
- de color miel

GRAMÁTICA		
	tener	to have
yo	tengo	I have
tú	tienes	you (informal) have
usted	tiene	you (formal) have
él/ella	tiene	he/she has

2b. Relaciona las siguientes frases con las fotografías.
Match the following statements with photographs.

A. Tengo el pelo liso, negro y largo.
B. Tengo el pelo liso, pelirrojo y corto.
C. Tengo el pelo moreno, liso y muy corto.
D. No tengo pelo. Soy calvo.
E. Tengo el pelo rubio y liso. No tengo el pelo ni largo ni corto.
F. Tengo el pelo rizado, largo y negro.

> **¡DESCUBRE!**
> **No tengo pelo.**
> **Soy calvo/a.**

> ¡Hola! Me llamo Paula. Soy morena, delgada y guapa. Soy simpática, optimista y trabajadora. Tengo el pelo moreno, largo y ondulado. Tengo los ojos negros. ¿Y tú? ¿Cómo eres?

2c. Escribe un texto similar al ejemplo de arriba sobre ti mismo/a y compártelo con tus compañeros/as. Write a similar paragraph, like the example above of Paula, about yourself and share it with your classmates.

3. LLEVO. I WEAR

Audio 38

Escucha y repite. Listen and repeat.

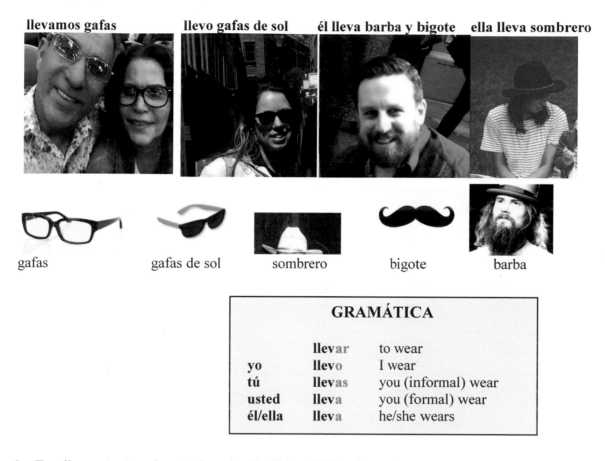

llevamos gafas   **llevo gafas de sol**   **él lleva barba y bigote**   **ella lleva sombrero**

gafas   gafas de sol   sombrero   bigote   barba

GRAMÁTICA

	llevar	to wear
yo	**llevo**	I wear
tú	**llevas**	you (informal) wear
usted	**lleva**	you (formal) wear
él/ella	**lleva**	he/she wears

3a. Escribe un texto sobre tu descripción física. Utiliza los verbos del recuadro.
Write a paragraph about your physical description. Use the verbs in the box.

¿Cómo eres? (What do you look like?)   **ser tener llevar**

**3b. Escribe un párrafo donde describes dos miembros de tu familia un hombre y una mujer.
Utiliza los verbos del recuadro.** Write a paragraph describing two members of
your family, a man and a woman. Use the verbs in the box.

ser tener llevar

¿Cómo es él/ella? (What does he/she look like?)

89

3c. Piensa en una persona famosa. No digas su nombre. Tu compañero/a te va a hacer preguntas, solamente puedes contestar sí o no. Think of a famous person. Do not say his/her name. Your partner will ask you questions. You can only answer yes or no.

- o ¿Es hombre?
- o ¿Lleva bigote?
- o ¿Es mujer?
- o ¿Tiene el pelo largo?
- o ¿Tiene el pelo corto?
- o ¿Es blanco/a?
- o ¿Es negro/a?
- o ¿Tiene los ojos verdes?
- o ¿Lleva gafas?

> **Ejemplo**:
>
> A: ¿Es hombre?
> B: Si.
> A: ¿Lleva bigote?
> B: No
> …
> B: ¿Quién es él?

Audio 39

3d. Escucha el correo electrónico que Laura manda a su amiga Rosa y escribe el nombre de cada amigo. Listen to the email Laura sent to her friend, Rosa, and write the name of each friend.

1 **2** **3** **4**

1…………………………………………………

2………………………………………………..

3………………………………………………...

4…………………………………………………

Audio 40

3e. Escucha y rellena la siguiente ficha con los datos que se piden.
Listen and fill in the form below with the information requested.

Nombre(s) _____
Apellidos _____
Nacionalidad _____ Edad _____ años.
Profesión _____
Teléfono _____ Teléfono móvil _____
Dirección:
    Calle _____
    Número _____
    Ciudad _____ Código postal _____
    País _____
Correo electrónico _____
Breve descripción física _____

4. ¿CÓMO ES? HOW IS IT?

Audio 41

4a. Relaciona las frases con las fotografías. Match the sentences with the pictures.

1. El centro comercial es moderno, grande y bonito.
2. El sofá es nuevo, grande y azul.
3. El faro es blanco, pequeño, bonito y antiguo.
4. La casa es moderna, nueva y grande.
5. La silla es vieja, blanca y fea.
6. La casa es vieja, bonita y crema.
7. El coche es rojo, pequeño y nuevo.
8. La mesa es pequeña, vieja, azul y fea.

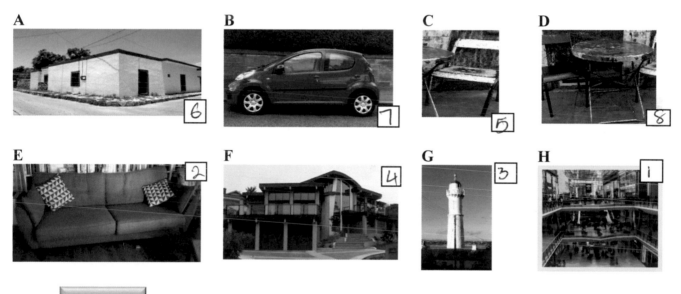

Audio 42

4b. Escribe en los espacios vacíos el verbo adecuado. Fill in the blanks with the correct verb.

Mario (**1**) _____ un chico moreno y un poco bajo. (**2**) _____ muy guapo e inteligente. (**3**) _____ el pelo corto, liso y moreno. (**4**) _____ los ojos marrones. (**5**) _____ gafas y bigote. Mario (**6**) _____ en una casa pequeña y moderna. Su casa (**7**) _____ blanca con marrón y su coche (**8**) _____ rojo y nuevo. Él (**9**) _____ soltero pero tiene pareja. Su pareja se llama Marta. Marta (**10**) _____ una chica alta, rubia y trabajadora. (**11**) _____ el pelo largo y (**12**) _____ gafas.

> **¡DESCUBRE!**
> The adjective `**viejo/a**´ is used for people, animals and objects, but the adjective `**mayor**´ is used only for people.

4c. Describe los siguientes objetos como en el ejemplo. Trabaja en tu grupo.
Describe the following items as in the example. Work in your group.
Ejemplo: Es rosa, nuevo y bonito. ¿Qué es? ⟶ Es un bolso.

una bicicleta   un libro   un bolígrafo   un coche

un tren   un ordenador portátil   un bolso   una mochila

5. SOY MÁS ALTO/A QUE TÚ. I AM TALLER THAN YOU.

5a. Escribe las frases completas con los verbos adecuados como en el ejemplo.
Write complete sentences with the appropriate verb, as in the example.

Ejemplo: Alberto 50 años/75kg/1,80m.
Alberto tiene 50 años, pesa 75 kilogramos y mide 1,80 metros.

1. Juan/50 años/70kg/1,72m
2. Lorenzo/34 años/65kg/1,52m
3. Megan/25 años/65kg/1,70m
4. Isabel/24 años/63kg/1,60m
5. Rodrigo/18 años/78kg/1,80m
6. Luis/21 años/80kg/1,80m

> **GRAMÁTICA**
> **Los comparativos**
>
> **más.......que**............more.....than
> **menos....que**............less......than
> **tan........como**..........as.........as

1..
2..
3..
4..
5..
6..

5b. Utiliza la información anterior y escribe frases utilizando los comparativos.
Use the above information and write sentences using comparatives.
Ejemplos: Juan es **más** alto **que Lorenzo**.   Rodrigo es **tan** alto **como** Luis.

a.
b.
c.
d.
e.

5c. Estudia las siguientes frases de comparativos y superlativos y practica con tus compañeros/as ejemplos similares. Study the following comparatives and superlative phrases and practise with your partners similar examples.

1. Rosario es **más** alta **que** Rosa.
2. Pablo es menos organizado que Pedro.
3. Mi padre es **tan** alto **como** yo.
4. Arturo es **tan** guapo **como** Antonio.
5. Juan es **el** chico **más** inteligente de la clase.
6. Laura es **la** chica **más** habladora de la clase.
7. Los estudiantes de español son los **más** inteligentes de la universidad.

6. LOS COLORES. COLOURS.

Audio 43

6a. Escucha, lee y repite.
Listen read and repeat.

- **azul**
- **verde**
- **marrón/café**
- gris
- **rosa**
- **naranja**

Ejemplos:

La mesa es **verde**.   El libro es **verde**.
La casa es **marrón**.   El escritorio es **marrón**.
La silla es **azul**.   El coche es **azul**.

- roj**o** --------------roj**a**
- negr**o**-----------negr**a**
- *blanco*……… *blanca*
- morad**o**---------morad**a**
- amarill**o**--------amarill**a**

Ejemplos:

El libro es rojo.   La silla es roja.
El bolígrafo es **negro**.   La cámara es **negra**.
El apartamento/piso es *blanco*.   La casa es *blanca*.
El teléfono es amarillo.   La carpeta es amarilla.

6b. Relaciona las siguientes dos columnas. Match the Spanish with the English.

1. amarillo   a) red
2. naranja   b) grey
3. azul   c) white
4. blanco   d) brown
5. dorado   e) pink
6. gris   f) purple
7. marrón   g) green
8. negro   h) yellow
9. morado/púrpura   i) orange
10. rojo   j) black
11. rosa   k) gold
12. verde   l) blue

6c. Trabaja con tu compañero/a y traduce al inglés las siguientes palabras.
Work with your partner and translate the following words into English.

1. La casa
2. El piso
3. La bicicleta
4. El ordenador portátil
5. La cámara
6. El teléfono móvil/celular
7. El coche
8. El dormitorio
9. El cuarto de baño
10. La carpeta
11. La mochila
12. El bolígrafo
13. El escritorio
14. La tableta

6d. Escribe de qué color es tu _____ .
Write the colour of your _____ .

1. bicicleta   ....
2. ordenador portátil ....
3. cámara   ....
4. teléfono móvil   ....
5. escritorio   ....
6. coche   ....
7. dormitorio   ....
8. cuarto de baño   ....
9. carpeta   ....
10. mochila   ....
11. bolígrafo   ....
12. tableta   ....

6e. Pregunta y responde las siguientes preguntas a tu compañero/a. Ask and answer the following questions to your partner.

Ejemplo:

A. ¿De qué color es **tu casa**?
B. Mi casa es blanca.

A. ¿De qué color es tu _____ ?
B. Mi _____ es _____

6f. Comparte con otro compañero/a la información del ejercicio anterior 6d.
Tienes que utilizar los posesivos «mi» y «su». Share with another partner the previous information from exercise 6d. You have to use the possessives: 'my' and 'his/her'.

Mi casa es *verde.*	**Su** casa es *azul.*	Mi...	Su...
1........................	_____	7.................	_____
2........................	_____	8.................	_____
3........................	_____	9.................	_____
4........................	_____	10.................	_____
5........................	_____	11.	_____
6........................	_____	12.................	_____

6g. Completa los colores de estos objetos utilizando el verbo «ser» en la 3ª persona del singular o del plural (es/son).
Fill out the colours of these objects using the verb 'to be' in the 3rd person singular or plural (is/are).

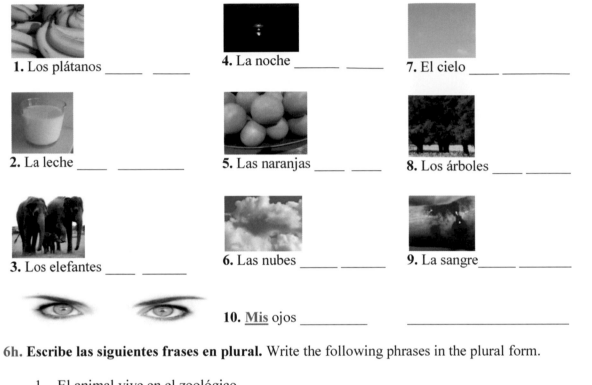

1. Los plátanos _____ _____

4. La noche _____ _____

7. El cielo ____ _____

2. La leche ____ _____

5. Las naranjas ____ ____

8. Los árboles ____ _____

3. Los elefantes ____ _____

6. Las nubes _____ _____

9. La sangre_____ _____

10. <u>Mis</u> ojos _____ _____

6h. Escribe las siguientes frases en plural. Write the following phrases in the plural form.

1. El animal vive en el zoológico. ....
2. El coche negro es nuevo y grande. ....
3. La chica es más alta que el chico. ....
4. El hombre es guapo, rubio y alto. ....
5. El niño es simpático e inteligente. ....
6. El teléfono es viejo. ....
7. La mochila es grande. ....
8. El profesor es organizado. ....
9. El pez vive en el agua. ....
10. El país es pequeño. ....

GRAMÁTICA
Plural form:
- Add a final **s**: when the singular noun ends in a vowel (a, e, i, o and u)
- Add a final **es**: when the singular noun ends in a consonant

- For more information about the plurals, see the Gramática section.

7. LECTURA Y COMPRENSIÓN READING COMPREHENSION.

Lee el siguiente texto y contesta en español a las siguientes preguntas sobre María.
Read the following text and answer the questions about María in Spanish.

María es española de un pueblo pequeño que se llama Aranjuez pero no vive allí, ahora vive en Londres. Londres es una ciudad muy grande, turística e interesante. Aranjuez está en el centro de España muy cerca de Madrid a 30 kilómetros exactamente. Es un pueblo pequeño, bonito y viejo. María tiene una familia muy grande. Tiene seis hermanos, ella es la única hija mujer. No tiene hermanas. Su madre tiene 80 años y es ama de casa. María habla dos idiomas español e inglés. Es profesora y artista, le gusta mucho la pintura. Es bastante alta, morena, guapa y muy simpática. Tiene los ojos marrones y el pelo castaño y corto. Junto con uno de sus hermanos es la dueña de un pequeño restaurante que se llama Macondo y está en Aranjuez. En Macondo hay tapas, bocadillos, sándwiches y bebidas de todo tipo. El restaurante es pequeño, bonito e interesante. Cuando María va de vacaciones a su pueblo, trabaja en su restaurante como camarera. Está casada y su marido se llama David, él es sudafricano y es doctor y trabaja en un hospital. Él vive en Gran Bretaña también junto con María pero toda su familia vive en Sudáfrica. Habla tres idiomas, español, inglés y zulú. Es alto, negro, guapo y trabajador. Tiene los ojos negros. Tiene el pelo negro, rizado y corto.

1. ¿Cuál es la nacionalidad de María?
2. ¿Cómo es Aranjuez y dónde está?
3. ¿Dónde vive y cómo es ese lugar?
4. ¿A qué se dedica?
5. ¿Cuántos hermanos tiene?
6. ¿Cuál es la profesión de su madre?
7. ¿Cómo se llama su restaurante?
8. ¿Cuál es la profesión de María cuando va a Aranjuez?
9. ¿Cuál es la nacionalidad de su marido?
10. ¿Cuántos idiomas habla su marido?
11. ¿Dónde trabaja su marido?
12. ¿Cómo es María?
13. ¿Cómo es su marido?
14. ¿Qué hay en el restaurante? ¿Cómo es?

8. VAMOS A ESCRIBIR. LET'S WRITE.

> va..............he/she goes
> de + el== del

Escribe un texto similar sobre ti mismo. Debes de incluir lo siguiente:
Write a similar paragraph about yourself. You have to add the following points:

- Nombre completo (nombre y apellido), nacionalidad y profesión
- Lugar de trabajo y descripción de donde trabajas
- Edad, descripción física y de personalidad
- Lugar de residencia y descripción de este lugar
- Familia (nombre, edad, profesión, descripción física y de personalidad de **dos** familiares [uno femenino y otro masculino]).

GRAMÁTICA

- **Los colores y la estructura gramatical.** Colours and grammar structure.
  The form changes depending on the number and gender of what's being described. In Spanish, the adjectives go after the noun, except in some situations.

Tengo un coche **verde**.	I have a **green** car.
Hay dos coches **amarillos**.	There are two **yellow** cars.
Tengo tres casas *blancas*.	I have three *white* houses.
Tienes un perro **negro**.	You have a **black** dog.
Mis zapatos son **rojos**.	My shoes are **red**.

- **Los comparativos.** Comparatives.

  o **más.........que**....................more.....than
  o **menos......que**....................less......than
  o **tan..........como**..................as.........as

- **Los superlativos.** Superlatives.

  Juan es el chico **más** inteligente de la clase.   Juan is <u>the most</u> intelligent boy in the class.
  Marcelo y Carlos son los **más** altos de la familia. Marcelo and Carlos are <u>the tallest</u> in the family.
  Madrid es la ciudad **más** grande de España.   Madrid is <u>the largest</u> city in Spain.

- **Formación de los plurales.** Forming the plurals.

  o Add a final s: When the singular noun ends in a vowel (a, e, i, o and u)
    e.g: casas, padres, bicis, libros.
  o Add a final es: When the singular noun ends in a consonant
    e.g: ustedes, profesores, escritores, leones, países.
  o Add a final es: When the singular noun ends in z, the z needs to change to c
    e.g: pez…peces, lápiz…lápices.
  o Add a final es : When the singular noun ends in a vowel with an accented
    e.g: maniquíes, colibríes.
  o Words that end in a vowel (a, e, i, o and u) + s remain the same
    e.g: lunes, martes, cumpleaños.
  o There are nouns that exist in plural form only **e.g**: gafas, pantalones, tijeras.

- **El verbo llevar.** To wear.

	llevar	to wear/to take (away)
yo	llevo	I wear
tú (informal)	llevas	you (informal singular) wear
usted (formal)	lleva	you (formal singular) wear
él/ella	lleva	he/she wears
nosotros/nosotras	llevamos	we wear
vosotros/vosotras (informal)	lleváis	you (informal plural) wear
ustedes (formal)	llevan	you (formal plural) wear
ellos/ellas	llevan	they wear

EJERCICIOS

1. Completa cada pregunta con una de las palabras del recuadro (con las mayúsculas necesarias). Complete each question with the words in the box (with the necessary uppercase letter).

quién	cómo	cuál	dónde	cuántos	qué

1. ¿_____ se llama tu hermano?
2. ¿_____ años tiene tu madre?
3. ¿A _____ te dedicas tú?
4. ¿_____ es esta chica de la foto?
5. ¿_____ es la profesión de tu padre?
6. ¿De _____ es?

2. Relaciona el español con el inglés. Match the Spanish with the English.

1. Soy una mujer morena, simpática y tranquila.
2. Soy una chica baja, activa y nerviosa.
3. Soy negro, alto, trabajador y optimista.
4. Soy rubio, un poco perezoso pero simpático.

a) I am blonde, a little lazy but a nice man.
b) I am a dark, nice and quiet woman.
c) I am a black, tall, optimistic and hard-working man.
d) I am a small, active and nervous girl.

3. Completa las frases con los comparativos y los superlativos adecuados: más, que, menos o tan.
Fill the blanks with the correct comparatives and superlatives: more, than, less and as.

1. Rita es _____ alta _____ Rosa.
2. Miguel es _____ organizado _____ Pedro.
3. Mi hermano es _____ alto _____ yo.
4. Lorenzo es _____ guapo _____ Antonio.
5. Jacinto es el chico _____ inteligente de la clase.
6. Luisa es la chica _____ habladora de la clase.
7. Los estudiantes de matemáticas son los _____ inteligentes de la universidad.

4. Escribe cada una de las siguientes palabras en la columna correspondiente (singular o plural).
Write each of the following words in the appropriate column (singular or plural).

blanco hijo tienen sobrinos morenos viven estudiante doctores ojos optimista amigas grandes es simpático cantante españoles cafés altos tranquila camareros gaseosas tiene azul leche gorda vive casados hermanos rubios

Singular	Plural

5 Lee los siguientes diálogos y subraya la forma verbal correspondiente.
Read the following dialogues and highlight the corresponding verbal form.

1. A. ¿Cuántos años **tiene/tienen** tus hermanos?
   B. 20 y 25 años.

2. A. ¿Tus amigas **está/están** casadas o solteras?
   B. Solteras excepto una.

3. A. Tu hermano **es/son** bastante alto ¿no?
   B. Sí bastante.

4. A. ¿Dónde **vive/viven** tus abuelos?
   B. En Andalucía.

5. A. ¿Qué idioma **habla/hablan** Mario?
   B. Español.

6. A. ¿Dónde **trabaja/trabajan** tu marido?
   B. En una oficina de turismo.

6. Escribe los verbos que faltan en los espacios vacíos. Write the missing verbs in the gaps.

¡Hola! _____ _____ (**1. llamarse**) Marta, _____ (**2. ser**) española de Sevilla pero _____ (**3. vivir**) en Londres. _____ (**4. ser**) estudiante de psicología y _____ (**5. trabajar**) en una biblioteca. _____ (**6. tener**) 38 años y _____ (**7. estar/ser**) casada. Mi marido _____ _____ (**8. llamarse**) David, _____ (**9. ser**) inglés de Londres. _____ (**10. ser**) profesor de matemáticas en un instituto. Nosotros _____ (**11. tener**) dos hijos y un perro. Alison _____ (**12. ser**) nuestra hija mayor, _____ (**13. tener**) 10 años. Adam nuestro hijo menor _____ (**14. tener**) 7 años. Alison _____ (**15. ser**) muy guapa, delgada, alta, rubia y muy simpática. _____ (**16. tener**) el pelo largo y rubio. Tiene los ojos azules. Adam _____ (**17. ser**) muy diferente, _____ (**18. ser**) blanco pero _____ (**19. tener**) el pelo negro corto y liso. Él_____ (**20. ser**) bastante desorganizado y un poco perezoso pero también _____ (**21. ser**) muy simpático. Nuestro perro _____ (**22. tener**) 8 años, _____ (**23. ser**) pequeño, feo y nervioso.

Mis padres _____ (**24. vivir**) en Madrid pero _____ (**25. estar**) divorciados. Mi madre _____ (**26. tener**) 58 años, _____ (**27. ser**) recepcionista y _____ (**28. trabajar**) en un hospital. Mi padre _____ (**29. tener**) 60 años _____ (**30. ser**) electricista y _____ (**31. trabajar**) en una compañía de electricidad. Esta _____ (**32. ser**) mi familia. Adiós.

7. Escribe las siguientes frases en plural. Write the following phrases in the plural form.

a.	El lápiz es nuevo y amarillo.	
b.	La biblioteca es grande, vieja y antigua.	
c.	Toda la familia vive en la casa grande y antigua.	
d.	El hombre es viejo, feo y perezoso.	
e.	La señora es morena, baja y simpática.	
f.	El pintor es joven y guapo pero desorganizado.	
g.	La piscina es pequeña y bonita pero está sucia.	
h.	El coche es moderno, bonito y rápido.	

VOCABULARIO

1. ¿CÓMO ERES? / *1. WHAT DO YOU LOOK LIKE?*

adulto/a	*adult*
alto/a	*tall*
antipático/a	*unfriendly*
bajo/a	*small*
blanco/a	*white*
bonito/a	*pretty/beautiful*
delgado/a	*slim*
dependiente (m/f)	*dependent*
desorganizado/a	*disorganized*
feo/a	*ugly*
guapo/a	*good-looking*
gordo/a	*fat*
independiente (m/f)	*independent*
inteligente (m/f)	*intelligent*
joven (m/f)	*young*
mayor (m/f)	*old*
moreno/a	*dark/brunette*
muy	*very*
negro/a	*black*
optimista (m/f)	*optimistic*
organizado/a	*organized*
pelirrojo/a	*redheaded*
perezoso/a	*lazy*
pesimista	*pessimistic*
rubio/a	*blonde*
simpático/a	*nice*
tonto/a	*silly*
trabajador/trabajadora	*hard-working*
viejo/a	*old*

2. TENGO / *2. I HAVE*

castaño	*chestnut*
color	*colour (UK)/color (US)*
miel (f)	*honey*
ojo (m)	*eye*
pelo (m)	*hair*

3. LLEVO / *3. TO WEAR*

barba (f)	*beard*
bigote (m)	*moustache*
gafas (fpl)	*glasses*
gafas de sol (fpl)	*sunglasses*

4. ¿CÓMO ES? / *4. HOW IS IT?*

antiguo/a	*old/ancient/vintage*
casa (f)	*house*
centro comercial (m)	*shopping centre*
coche (m)	*car*
faro (m)	*lighthouse*
grande (m/f)	*big*
moderno/a	*modern*
nuevo/a	*new*
pequeño/a	*little/small*
poco	*a little*
silla (f)	*chair*
sofá (m)	*sofa*

5. SOY MÁS ALTO/A QUE TÚ / *5. I AM TALLER THAN YOU*

kilogramo (m)	*kilogram*
metro (m)	*metre (UK)/meter (US)*
mide	*measures*
(él/ella) pesa	*he/she weighs*

6. LOS COLORES / *6. THE COLOURS*

amarillo/a	***yellow***
azul (m/f)	***blue***
bicicleta (f)	*bicycle*
blanco/a (m/f)	*white*
bolígrafo (m)	*pen*
bolso (m)	*bag*
carpeta (f)	*folder*
cuarto de baño (m)	*bathroom*
dorado/a	*gold*
dormitorio (m)	*bedroom*
gris (m/f)	*grey (UK)/gray (US)*
marrón/café (m/f)	***brown***
mochila (f)	*backpack*
morado/a	*purple*
naranja (m/f)	***orange***
negro/a	***black***
ordenador portátil (m)	*laptop*
piso (m)	*flat(UK)/apartment(US)*
rojo/a	***red***
rosa (m/f)	*pink*
tableta (f)	*tablet*
teléfono móvil (m)	*mobile/cell (US) phone*
verde (m/f)	*green*

7 ¿DÓNDE ESTÁ?

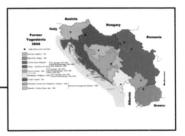

TEMAS TOPICS	OBJETIVOS COMUNICATIVOS COMMUNICATIVE OBJECTIVES	GRAMÁTICA GRAMMAR
Lugares de interés. Geografía de lugares. Más números.	**Describir lugares.** Describing location. **Preguntar y responder:** **¿De dónde eres? ¿Dónde está?** Asking and answer: Where do you come from? Where is it? **Hablar de la situación geográfica de una población.** Talking about geographical situation of a location. **Hablar del número de habitantes de una población.** Talking about the number of inhabitants of a city or town/village. **Contar desde 100…**Counting from 100…	**Contraste entre los verbos irregulares: ser y estar.** The contrast between: ser (to be)/ estar (to be in a place). **Diferencia entre: está en el/está al.** Differentiation between: It is in/It is to the. **Preposiciones: cerca y lejos.** Prepositions: near and far. **Los números a partir del 100.** Numbers from 100. **Interrogativos: ¿Dónde? ¿Cuál? ¿Qué? ¿Cuántos/as?** Interrogatives: Where? Which? What? How many?

1. ¿DÓNDE ESTÁ Y CÓMO ES? WHERE IS IT AND WHAT DOES IT LOOK LIKE?

¿Dónde está?

Norte, sur, este, oeste, noreste, sureste, suroeste, noroeste, centro.

¡Hola! Me llamo Rosa. Soy peruana de Tabaconas ¿Y tú?

¿Qué tal Rosa? Yo me llamo Luisa. Soy de Sevilla, España.

Audio 45

1a. Rosa y Luisa hablan de sus lugares de origen. Escucha y lee el siguiente diálogo.
Rosa and Luisa talk about their home town. Listen and read.

Rosa	**¡Hola! ¿Cómo estás Luisa?**
Luisa	¿Qué tal Rosa? Estoy bien pero tengo mucho trabajo.
Rosa	**¿De dónde eres?**
Luisa	Soy de Sevilla pero vivo aquí en Londres. ¿Y tú?
Rosa	**Yo soy de Tabaconas Perú, pero vivo en Londres también. ¿Dónde está Sevilla?**
Luisa	Está en el sur de España. ¿Dónde está Tabaconas?
Rosa	**Está en el norte del Perú al norte de Lima. ¿Es grande Sevilla?**
Luisa	Sí, es muy grande.
Rosa	**¿Cuántos habitantes tiene?**
Luisa	Hay setecientos mil habitantes aproximadamente. ¿Cuántos habitantes hay en Tabaconas?
Rosa	**Es un pueblo muy pequeño tiene dieciséis mil habitantes más o menos. ¡Luisa! ¿Qué quieres tomar?**
Luisa	Quiero un café con leche.
Rosa	**Yo quiero un té con limón. ¡Camarero! Un café con leche y un té con limón, por favor.**

GRAMÁTICA

In Spanish, there are two verbs meaning to be: ser and estar.

Estar: Is used to explain where something or someone is.

Madrid **está** en España. Madrid is in Spain.

103

1b. Lee una vez más el diálogo anterior y contesta a las preguntas siguientes.
Read the previous dialogue again and answer the following questions.

Suramérica

España

1. ¿Dónde vive Rosa?
2. ¿De dónde es Rosa?
3. ¿Dónde está Tabaconas?
4. ¿Es Tabaconas un pueblo o una ciudad?
5. ¿Cuántos habitantes hay?
6. ¿Dónde vive Luisa?
7. ¿De dónde es Luisa?
8. ¿Dónde está su ciudad?
9. ¿Cómo es su ciudad?
10. ¿Cuántos habitantes tiene Sevilla?

1c. Relaciona las expresiones del español con el inglés.
Match the Spanish expressions with the English ones.

1. ¿Dónde vive Rosa?	a) Where does Rosa come from?
2. ¿De dónde es Rosa?	b) How many inhabitants are there?
3. ¿Dónde está Tabaconas?	c) What does Tabaconas look like?
4. ¿Cómo es Tabaconas?	d) Where does Rosa live?
5. ¿Cuántos habitantes hay?	e) Where is Tabaconas?

¡DESCUBRE!

¿Dónde está?	Where is it?
¿Cómo es?	What does it look like?
grande	big
pequeño/a	small
muy	very

1d. Lee la conversación en la sección «a» una vez más y contesta Sí o No a las siguientes preguntas. Read the conversation in section "a" again and answer Yes or No to the following questions.

1. ¿Luisa es de Sevilla?
2. ¿Rosa es de Londres?
3. ¿Tabaconas está en Inglaterra?
4. ¿Sevilla está en Escocia?

5. ¿Sevilla es una ciudad grande?
6. ¿Tabaconas es un pueblo?
7. ¿En Sevilla hay setecientos mil habitantes?
8. ¿En Tabaconas hay diecisiete mil habitantes?

Practica con tu compañero/a el siguiente diálogo (ver el mapa de Europa).
Practise with your partner the following dialogue (see the Europe map).

A. ¿Dónde está **Noruega**?
B. Está en el **norte** de **Europa**.

A. ¿Dónde está _____?
B. Está en el _____ de _____.

Audio 46

1e. Escucha y lee las siguientes frases. Localiza en el siguiente mapa de Latinoamérica la capital que le corresponde a cada país. Comprueba tus respuestas con tu profesor. Listen and read. Locate the capital city of each country on the following map of Latin America. Verify your answers with your teacher.

1. La Habana está en el noroeste de Cuba.
2. Santiago está en el centro de Chile.
3. Caracas está en el norte de Venezuela.
4. Ciudad de México está en el sur de México.
5. Asunción está en el suroeste de Paraguay.
6. Quito está en el norte de Ecuador.
7. Lima está en el oeste de Perú.
8. Buenos Aires está en el este de Argentina.
9. Bogotá está en centro de Colombia.
10. Montevideo está en el sur de Uruguay.
11. La Paz está en el oeste de Bolivia.
12. Ciudad de Panamá está en el centro de Panamá.

LATINOAMÉRICA

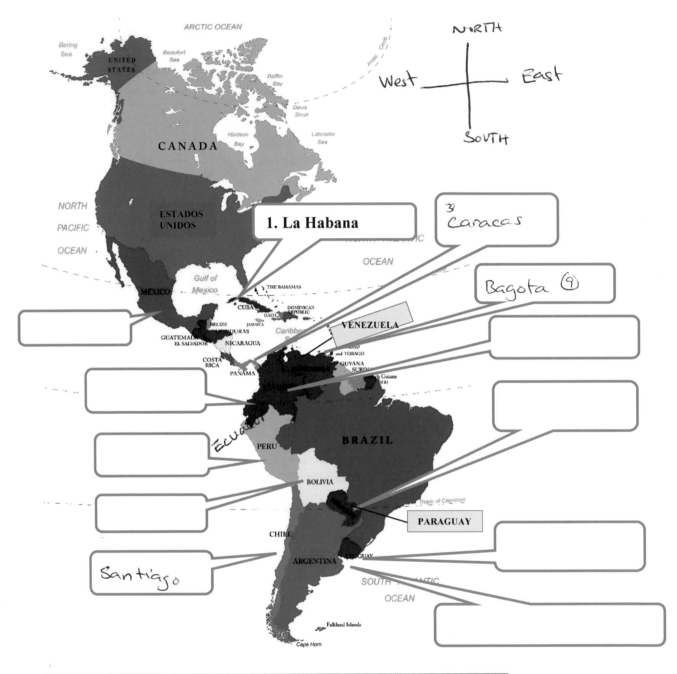

1. La Habana

Caracas

Bagota (9)

Santiago

1f. **Practica con tu compañero/a.**

     A. ¿Dónde está **Chile**?
     B. Está en el **suroeste** de **Suramérica**. Está al **oeste** de **Argentina**.

     A. ¿Dónde está _____?
     B. Está al_____ de _____.

1g. Mira el mapa de España y escribe la ciudad correspondiente en el espacio vacío.
Look at the map of Spain and fill in the blanks with the names of the appropriate cities.

Ejemplo:

A. ¿Dónde está **Valencia**?

B. **Valencia** está **en el** **este** de España*(está) **al norte** de Alicante.

1. _____ está en el **centro** de España,*(está) al **noroeste** de Madrid y cerca de Valladolid.

2. _____ está en el **noreste** de España, *(está) al **sur** de Barcelona.

3. _____está en el **sur** de España, *(está) al **suroeste** de Córdoba y al **este** de Huelva.

4. _____ está en el **norte** de España, *(está) al **oeste** de Bilbao.

5. _____ está en el **sur** de España, *(está) al **este** de Sevilla.

6. _____ está en el **centro** de España, *(está) al **norte** de Toledo.

Nota: *(está) es opcional.

MAPA DE ESPAÑA

¡DESCUBRE!

Está en el sur de. It's in the south of...
Está al sur de... It's to the south of...

Estudiante A ¿Dónde está **Sevilla**?
Estudiante B Está **en el** **sur** de España, *(está) **al suroeste** de **Córdoba**.

1h. Practica con tu compañero/a. Practise with your partner.

Estudiante A ¿Dónde está _____?
Estudiante B Está **en el** _____ de España **al** _____ de _____.

2. MÁS NÚMEROS. MORE NUMBERS.

Audio 47

2a. Escucha y repite los siguientes números. Listen and repeat.

100 cien
110 cien**to** diez
200 doscient**os/as**
300 trescient**os/as**
400 cuatrocient**os/as**
500 quinient**os/as**
600 seiscient**os/as**
700 setecient**os/as**
800 ochocient**os/as**
900 novecient**os/as**

1.000 mil
2.000 dos mil
3.000 tres mil
4.160 cuatro mil ciento sesenta
5.680 cinco mil seiscientos ochenta
8.231 ocho mil doscientos treinta y uno
1.000.000 un millón
2.000.000 dos millon**es**
3.130.200 tres millon**es** ciento treinta
mil doscientos.
12.000.143 doce millon**es** ciento
cuarenta y tres

Ejemplos de números donde cambia el género:

el euro €   £ **la** libra
doscientos euros   doscientas libras

2b. En una hoja de papel escribe 10 números diferentes. Compártelos con tu compañero/a y en otra hoja escribe sus números. On a sheet of paper, write down 10 different numbers. Show them to your partner and on another sheet, write down the numbers of his/her choice.

| Escribe **tus** números 130   1.400   .... | Escribe los números **de tu** compañero/a 490   .... |

Audio 48

2c. Escucha la conversación entre Felipe y Laura y rellena los cuadros con la información que se pide. Listen to the conversation between Felipe and Laura and complete the table with the information required.

	Felipe	Laura
a) Nacionalidad		
b) Lugar de residencia actual		
c) Lugar de origen		
d) Dónde está el lugar de origen		
e) Número de habitantes del lugar de origen		
f) Descripción del lugar de origen		
g) ¿Qué quieren tomar?		

3. ¿DÓNDE ESTÁ EXACTAMENTE? WHERE IS IT EXACTLY?

3a. Mira el mapa de abajo y practica en parejas las siguientes preguntas (dónde está y cuántos habitantes tiene). Practise the following dialogues with reference to the map below.

Estudiante A	**¿Dónde está <u>México</u>?**
Estudiante B	<u>México</u> está en el <u>sur</u> de Norteamérica. Al <u>sur</u> de los Estados Unidos.
Estudiante A	**¿Cuántos habitantes hay (<u>En México</u>)?**
Estudiante B	(<u>En México</u>) hay <u>ciento treinta millones, novecientos noventa y dos mil ciento treinta</u> habitantes.

MAPA DE AMÉRICA

Población aproximada de los países de América.

Estudiante A

- Argentina 44.411.000
- Belice 677.000
- Bolivia 14.550.099
- Brasil 214.999.911
- Canadá 32.211.000
- Chile 18.990.002
- Colombia 48.122.000
- Costa Rica 8.811.990
- Cuba 12.120.000
- Ecuador 16.600.000
- El Salvador 9.911.990
- Estados Unidos 385.899.110

Estudiante B

- Guatemala 13.311.900
- Honduras 7.711.990
- Jamaica 106.599
- Honduras 106.599
- México 130.992.130
- Nicaragua 8.110.000
- Panamá 4.980.990
- Paraguay 21.211.000
- Perú 32.200.900
- República Dominicana 10.500.000
- Uruguay 5.511.000
- Venezuela 33.766.192

3b. **Practica con tu pareja la siguiente conversación. Cambia los datos que están subrayados por tus datos personales.** Practise the following dialogue with your partner, substituting your own personal details for the underlined words.

Estudiante A	**¡Hola! ¿Cómo estás?**
Estudiante B	¿Qué tal? Estoy fenomenal, tengo un trabajo nuevo.
Estudiante A	**¿De dónde eres?**
Estudiante B	Soy de Bogotá, Colombia pero vivo en Madrid ¿Y tú?
Estudiante A	**Yo soy de Toledo pero vivo aquí en Madrid también. ¿Dónde está Bogotá?**
Estudiante B	Está en el centro de Colombia. ¿Dónde está Toledo? y ¿Cómo es?
Estudiante A	**Está en el centro de España al sur de Madrid. Es una ciudad pequeña, histórica y muy turística. ¿Cómo es Bogotá?**
Estudiante B	Es una ciudad grande y muy bonita.
Estudiante A	**¿Cuántos habitantes tiene?**
Estudiante B	Hay aproximadamente siete millones de habitantes.
Estudiante A	**¿Cuántos habitantes hay en Toledo?**
Estudiante B	Hay más o menos noventa mil habitantes.
Estudiante A	**Adiós.**
Estudiante B	Hasta luego.

3c. **Contesta las siguientes preguntas y practica con dos compañeros/as.**
Answer the following questions and ask two other people the same questions.

	Tú	Compañero/a	Compañero/a
¿Cómo te llamas?			
¿Cuál es tu nacionalidad?			
¿Cuál es tu profesión?			
¿De dónde eres?			
¿Dónde está tu ciudad/pueblo?			
¿Cómo es tu ciudad/pueblo?			
¿Cuántos habitantes tiene tu ciudad/ pueblo?			

4. LECTURA Y COMPRENSIÓN. READING AND COMPREHENSION.

4a. Lee el siguiente texto sobre Perú y marca verdadero o falso enfrente de cada texto.
Read the following text about Peru and tick true or false.

PERÚ

Perú tiene una población aproximada de treinta y dos millones doscientos mil novecientos noventa habitantes. Es un país que está situado en el oeste de América del Sur y bordea su costa con el océano Pacifico. Está al sur de Colombia y Ecuador, al oeste de Brasil y Bolivia y al norte de Chile. Su territorio se compone de diversos paisajes: los valles, las mesetas y las montañas de los Andes. Entre sus principales actividades económicas se incluyen: la agricultura de exportación como la quinua y el espárrago fresco, la pesca, la minería y la manufactura de productos como los textiles.

La población peruana es mestiza entre españoles e indios y posteriormente, por influencia de inmigrantes, de China, Japón y Europa. El idioma principal y más hablado es el español, aunque un número significativo de peruanos habla diversas lenguas nativas, siendo la más extendida el quechua sureño. Políticamente, el país es una república presidencialista. Perú es bastante popular para los turistas no solamente por las ruinas del complejo arqueológico de Machu Picchu sino porque cuenta con diversos destinos que ofrecen un sinfín de actividades, tesoros milenarios y modernos, y la belleza espectacular de selvas, sierras y costas. Allí encontrarás una travesía única por el Río Amazonas y un recorrido por el lago Titicaca que es el lago navegable más alto del mundo.

Sacado y adaptado de: https://es.wikipedia.org/wiki/Per%C3%BA

		V	F
1.	Perú es un país que está situado en el este de América del Sur y bordea su costa con el océano Pacifico. Está al sur de Colombia y Ecuador.		
2.	Entre sus principales actividades económicas se incluyen: la agricultura de exportación como la quinua y el espárrago fresco, la pesca y la minería.		
3.	Perú es bastante popular para los turistas solamente por las ruinas del complejo arqueológico de Machu Picchu.		
4.	El idioma principal y más hablado es el quechua.		

4b. Lee el siguiente texto sobre Isabel Allende y contesta a las preguntas.
Read the following text about Isabel Allende and answer the questions.

1. ¿Cuál es su profesión?
2. ¿Cuál es su nacionalidad?
3. ¿Cuál es su ciudad natal?
4. ¿Cómo es físicamente?
5. ¿Qué idiomas habla?
6. ¿Está casada?

7. ¿Cómo se llaman sus nietas?
8. ¿Cuál es su novela más famosa?
9. ¿Qué géneros literarios escribe?
10. ¿Dónde está Lima?
11. ¿Cómo es Lima?
12. ¿Cuántos habitantes tiene Lima?

Isabel Allende

Me llamo Isabel Allende. Tengo dos nacionalidades. Soy chilena y estadounidense pero mi ciudad natal es Lima, Perú. Vivo en los Estados Unidos. Soy periodista y escritora de novelas, cuentos y memorias. Mi fecha de nacimiento es el 2 de agosto de 1942. Soy baja, delgada y muy trabajadora. Tengo el pelo moreno y corto. Llevo gafas para leer. Hablo español e inglés. Soy la mayor de tres hermanos. Estoy divorciada y casada por segunda vez. De mi primer matrimonio *tuve un hijo y una hija. Mi hijo se llama Nicolás, pero mi hija **murió en 1991 a la edad de 28 años de una enfermedad hereditaria. Estoy casada por segunda vez, mi marido se llama Willie Gordon y es estadounidense. Tengo dos nietas que se llaman Andrea y Nicole.

De todas mis novelas la más famosa se llama «La casa de los espíritus» pero mi novela preferida se llama «Paula» porque es la historia de mi vida, mi familia y la de mi hija Paula.

Lima es mi ciudad natal, está en el oeste de Perú en América del Sur. Lima es una ciudad grande, moderna y antigua también. Tiene una población aproximada de ocho millones de habitantes.

Sacado y adaptado de:
- http://www.elresumen.com/biografias/isabel_allende.htm
- http://es.wikipedia.org/wiki/Isabel_Allende_Llona
- http://es.wikipedia.org/wiki/Lima

*tuve: I had ** murió: he/she died

4c. Vuelve a leer el texto de Isabel Allende y subraya todos los verbos.
Read the text about Isabel Allende over again and underline all the verbs.

4d. Escribe el texto en la 3ª persona del singular. Write out the text in the 3rd person singular.
Se llama Isabel Allende.

5. VAMOS A ESCRIBIR. LET'S WRITE.

5a. Lee la información sobre Enrique Iglesias y su amigo y contesta a las preguntas del recuadro. Read the information about Enrique Iglesias and his friend and answer the questions in the table below.

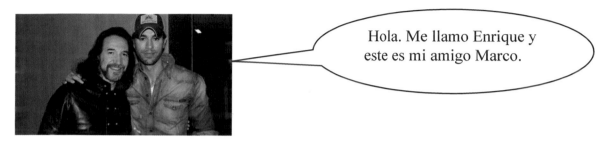

Hola. Me llamo Enrique y este es mi amigo Marco.

¡Hola! Me llamo Enrique Iglesias. Soy español. Soy cantante y escritor de música. Soy alto, moreno y tengo el pelo corto y moreno. Soy de Madrid. Madrid es una ciudad muy grande e interesante que está en el centro de España. Tiene tres millones cuatrocientos mil habitantes aproximadamente.

Este es mi amigo Marco Antonio Muñiz. Es mexicano. Es cantante. Es bajo y simpático. Tiene el pelo moreno y largo. Lleva barba y bigote. Es de Guadalajara México. Guadalajara es una ciudad grande, bonita, moderna, antigua e histórica que está en el oeste de México. Tiene un millón quinientos mil habitantes más o menos.

	Enrique	Marco Antonio
1. ¿Cuál es su nacionalidad?		
2. ¿Cuál es su profesión?		
3. ¿Cómo es físicamente?		
4. ¿De dónde es?		
5. ¿Dónde está su ciudad?		
6. ¿Cómo es su ciudad?		
7. ¿Cuántos habitantes tiene su ciudad?		

5b. Lee una vez más el texto anterior sobre Enrique Iglesias y su amigo (5a). Escribe un texto similar sobre tu persona y un/a amigo/a.
Read the above text about Enrique Iglesias and his friend again (5a). Write a similar text about yourself and a friend.

5c. Busca en la web la información de dos personajes famosos y escribe un texto sobre él y ella. Debes incluir los siguientes puntos:
Search the web for some information about two celebrities and write a text about him and her. You must include the following points:

- Nombre, profesión, nacionalidad, descripción física e idiomas que habla.
- Familia y estado civil
- Su ciudad natal:
    - ¿Dónde está exactamente?
    - ¿Cómo es?
    - ¿Cuántos habitantes tiene?

GRAMÁTICA

- **Ser y estar** – 'to be'. In Spanish there are two verbs meaning, 'to be': **ser and estar**

  o **Estar**: is used to explain where something or someone is.
    - **Estoy** en la universidad.
    - No **estoy** en casa, estoy en el restaurante Pepe.
    - Madrid **está** en Europa.
    - **Estamos** en la clase de español.

  o **Ser**: is used for names, nationalities, professions, descriptions and adjectives (for permanent qualities).
    - **Soy** Luis, soy español de Barcelona, soy arquitecto. Soy alto moreno y guapo.
    - **Eres** María, eres italiana de Roma, eres actriz. Eres baja, guapa y simpática.
    - **Es** Pedro, es argentino de Buenos Aires, es ingeniero. Es alto, rubio y trabajador.
    - ¿**Sois** vosotros Luis y Carolina, los estudiantes españoles?

  *Note: to indicate marital states, it is possible to use either: **ser** or **estar**
  estoy/soy casado/a: I'm married
  estoy/soy soltero/a: I'm single

- **Gramática de los verbos irregulares: ser y estar**. Conjugation of the verb: 'to be'.

	ser	estar	to be
yo	soy	estoy	I am/I'm
tú (informal)	eres	estás	you are (informal singular)
usted (formal)	es	estás	you are (formal singular)
él/ella	es	está	he/she is
esto	es	está	it is/it's
nosotros/nosotras	somos	estamos	we are
vosotros/vosotras (informal)	sois	estáis	you are (informal plural)
ustedes (formal)	son	están	you are (formal plural)
ellos/ellas	son	están	they are

- **Diferencia entre: Está en el/Está al...** Diferentiation between: It is in/It is to the…

Está en el …….It is in…	Está al …….It is to the…
Brighton **está en el** sur de Inglaterra.	Brighton **está al** sur de Londres.
Edimburgo **está en el** este de Escocia.	Edimburgo **está al** este de Glasgow.
Barcelona **está en el** noreste de España.	Barcelona **está al** norte de Tarragona.

- **Números cardinales.** Cardinal numbers.

The cardinal numbers indicate a specific number of a noun but don't have to match that noun in gender or number except for some cases: **uno** → **una** and between 200-900.

1 chair - **una silla**	200 people - **doscientas personas**
21 weeks - **veintiuna semanas**	500 cities - **quinientas ciudades**
41 tables - **cuarenta y una mesas**	900 pounds – **novecientas libras**

EJERCICIOS

1. **Escribe el verbo correcto (ser/estar) en los espacios vacíos.**
   Fill in the blanks with a conjugated part of verbs (ser/estar), as appropriate.

   1. La ciudad _____ grande y bonita.
   2. Barcelona _____ en el noreste de España.
   3. Mi madre _____ baja y guapa.
   4. Tú _____ arquitecto.
   5. Yo _____ estudiante de medicina.
   6. Nosotros _____ europeos.
   7. Vosotros _____ en casa siempre.
   8. Juan y María _____ morenos, guapos y simpáticos.
   9. Barcelona _____ una ciudad bonita y grande que _____ en el noreste de España.

2. **Escribe el verbo correcto en los espacios vacíos.** Write the correct verb in the blanks.

   Mi primo _____ _____ (**1. llamarse**) Javier. _____ (**2. ser**) ingeniero y _____ (**3. vivir**) en Sevilla. _____ (**4. tener**) 30 años. _____ (**5. estar**) soltero pero _____ (**6. tener**) pareja y un hijo de dos años. Su pareja _____ _____ (**7. llamarse**) Rosa y su hijo Roberto. Javier _____ (**8. ser**) alto y moreno, _____ (**9. tener**) el pelo corto y _____ (**10. llevar**) gafas.

   Sevilla _____ (**11. ser**) una ciudad grande y turística. _____ (**12. estar**) en el sur de España. _____ (**13. tener**) aproximadamente ochocientos mil habitantes.

3. **Escribe los siguientes números en cifra.** Write out the following numbers in full.
   Ejemplo:
   300.250 = trescientos mil doscientos cincuenta.

   a) 267...
   b) 5.548..
   c) 78.370...
   d) 157.478...
   e) 2.600.581..

4. **Escribe las siguientes frases en números.** Write out the following phrases in numbers.
   Ejemplo: un millón doscientos cincuenta mil = 1.250.000.

   a) Ciento cuarenta mil. ....
   b) Trescientos mil ochocientos noventa. ....
   c) Quinientos millones cien mil
      doscientos treinta. ....
   d) Doscientos ochenta y cinco. ....
   e) Setecientos mil cuatrocientos
      cuarenta. ....

VOCABULARIO

1. ¿DÓNDE ESTÁ?	1. *WHERE IS IT?*	2. NÚMEROS	2. *NUMBERS*
actual	*actual*	cien	*one hundred*
al	*to*	doscientos/**as**	*two hundred*
aproximadamente	*about*	trescientos/**as**	*three hundred*
ciudad (f)	*city*	cuatrocientos/**as**	*four hundred*
de	*of*	quinientos/**as**	*five hundred*
el	*the*	seiscientos/**as**	*six hundred*
en	*in/on*	setecientos/**as**	*seven hundred*
Está al sur de…	*It's to the south of…*	ochocientos/**as**	*eight hundred*
Está en el sur de…	*It's south of…*	novecientos/**as**	*nine hundred*
este	*this*	mil	*one thousand*
este (m)	*east*	dos mil	*two thousand*
grande (m/f)	*big/large*	un millón	*one million*
habitantes (mpl)	*inhabitants*	dos millones	*two million*
lugar (m)	*place*	el euro (m)	*the euro*
muy	*very*	la libra (f)	*the pound*
nacionalidad (f)	*nationality*		
norte (m)	*north*		
o	*or*		
oeste (m)	*west*		
origen (m)	*origin*		
pequeño/a	*small*		
población (f)	*population*		
pueblo (m)	*town*		
residencia (f)	*residence*		
siempre	*always*		
sur/sud (m)	*south*		
¿Cuántos habitantes tiene?	*How many inhabitants does it have?*		
¿Cuántos habitantes hay?	*How many inhabitants are there?*		
¿Cómo es?	*What does it look like?*		
¿Dónde está?	*Where is it?*		
¿Es grande?	*Is it big?*		

8 MI CIUDAD/MI PUEBLO

Monterrey es una ciudad moderna, grande, industrial y bonita.

TEMAS TOPICS	OBJETIVOS COMUNICATIVOS COMMUNICATIVE OBJECTIVES	GRAMÁTICA GRAMMAR
La vida en mi ciudad/pueblo. **¿Dónde está exactamente?** **Mi ciudad es más pequeña que tu ciudad.**	**Describir cómo es tu ciudad/pueblo.** Describing what your hometown is like. **Expresar ubicación.** Indicating location. **Decir qué hay en tu ciudad/pueblo.** Saying what there is in your hometown. **Usar los comparativos y los superlativos.** Using the comparative.	**Adjetivos calificativos: grande, bonito/a, feo/a...** Qualifying adjective: large/big, nice/pretty, ugly... **Adjetivos posesivos: mi/mis, tu/tus, su/sus...** Possessive adjectives: my, your, his/her/their... **Preposiciones indicando un lugar específico.** Prepositions indicating the exact location. **Algunos usos del verbo 'hay' con el vocabulario de lugares.** Some uses of 'There is/are' with location vocabulary. **Preposiciones: de/a+ artículo determinado.** Prepositions: from/to+ definite article. **Adverbios de cantidad: muy, mucho/a, muchos/as.** Adverbs of quantity: very, a lot of/many.

1. ¿CÓMO ES? WHAT DOES IT LOOK LIKE?

1a. Escucha y traduce al inglés o a tu primer idioma los siguientes adjetivos calificativos.
Listen and translate the following adjectives into English or into your native language.

- grande
- bonito/a
- nuevo/a
- moderno/a
- dinámico/a
- tranquilo/a
- hermoso/a
- turístico/a

- pequeño/a
- feo/a
- viejo/a
- antiguo/a
- aburrido/a
- peligroso/a
- horrible
- no turístico/a

1b. Escribe una descripción de cada fotografía en los siguientes recuadros y comprueba con tu profesor. Write a description of each photograph in the boxes below and verify with your teacher.

1 _____

2 _____

3 _____

1c. Contesta a las siguientes preguntas y practícalas con tus compañeros/as.
Answer the following questions and practise with your partner.

- ¿De dónde eres?
- ¿Dónde está?
- ¿Cómo es tu ciudad/pueblo? *What does your home town look like?*

2. ¿QUÉ HAY EN TU CIUDAD/PUEBLO? WHAT IS THERE IN YOUR HOMETOWN?

2a. Relaciona las dos columnas. Match the two columns.

1. edificios   c
2. un río   k
3. muchas tiendas   d
4. un centro comercial   a
5. muchos bares   h
6. una piscina   b
7. una plaza de toros   j
8. una plaza   i
9. una iglesia   f
10. correos   g
11. playa   e
12. un ayuntamiento   l

a) a shopping centre/mall
b) a swimming pool
c) buildings
d) lots of shops
e) beach
f) a church
g) a post office
h) lots of pubs
i) a city/town square
j) a bull ring
k) a river
l) a town hall

3. DESCRIPCIÓN DEL LUGAR DONDE NACISTE.
DESCRIPTION OF YOUR HOME TOWN.

3a. **Lee las descripciones de cada fotografía y contesta a las preguntas.**
Read the descriptions below and answer the questions.

Monterrey

Ciempozuelos

Monterrey está en el noreste de México cerca de Texas pero lejos de ciudad de México, a 1.000 kilómetros. Es una ciudad bonita, grande, interesante, moderna e industrial. No es turística. Hay montañas, parques y un zoológico. Hay muchas tiendas, muchos centros comerciales y restaurantes. Hay un metro nuevo y bonito y muchos museos. Hay un río muy grande sin agua. No hay playa. Tiene tres millones de habitantes.

Ciempozuelos está en el centro de España muy cerca de Madrid, a 35 kilómetros. Está lejos de Francia. Es un pueblo muy bonito, grande, antiguo y moderno. Es turístico. Hay una plaza, un ayuntamiento, una estación de trenes muy moderna, una plaza de toros, un campo de fútbol, cuatro conventos y una ermita. No hay castillo. Tiene veinticuatro mil habitantes.

1. ¿Dónde está Monterrey?
2. ¿Cómo es?
3. ¿Qué hay?
4. ¿Qué no hay?
5. ¿Cuántos habitantes tiene?

6. ¿Dónde está Ciempozuelos?
7. ¿Cómo es?
8. ¿Qué hay?
9. ¿Qué no hay?
10. ¿Cuántos habitantes tiene?

GRAMÁTICA

¿Dónde está?	Where is it?
¿Cómo es?	What does it look like?
¿Qué hay?	What's there?
Hay	There is/are
Tengo que	I have to
Está cerca/lejos de aquí	It's <u>nearby/far</u> from here
mucho/a	a lot of/lots of/many
muchos/as	a lot of/lots of/many
muy	very

Audio 50

3b. Escucha y escribe en los espacios vacíos la palabra adecuada.
Listen and fill in the blanks.

Monterrey

Ciempozuelos

Susana	**¡Hola Isabel! ¿Qué quieres tomar?**
Isabel	¿Qué tal Susana? Quiero un expreso y un sándwich de queso.
Susana	**¡Camarero! Un expreso y un sándwich de queso y para mí un zumo de naranja y una tortilla de patata. Isabel no (1) _____ española. ¿Verdad?**
Isabel	No, no (2) _____ española. (3) _____ mexicana de Monterrey.
Susana	**¿Dónde está Monterrey?**
Isabel	Monterrey (4) _____ en el noreste de México, cerca de Texas pero lejos de Ciudad de México.
Susana	**¿A cuántos kilómetros está de Ciudad de México?**
Isabel	(5) _____ a mil kilómetros más o menos. ¿Y tú? ¿De dónde eres?
Susana	**Yo (6) _____ de Ciempozuelos.**
Isabel	¿Dónde está Ciempozuelos?
Susana	**Ciempozuelos. (7) _____ en el centro de España muy cerca de Madrid.**
Isabel	¿A cuántos kilómetros está de Madrid?
Susana	**(8) _____ a treinta y cinco kilómetros. ¿Cómo es tu ciudad? ¿Cuántos habitantes hay?**
Isabel	Mmmm bueno, Monterrey (9) _____ una ciudad muy grande, moderna. (10) _____ tres millones de habitantes. ¿Cómo es Ciempozuelos? ¿Cuántos habitantes tiene?
Susana	**Ciempozuelos (11) _____ un pueblo grande, bonito, viejo y turístico. (12) _____ veinticuatro mil habitantes. ¿Qué hay en tu ciudad Isabel?**
Isabel	En mi ciudad Monterrey (13) _____ tiendas, restaurantes, cines, teatros, montañas, edificios grandes y modernos. También (14) _____ muchas fábricas, un río sin agua, un parque acuático y un zoológico, pero no (15) _____ castillo ni playa. ¿Qué hay en tu pueblo Susana?
Susana	**Pues en mi pueblo (16) _____ monumentos históricos, iglesias,… cuatro conventos, dos hospitales, una plaza, una plaza de toros, muchos bares y restaurantes, una piscina y una ermita. Vale (17) _____que ir a casa. Adiós.**
Isabel	Hasta luego yo (18) _____ que trabajar.

- **Contesta a las preguntas y practica con tu compañero/a.**
  Answer the questions and practise with your partner.

a)	¿De dónde eres tú?	e)	¿Qué no hay?
b)	¿Dónde está?	f)	¿Cuántos habitantes tiene?
c)	¿Cómo es tu ciudad/pueblo?	g)	¿Está cerca o lejos de la montaña?
d)	¿Qué hay?	h)	¿Está cerca o lejos del mar?
		i)	¿A cuántos kilómetros está de la frontera?

3c. Mira el siguiente mapa de España y trabaja con tu compañero/a.
Look at the following map of Spain and work with your partner.

Estudiante A ⟶	Estudiante B
¿Dónde está <u>Madrid</u>?	(<u>Madrid</u>) Está en el <u>centro</u> de España.
¿Está cerca o lejos de <u>Santander</u>?	No está cerca, está lejos de <u>Santander</u>
¿A cuántos kilómetros está de <u>Santander</u>?	Está a <u>400</u> km más o menos.

Estudiante A ⟶	Estudiante B
¿Dónde está(n) _____ ?	¿Dónde está(n) _____ ?
¿Está/n cerca de/lejos de _____ ?	¿Está/n cerca de/lejos de _____ ?
¿A cuántos kilómetros está de _____ ?	¿A cuántos kilómetros está de _____ ?

Estudiante A	Estudiante B
• Valencia	• León
• Gijón	• Tarragona
• Barcelona	• Granada
• Vigo	• Alicante
• Cadiz	• La Coruña
• Málaga	• Valladolid
• Toledo	• Huelva
• Ceuta	• Gibraltar
• Bilbao	• Portugal
• Las Islas Baleares	• Los Pirineos

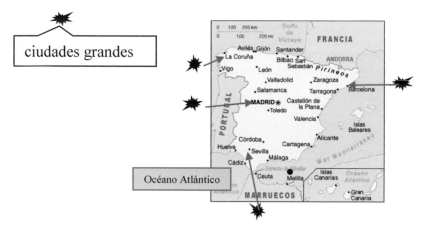

ciudades grandes

Océano Atlántico

3d. En grupos de dos o tres, cada estudiante piensa en una ciudad y los otros le hacen preguntas para adivinar cuál es. Solamente se puede responder «Sí» o «No».
In groups of three or four, each student takes it in turn to think of a city. The others ask questions (which can only be answered, 'Yes' or' No'), in order to find the right answer.

☺	☹
• ¿Está en España?	Sí
• ¿Es grande?	Sí
• ¿Es pequeña?	No
• ¿Está en el norte España?	No
• ¿Es moderna y turística?	Sí
• ¿Tiene costa?	No
• ¿Tiene playa?	No
• ¿Está al lado del Mar Mediterráneo?	No
• ¿Es Madrid?	Si.

Audio 51

3e. Escucha el siguiente texto sobre Santander y contesta a las preguntas.
Listen to the following text about Santander and answer the questions.

Santander

1. ¿Dónde está?
2. ¿Cómo es?
3. ¿Qué hay en la ciudad?
4. ¿Por qué es famosa?
5. ¿A cuántos kilómetros está de Madrid?
6. ¿Cuántos habitantes hay?
7. ¿Cómo es el transporte?

3f. Escucha otra vez la grabación sobre Santander y marca verdadero o falso.
Listen again to the recording about Santander and tick true or false.

	V	F
1. Santander es una ciudad grande y muy moderna.		
2. Está en el norte de España, al lado del mar Cantábrico.		
3. Hay una playa donde se practica el surf y también hay una escuela de surf.		
4. Santander es una ciudad famosa por sus monumentos y teatros.		
5. Hay una estación de esquí muy famosa para los turistas.		

3g. Completa los comparativos y los superlativos con «más», «menos» o «tan».
Fill the blanks with the correct comparatives and superlatives.
1. El pueblo es _____ tranquilo que la ciudad.
2. La plaza del pueblo es _____ peligrosa que la plaza de toros.
3. La casa es _____ pequeña **como** el piso.
4. Madrid es la ciudad _____ grande de España.

4. ¿DÓNDE ESTÁ? WHERE IS IT?

4a. Escucha y lee las siguientes preposiciones de lugar.
Listen and read.

al lado de

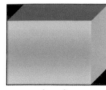

el cubo   el lápiz

¿Dónde está **el lápiz**?
El lápiz está **al lado del** cubo

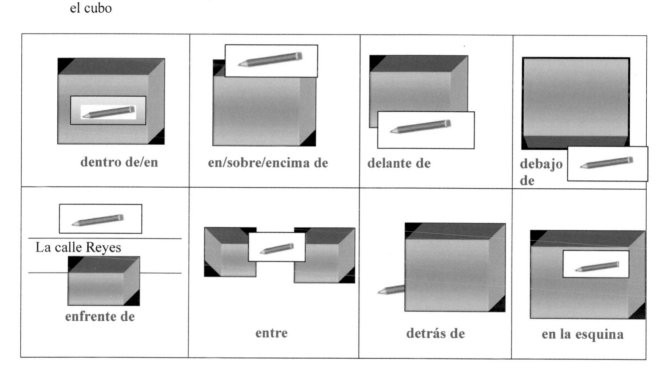

dentro de/en	en/sobre/encima de	delante de	debajo de
La calle Reyes enfrente de	entre	detrás de	en la esquina

4b Relaciona las dos columnas. Match the two columns.

1. al lado de _b_
2. dentro de/en _i_
3. detrás de _d_
4. delante de _a_
5. debajo de _f_
6. enfrente de _g_
7. entre _c_
8. en/sobre/encima de _e_
9. en la esquina _h_

   a. in front of
   b. next to
   c. between
   d. behind
   e. on
   f. under
   g. opposite
   h. on the corner
   i. inside/in

GRAMÁTICA

de + el = del
de la = de la

4c. Practica con tu compañero/a: ¿Dónde está el libro?
Practise with your partner: 'Where's the book?'

123

5. SER O ESTAR. TO BE.

5a. Completa las siguientes frases con la forma verbal adecuada (ser o estar).
Complete the following sentences with the appropriate form of the verb 'to be' (ser or estar).

1. **Es** muy antigua.
2. _____ en el norte de España.
3. _____ cerca de Madrid.
4. _____ al sur de Buenos Aires.
5. _____ grande bonita e interesante.
6. _____ viejo y aburrido.
7. No _____ lejos de aquí.
8. _____ famosa por su vida nocturna.
9. _____ en la costa del Mar Mediterráneo.
10. No _____ bonita ni interesante.

5b. Marca verdadero o falso. Tick true or false.

	V	F
1. La ciudad **está** grande.		
2. El pueblo **es** interesante.		
3. La casa **es** al norte de la ciudad.		
4. La película **es** muy divertida.		
5. El restaurante **está** en el centro de la ciudad.		
6. Luis **está** en la biblioteca.		
7. María **está** española de Barcelona.		

5c. Rellena los espacios vacíos con la forma verbal correspondiente: hay, ser o estar.
Fill the blanks with the appropriate form of the verb: there is/are (**hay**), to be (**ser** or **estar**).

María _____ una chica muy simpática. _____ profesora de primaria. _____ alta morena y guapa. Vive en una casa, su casa _____ vieja y _____ cerca de la plaza pero lejos del río. En su casa _____ una cocina, un dormitorio, un salón comedor y un jardín pequeño. Pero no _____ garaje. María _____ soltera pero vive con su pareja que se llama Jorge, él _____ carpintero y trabaja en una fábrica de muebles. María vive en Laredo. Laredo _____ un pueblo pequeño y bonito pero _____ turístico. _____ muy cerca de la playa y lejos de la montaña.

Los padres de María _____ profesores también pero viven en la ciudad. María tiene dos hermanos, ellos _____ casados y _____ funcionarios.

5d. Marca la frase correcta: a o b. Tick the correct sentence: a or b.

a)   a) Toda la familia está en Barcelona.   b) Toda la familia es en Barcelona.
b)   a) Mario está alto y guapo.   b) Mario es alto y guapo.
c)   a) El pueblo está al norte de Madrid.   b) El pueblo es al norte de Madrid.
d)   a) La ciudad está bonita y grande.   b) La ciudad es bonita y grande.
e)   a) El banco está al lado de la plaza.   b) El banco es al lado de la plaza.
f)   a) El teatro es enfrente del cine.   b) El teatro está enfrente del cine.
g)   a) La catedral es antigua y vieja.   b) La catedral está antigua y vieja.

6. LECTURA Y COMPRENSIÓN. READING AND COMPREHENSION.

6a. Lee los siguientes textos y rellena los recuadros de abajo.
Read the following texts and fill in the table below.

Madrid

Madrid es la capital de España, está en el centro del país y tiene una población de tres millones trescientos mil habitantes. Es una ciudad muy grande, turística, moderna y antigua. Es una ciudad muy cosmopolita y su vida nocturna es muy activa. También tiene muy buenas universidades. Hay muchos teatros y lugares para divertirse. Lo malo es que es demasiado grande para recorrer la ciudad, la gente no es muy amable y en verano hace mucho calor.

Cancún

Es una ciudad pequeña, bonita, moderna y muy turística. Está en el sureste de México junto al mar Caribe. Tiene muchas playas muy hermosas. Hay muchos sitios para que toda la familia se pueda divertir durante el día y por la noche. Normalmente el clima es muy bueno y hace sol casi todos los días del año. Lo malo es que es una ciudad para el turismo, todo es muy caro, no hay universidades y además puede haber huracanes.

Higueras

Es un pueblo muy pequeño, antiguo y tranquilo. Está en el noreste de México al pie de la sierra de Picachos. La gente es muy amable y el clima es muy bueno, por lo general siempre hace calor. Lo malo es que no hay muchas facilidades, no hay institutos ni academias. No hay muchas tiendas, no hay cines ni restaurantes ni bancos.

	Madrid	Cancún	Higueras
Lo bueno			
Lo malo			

6b. Lee el siguiente artículo y contesta en inglés a las preguntas sobre Maggie y su pueblo en inglés. Read the following article and answer the questions about Maggie and her hometown in English.

Huntly

Me llamo Maggie, soy escocesa de Huntly. Huntly está en el norte de Escocia.

Me llamo Maggie. Soy escocesa, de Huntly pero vivo cerca de Perth y trabajo en Dundee. En mi familia somos cinco: mi madre, mis dos hermanas, mi hijo y yo. Mi padre murió[1]. Todos vivimos en Escocia. Mi hijo se llama Max, es estudiante de política y es músico. Es alto y delgado, tiene el pelo castaño. Tiene 24 años.

Huntly es un pueblo bastante pequeño. Tiene una población de 5.000 habitantes más o menos. Huntly está en el noreste de Escocia, cerca de Aberdeen. Está cerca de las montañas famosas de Escocia llamadas Tierras Altas «The Highlands» pero está muy lejos de Londres, Inglaterra, a 1.000 kilómetros más o menos. Huntly es un pueblo bonito, pequeño, turístico e interesante. Hay mucha cultura, arte, un castillo famoso, tiendas, museos, una plaza muy pequeña, un ayuntamiento y un campo de golf. Hay un centro de cultura y arte nuevo que se llama Deveron, como el río. El río es famoso por la pesca del salmón. Las principales actividades turísticas al aire libre del pueblo son: la pesca y la equitación y el Castillo el cual atrae a muchos turistas cada año. Este pueblo es también el hogar de los panaderos de Dean, que son famosos por trabajar en la fábrica de pan que produce galletas de mantequilla. Pero en Huntly no hay un centro comercial ni una universidad. Sin embargo, el colegio tiene una excelente reputación. En la mayoría de los pueblos de las afueras de Aberdeen se habla el doric, que es un dialecto muy antiguo. Casi toda mi familia habla doric e inglés.

Recuerdo con cariño[2] a mi abuela, Christina, una mujer baja y un poco delgada y morena con pelo negro, parecía española. Era muy simpática y tuvo una vida muy dura. Antes de casarse, era modista y luego tuvo seis hijos. La recuerdo con todos sentados alrededor del fuego, en la casa construida por su padre, con sus amigas y parientes. Me acuerdo de sus historias y del cotilleo[3].

[1] **murió** he died   [2] **con cariño** fondly   [3] **cotilleo** gossip

El Castillo de Huntly

El pueblo de Huntly también es famoso por su castillo, el cual está situado en las afueras de la ciudad de Huntly. El castillo es uno de los edificios de la Escocia medieval más impresionante. *Fue construido alrededor del año 1450 por el recién ennoblecido conde de Huntly. Está en ruinas desde el siglo XVIII pero es bonito de visitar; puedes subir a las torres, pasear por las habitaciones y mantiene un sabor real y misterioso.

*fue… it was

Sacado de: http://www.viajesylugares.es/reino-unido/escocia/03-huntly-castle.html

1. Where does Maggie live and work?
2. Where exactly is Huntly?
3. What does Maggie's son look like?
4. What is Maggie's town like?
5. What is there to see and do?
6. How many inhabitants are there?
7. What kind of biscuit is produced in the town?
8. What kinds of activities are there for tourists?
9. How does Maggie remember her grandmother?
10. What kind of castle does Huntly have?
11. In which year was the castle built?

7. VAMOS A ESCRIBIR. LET'S WRITE.

Escribe un texto sobre tu ciudad o pueblo, tienes que incluir los siguientes puntos:
Write a paragraph about your hometown, including the following points:

- Tu nombre y nacionalidad y una breve descripción de tu familia.
- Descripción de lugar de origen.
- Dónde está.
- Cómo es.
- Qué hay.
- Qué no hay.
- Número de habitantes.
- Tipo de transporte.
- Está cerca o lejos la montaña/frontera.
- A cuántos kilómetros está de la costa.
- Lo bueno y lo malo de tu ciudad/pueblo.

GRAMÁTICA

- **Adjetivos calificativos.** Qualifying adjectives.
  The adjective normally goes after the noun and is in agreement with number and gender with the noun it is qualifying.

○	**grande**	Es una ciudad grande. Es un pueblo pequeño.
○	**bonito/a**	Es un castillo bonito. Es una plaza bonita.
○	**feo/a**	Es una casa fea. Es un piso feo.
○	**viejo/a**	Es un libro viejo. Es una mesa vieja.
○	**interesante**	Es un libro interesante. Es una película interesante.

- **Preposiciones indicando un lugar específico.** Prepositions indicating exact location.

• **al lado de**.......... next to	• **en la esquina** ......on the corner
• **debajo de** .... under	• **enfrente de**.........opposite
• **delante de** ....in front of	• **entre** ....between
• **dentro de/en**...... inside	• **en/sobre**........... on
• **detrás de**........... behind	

- **El uso de las preposiciones «de» y «a» + artículo determinado.**
  Use of the prepositions 'de' and 'a' + article.

*el banco (*m*)
*la librería (*f*)

  ○ **de + el = del pero** (but) **de la = de la**

  Ejemplo: Está cerca **del** banco (el banco) ....It is near the bank.
  Está cerca **de la** librería....................It is near the bookshop.

*el parque (*m*)
*la biblioteca (*f*)

  ○ **a + el = al pero** (but) **a la = a la**

  Ejemplo: (Nosotros) vamos **al** *parque .... We go to the park.
  (Nosotros) vamos **a la** *biblioteca........... We go to the library.

- **Adverbios de cantidad.** Adverbs of quantity.

muy	very	**La ciudad es muy grande.**	The city is very big.
mucho/a	a lot of	**Hay mucho tráfico.**	There is a lot of traffic.
		Hay mucha comida en casa.	There is a lot of food at home.
muchos/as	many	**Hay muchos coches.**	There are many cars.
		Hay muchas bicicletas.	There are many bicycles.

- **Comparativos y superlativos.**

más......que	more.....than
menos...que	less.......than
tan.......como	as.........as
el/la...más...de	the biggest/largest...of

- **Adjetivos posesivos.**

mi/mis	my	**nuestro/nuestra/ nuestros/nuestras**	our
tu/tus	yours	**vuestro/vuestra/ vuestros/vuestras**	yours
su/sus	their	**sus**	their

EJERCICIOS

1. Escribe en los espacios vacíos la forma correcta de los verbos «ser» o «estar».
Fill in the blanks with the correct form of the verb 'to be' (**ser** or **estar**).

    A. Me llamo Pablo González. (**1**) _____ ingeniero civil. (**2**) _____ casado. (**3**) _____ alto, delgado y moreno. (**4**) _____ español de Barcelona. Barcelona (**5**) _____ en el norte de España. (**6**) _____ una ciudad grande y bonita.
    B. Bélgica (**1**) _____ un país muy bonito. (**2**) _____ en el oeste de Europa.
    C. Madrid (**1**) _____ en el centro de España. (**2**) _____ una ciudad grande e interesante.
    D. Londres (**1**) _____ una ciudad grande y muy turística. (**2**) _____ en el sur de Inglaterra.
    E. Mi amiga se llama Diana, (**1**) _____ estudiante de psicología. (**2**) _____ soltera. (**3**) _____ alta, guapa, morena y delgada. (**4**) _____ colombiana de Bogotá. Bogotá (**5**) _____ en el centro de Colombia y (**6**) _____ la capital del país. Bogotá (**7**) _____ una ciudad bonita e interesante pero (**8**) _____ muy peligrosa.

2. Completa las siguientes frases con la forma verbal adecuada de los verbos «ser» o «estar».
Complete the following sentences with the appropriate form of the verb 'to be'.

  1. _____ en el sur de Francia.
  2. _____ muy lejos de Sevilla.
  3. No_____ bonita.
  4. _____ grande y turística.
  5. _____ cerca de Barcelona.
  6. _____ muy interesante y hermosa.
  7. _____ famoso por su castillo.
  8. _____ en el centro de la plaza.
  9. No_____ cerca de la playa.

3. Completa las siguientes frases con el adjetivo posesivo adecuado.
Complete the following sentences with the appropriate possessive adjective.

  1. _____ (*my*) pueblo es pequeño y tranquilo. ¿Cómo es _____ (*your informal*) ciudad?
  2. _____ (*your informal*) pueblo tiene una la plaza de toros muy bonita. _____ (*my*) ciudad Barcelona ya no tiene plaza de toros. Ahora es un centro comercial.
  3. Ana tiene una casa muy bonita. _____ (*her*) casa está lejos de la ciudad porque es muy grande.
  4. _____ (*our*) padres son españoles de Madrid. ¿De dónde son _____ (*your informal*) padres?
  5. _____ (*our*) piscina es muy grande y bonita. ¿Cómo es _____ (*your informal*) piscina?
  6. Los López son _____ (*our*) vecinos. _____ (*their*) hijas son amigas de _____ (*our*) hijas. Pero _____ (*their*) perro no es amigo de _____ (*our*) perro.

4. Rellena los espacios vacíos con la forma verbal correspondiente: hay, ser o estar.
Fill the blanks with the appropriate form of the verb: 'there is/are' (**hay**), 'to be' (**ser** or **estar**).

Mario _____ un hombre muy trabajador. _____ alto y moreno. _____ granjero. Su granja _____ vieja y _____ cerca de un pueblo que se llama Torremolinos. En su granja _____ una cocina, tres dormitorios, un salón comedor y un corral grande. También hay muchos animales. Pero no _____ jardín. Mario _____ casado y vive con su mujer que se llama Laura, ella _____ profesora y trabaja en el colegio del pueblo. Torremolinos _____un pueblo grande y _____ muy turístico. _____ cerca de la playa pero lejos de las montañas.

Los padres de Mario _____ granjeros y viven en Torremolinos también. Mario tiene dos hermanos, ellos _____ solteros y _____ carpinteros.

VOCABULARIO

1. ¿CÓMO ES? / 1. WHAT DOES IT LOOK LIKE?

aburrido/a	boring
antiguo/a	old
bonito/a	pretty
dinámico/a	dynamic
feo/a	ugly
grande (m/f)	large/big
hermoso/a	beautiful
horrible (m/f)	horrible
moderno/a	modern
nuevo/a	new
peligroso/a	dangerous
pequeño/a	little
turístico/a	touristy
viejo/a	old
¿Cómo es tu ciudad/pueblo?	What does your hometown look like?
¿De dónde eres?	Where do you come from?
¿Dónde está?	Where is it?

2. ¿QUÉ HAY EN TU CIUDAD/PUEBLO? / 2. WHAT'S IN YOUR HOMETOWN?

ancho/a	wide
ayuntamiento (m)	town hall/city hall
bar (m)	bar
bastante	quite
calle (f)	street
centro comercial (m)	mall
correos (m)	post office
edificio (m)	building
estrecho/a	narrow
iglesia (f)	church
muchos/as	a lot of
piscina (f)	swimming pool
plaza (f)	square
plaza de toros (f)	bullfighting ring
río (m)	river
tienda (f)	shop

3. DESCRIPCIÓN DEL LUGAR DONDE NACISTE. / 3. DESCRIPTION OF YOUR HOME TOWN.

aquí	here
ciudad (f)	city
está cerca/lejos de	It's nearby/far from
habitante (m)	inhabitant
isla (f)	island
kilómetro (m)	kilometre/kilometer
pueblo (m)	town/village
tengo que	I have to
¿Qué hay?	What's there
¿Verdad?	Aren't you?

4. ¿DÓNDE ESTÁ? / 4. WHERE IS IT?

al lado de	next to
de	from
debajo de	under
delante de	in front of
dentro de/en	in/inside
detrás de	behind
en	in/on
en la esquina	on the corner
enfrente de	in front of
entre	between
esquina (f)	corner
sobre/encima	on/above

5. SER O ESTAR / 5. TO BE

carpintero/a	carpenter
divertido/a	fun
famoso/a	famous
frontera (f)	border
funcionario/a de gobierno	civil servant/government officer
vendedor/vendedora	salesman/saleswoman

VERBOS / VERBS

estar	to be (in a place)
hay	there is/are
ser	to be
tener	to have

9 HOGAR DULCE HOGAR

TEMAS TOPICS	OBJETIVOS COMUNICATIVOS COMMUNICATIVE OBJECTIVES	GRAMÁTICA GRAMMAR
El hogar. Los muebles de tu casa. ¿Cuál es tu dirección?	**Hablar de tu casa/piso.** Talking about your house/flat. **Explicar dónde está y cómo llegar a tu casa/piso.** Explain where it is and how to get there. **Aprender el vocabulario de la casa.** Learning vocabulary about the home. **Preguntar y decir «qué hay».** Asking and saying 'what is/are there'. **Usar los números ordinales: (1 º - 10 º).** Using ordinal numbers: (1st - 10th). **Usar interrogativos y exclamativos.** Using interrogatives and exclamations.	**Hay + artículo indeterminado + sustantivo.** There is/are + indefinite article + noun. **Artículo determinado + sustantivo +está/n.** Definite article + noun + to be (in a place). **Verbos irregulares en el presente: ir y hacer.** Irregular verbs in present tense: to go and to do/to make. **Presente de indicativo de verbos con irregularidad vocálica (e →ie): pensar, querer y preferir.** Verbs with vowel irregularity in present tense: to think, to want and to prefer. **Números ordinales: primero, segundo, tercero…** Ordinal numbers: first, second, third… **Interrogativos y exclamativos: ¿Qué? ¡Hola!** Interrogatives and exclamations: What? Hello!

1. ¿VIVES EN UN PISO O EN UNA CASA? DO YOU LIVE IN A FLAT OR IN A HOUSE?

1a. Mira las fotografías de la página anterior y junto con toda la clase, escribe el número correspondiente en los espacios vacíos. Look at the pictures from the previous page and, together with the whole class, write the corresponding number in the empty spaces.

1. un castillo	2. una casa	3. un piso/un apartamento
4. una habitación	5. una granja	6. un chalet adosado

Audio 53

1b. Conversación: Escucha y lee. Conversation: Listen and read.

GRAMÁTICA

¿Por qué?	Why?
porque	because
¡Qué suerte!	How lucky!
¡Qué pena!	What a shame!
querer	to want
preferir	to prefer
pensar	to think

Rosa **¡Hola Carlos! ¿Cómo estás?**

Carlos ¿Qué tal Rosa? Estoy muy feliz.

Rosa **¿Por qué?**

Carlos Porque tengo una casa nueva.

Rosa **¡Qué suerte! ¿Cómo es?**

Carlos Es nueva, grande, bonita y moderna. ¿Y tú Rosa? ¿Vives en una casa o en un piso?

Rosa **Prefiero vivir en una casa, pero vivo en un piso.**

Carlos ¿Cómo es tu piso?

Rosa **Mi piso es pequeño, feo y muy viejo. Está en el quinto piso y no hay ascensor.**

Carlos ¡Qué pena!

Rosa **¿Dónde está tu casa?**

Carlos Mi casa está en el sur de la ciudad, al lado de la piscina y enfrente del parque. ¿Y tu piso Rosa Dónde está?

Rosa **Mi piso está en el centro de la ciudad, enfrente del centro comercial, entre la oficina de correos y el café de internet.**

Carlos Bueno, quiero ir a nadar y pienso ir de compras. Adiós.

Rosa **Hasta luego Carlos, yo quiero ir al super porque tengo que comprar comida. No tengo nada en mi cocina.**

1c. Lee una vez más la conversación (1b) anterior y contesta a las siguientes preguntas. Read the conversation above (1b) again and answer the following questions.

1. ¿Por qué Carlos está muy feliz?
2. ¿Cómo es su casa?
3. ¿Dónde está la casa de Carlos?
4. ¿Cómo es el piso de Rosa?
5. ¿Dónde está el piso?
6. ¿Qué quiere hacer Carlos?
7. ¿Dónde quiere ir Rosa y por qué?
   ¿Y tú?
   a. ¿Vives en una casa o en piso?
   b. ¿Cómo es tu casa/piso?
   c. ¿Dónde está tu casa/piso?
   d. ¿Qué quieres hacer hoy?
   e. ¿Qué piensas hacer esta semana?

2. ¿QUÉ HAY EN TU PISO/CASA? WHAT'S IN YOUR FLAT/HOUSE?

Audio 54

2a. Escucha el siguiente vocabulario y relaciona las fotografías con las palabras.
Listen the following vocabulary and match the pictures with the words.

1. la cocina f
2. el salón L
3. el comedor a
4. el (cuarto de) baño b
5. el dormitorio g
6. el despacho/el estudio e

7. el aseo/el servicio i
8. el pasillo h
9. la escalera c
10. el balcón J
11. el garaje K
12. el jardín d

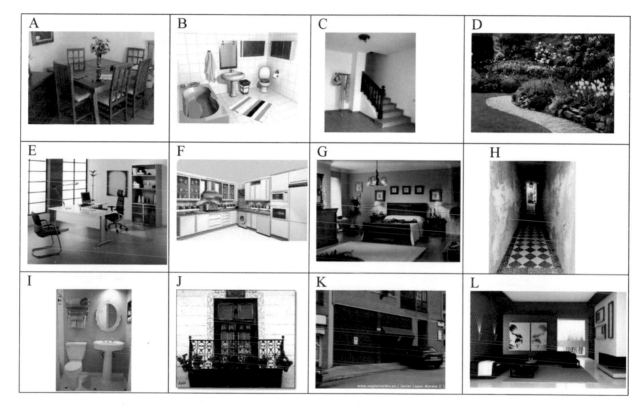

2b. Completa las siguientes frases con la forma verbal adecuada: ser o estar.
Complete the following sentences with the appropriate form of the verb 'to be' (ser or estar).

1. La casa _es_ muy grande y bonita. _Está_ en el sur de la ciudad.
2. La cocina _es_ vieja y grande. _Está_ al lado del salón - comedor.
3. Los dormitorios _son_ grandes y modernos. _Están_ al lado del baño.
4. El baño _es_ azul y pequeño. _Está_ enfrente del pasillo.
5. El piso de Pedro _está_ enfrente de correos. _Es_ pequeño y moderno.
6. Mi piso _está_ lejos de la universidad. _Es_ viejo y grande.
7. La casa de Rita _es_ muy bonita. No _está_ lejos de aquí.
8. Los balcones _están / Son_ muy grandes. _Están_ detrás del salón.

2c. Lee las siguientes descripciones e identifica qué plano es: A o B.
Read the following descriptions and identify which floor plan is: A or B.

A. En mi piso hay cuatro dormitorios, dos dormitorios dobles y dos individuales, un salón- comedor, una cocina muy grande y dos cuartos de baño. No hay balcón ni terraza.

B. En mi casa hay tres dormitorios dobles, dos baños, un salón-comedor muy amplio y bonito, una cocina grande y una terraza doble pero no hay balcón.

Plano 1   **Plano 2**

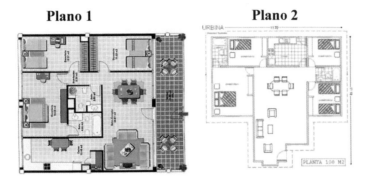

2d. Escribe las siguientes frases en plural. Write the plural of the following sentences.

1. La cocina es pequeña y fea. ....
2. El dormitorio doble es grande. ....
3. Hay un dormitorio individual. ....
4. El baño es grande y bonito. ....
5. La casa es muy pequeña pero es bonita. ....
6. El jardín está detrás de la casa. ....
7. El garaje es nuevo y moderno. ....
8. En el piso hay una piscina compartida. ....

2e. Contesta a las siguientes preguntas y practica con tus compañeros/as.
Answer the following questions and practise the dialogues with your partners.

	Ejemplo	Compañero/a 1	Compañero/a 2
¿Cómo te llamas?	Ricardo		
¿Vives en una casa o en piso?	Vivo en un piso.		
¿Dónde está?	Está en el este de la ciudad, enfrente del ayuntamiento.		
¿Cómo es?	Mi piso es grande, viejo y bonito.		
¿Qué hay en tu casa/piso?	Hay un salón-comedor, un baño, una cocina, dos dormitorios, un pasillo y un balcón.		
¿Qué no hay en tu casa/piso?	No hay garaje ni jardín.		

2f. Relaciona las palabras. Match the words.

1.	la ventana	a)	the washing machine
2.	la nevera	b)	the wardrobe
3.	la silla	c)	the mirror
4.	el espejo	d)	the armchair
5.	el armario	e)	the fridge
6.	la cama	f)	the shower
7.	la lavadora	g)	the kitchen/the cooker
8.	el sofá	h)	the window
9.	la ducha	i)	the chair
10.	la cocina	j)	the bookshelf
11.	la estantería	k)	the bed
12.	el sillón	l)	the sofa

2g. Mira la fotografía de abajo y en grupos de dos o tres practica las siguientes preguntas como en el ejemplo. Look at the picture below and in groups of two or three practise the following questions as in the example.

Estudiante A	Estudiante B
¿Qué hay en la foto 4?	Hay una **mesa.**
¿Cómo es?	(La mesa) es marrón, nueva y moderna.
¿Dónde está?	(La mesa) está enfrente de la nevera.

2h. Adivinar. Guessing.
  A. **¿En qué habitación hay dos camas individuales?**
  B. **En la cocina.**
  A. **No. En el dormitorio.**

2i. En una hoja de papel dibuja el plano de tu casa/piso y comparte con tu compañero/a.
  ¿Qué hay y dónde está cada habitación? On a piece of paper draw a floor plan of your house and share it with your partner. What's there and where are the rooms?

  Ejemplo: En mi casa hay una cocina. La cocina está entre el comedor y el cuarto de baño.

GRAMÁTICA
Hay **un** dormitorio   There is **one** bedroom
El dormitorio está…**The** bedroom is…

135

3. ¿CUÁL ES TU DIRECCIÓN? WHAT IS YOUR ADDRESS?

Audio 55

3a. Escucha y une las abreviaturas con las fotografías.
Listen and match the abbreviations with the pictures.

a.) P.º de los Álamos, 30
b.) Pza. Barcelona, 50
c.) C/Picasso, 53
d.) Ctra. San Augusto, 200
e.) Avda. del Rey, 85

1.   La avenida

2.   La carretera

3.   El paseo

4.   La calle

5.   La plaza

Audio 56

3b. Escucha y repite los números ordinales.
Listen and repeat the ordinal numbers.

1º primero/a (**primer**)
2º segundo/a
3º tercero/a (**tercer**)
4º cuarto/a
5º quinto/a
6º sexto/a
7º séptimo/a
8º octavo/a
9º noveno/a
10º décimo/a

Vivo en el quinto piso

Audio 57

3c. Escucha ¿A qué piso van estas personas?
Listen. What floor are they going to?

1. El _____ piso
2. El _____ piso
3. El _____ piso
4. El _____ piso
5. El _____ piso
6. El _____ piso

Traduce al inglés las siguientes frases.
Translate the following sentences into English.

a) El segundo día.
b) La quinta lección.
c) El tercer niño.
d) El primero de mayo.
e) (Nosotros) Vamos al noveno piso.

3d. Estudia las siguientes tarjetas de presentación y contesta a las preguntas.
Study the following business cards and answer the questions.

VIAJES MOLINA
ARNOLDO MOLINA MARTINEZ

Avenida Colón, No 1224
Colonia las Américas
Victoria, Tamaulipas.
MÉXICO
    Tel: 76 56 33
    Tel móvil: 073 23 45 67
    email: a.molinama@mex.com

Agencia de modas y diseño
LAURA ROMERO

C/ Reyes Católicos, 34 - 2º A
Código Postal: 29045
Madrid, ESPAÑA
Tel: 79 66 34
Tel móvil: 077 65 43 70
email: romero@hotmail.com

a) ¿Cuál es el teléfono fijo de Arnoldo?
b) ¿Cuál es el móvil de Laura?
c) ¿Cuál es la dirección del correo electrónico de la Agencia de VIAJES MOLINA?
d) ¿Cuál es la dirección de la Agencia de VIAJES MOLINA?
e) ¿Cuál es la dirección de la Agencia de modas y diseño?
f) ¿Cuál es el email de la agencia de modas y diseño?
g) ¿Cómo se llama la directora de la agencia de modas y diseño?

Audio 58

3e. Escucha y escribe la información que falta en cada tarjeta.
Listen and write the missing information on each card.

Tarjeta 1   **Tarjeta 2**

Mario [_____] [_____]

[_____]

Paseo [_____]

Teléfono: 92 [_____]

Código postal: [_____]

Madrid

Correo electrónico: [_____]

[_____] Ruiz

[_____] del Banco EUROLATINO

[_____]

Teléfono: 97 [_____]

Código postal: [_____]

Barcelona
Email: [_____]

3f. Escribe tu propia tarjeta de presentación y después preséntate a todos tus compañeros/as.
Write your own business card and then introduce yourself to all your classmates.

4. ¿CÓMO LLEGO? HOW DO I GET THERE?

Audio 59

4a. Escucha y repite. Listen and repeat.

a la derecha   a la izquierda   todo recto   al final de la calle   gira

Audio 60

4b. Estás en la oficina de turismo. Escucha y escribe en el plano de abajo el nombre de los lugares correspondientes. You are in the tourist office. Listen and write on the map below the name of the corresponding places.

1. El hospital	6. La estación de trenes	11. La universidad
2. La gasolinera	7. El parqueadero	12. La piscina
3. El restaurante	8. El centro comercial	13. El banco
4. El parque	9. El bar	14. La tienda
5. El colegio	10. El supermercado	

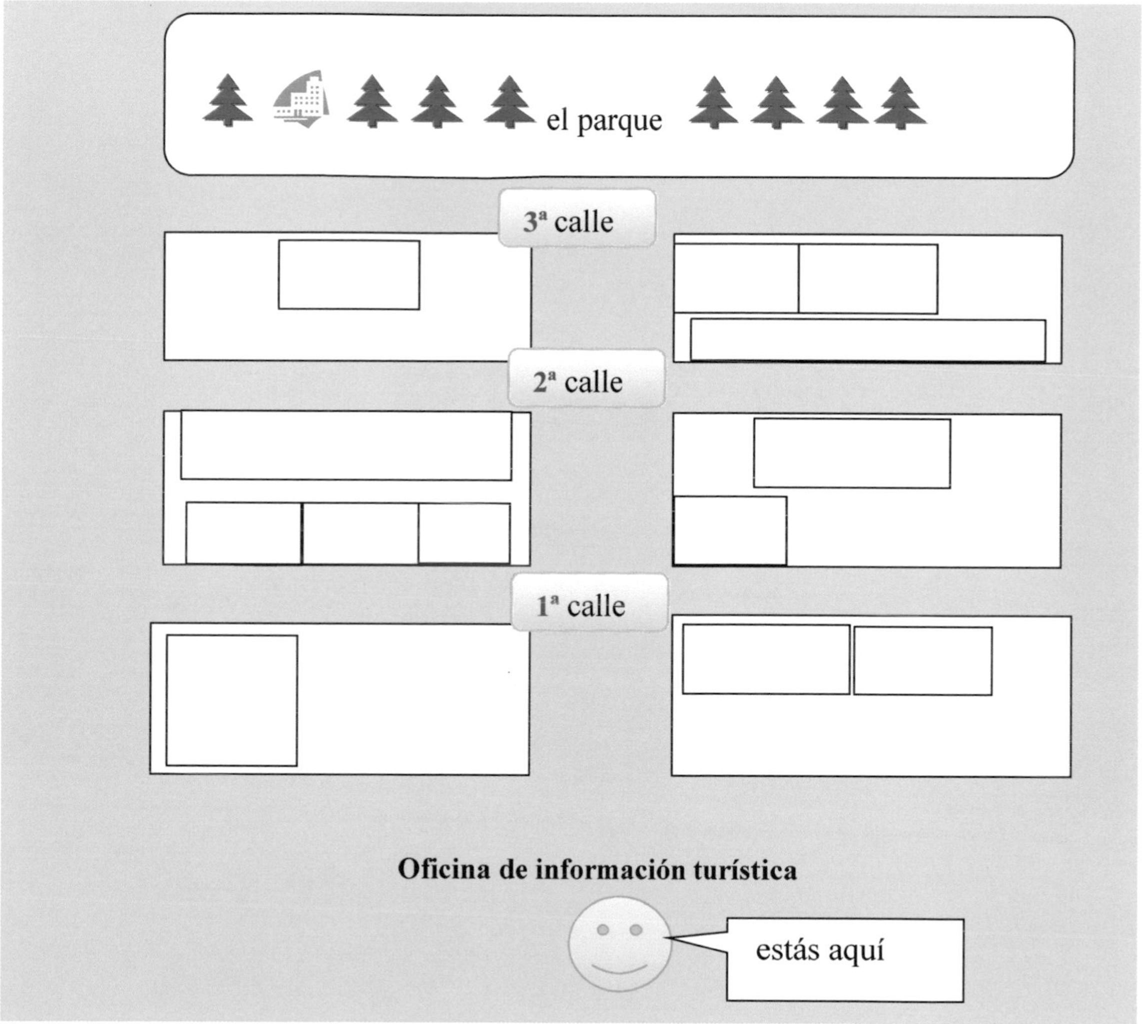

el parque

3ª calle

2ª calle

1ª calle

Oficina de información turística

estás aquí

5. QUÉ HAY EN TU BARRIO? WHAT'S IN YOUR NEIGHBORHOOD?

5a. Mira el plano y practica con tu compañero/a como en el ejemplo.
Look at the map and practise with your partner as in the example.

> **RECUERDA**
> una farmacia (f)
> un parqueadero (m)

Ejemplo:
A. ¿Hay una **farmacia cerca** de aquí?
B. Sí, sí hay una farmacia. Está en la calle **Colón, enfrente del hospital y al lado del bar**.

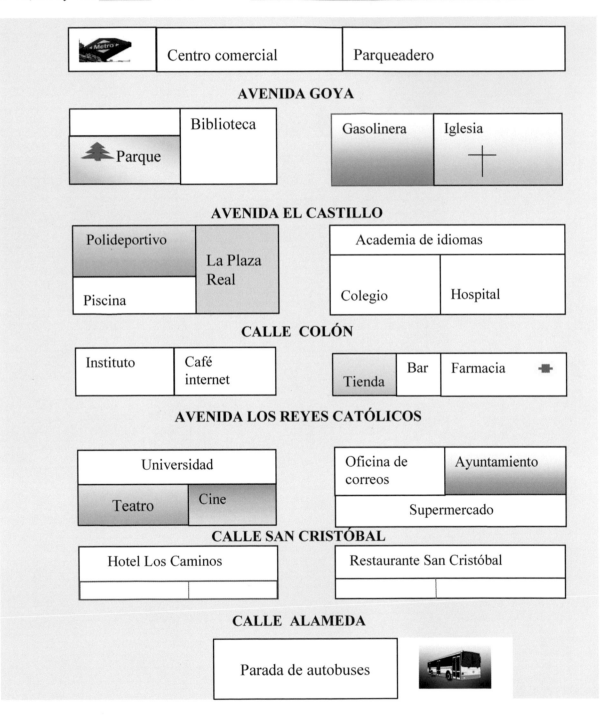

5b. Mira el plano anterio (5a) y practica con tu compañero/a cómo puedes llegar a los diferentes lugares. Look at the previous map (5a) and practise with your partner how you can get to the different places.

Ejemplo:

A. **¿Hay <u>un hospital</u> cerca de aquí?**
B. Sí, hay uno cerca aquí.
A. **¿Dónde está?**
B. Está <u>enfrente</u> de <u>la farmacia.</u>
A. **¿Podría decirme cómo puedo llegar por favor?**
B. Desde la parada de autobuses, <u>continúa todo recto hasta la calle Colón, gira a la derecha y el hospital está enfrente de la farmacia.</u>
A. **Muchas gracias.**
B. De nada.

¡DESCUBRE!	
toma/coge	take
continúa/sigue	continue
después	then
luego	then
¿Cómo puedo llegar?	How can I get to?

Mira una vez más el plano del ejercicio (5a) y practica con tu compañero/a la siguiente actividad. Estudiante A tiene los nombres de algunos lugares y Estudiante B tiene otros. Look at the previous map again (5a) and practise with your partner the following activity. Student A has the name of some of the places and Student B has others.

Estudiante A
Tú estás en la parada de autobuses. Explica a tu compañero/a dónde están los siguientes lugares:
You are at the bus stop. Explain to your partner where the following places are:

- El centro comercial
- El polideportivo
- La piscina
- El teatro
- El restaurante San Cristóbal
- El hospital
- El supermercado
- El bar

Estudiante B
Tú estás en el Centro comercial. Explica a tu compañero/a dónde están los siguientes lugares:
You are at the Los Caminos Hotel. Explain to your partner where the following places are:

- El metro
- El parque
- La Plaza Real
- El cine
- El ayuntamiento
- La farmacia
- La oficina de correos
- La iglesia

5c. Contesta a las siguientes preguntas y escribe un texto en base a tus respuestas.
Answer the following questions and write a paragraph based on your answers.
- ¿Vives en una casa o en un piso?
- ¿Cómo es tu casa/piso? (What does your house/flat look like?)
- ¿Qué hay en tu casa/piso? (What is there?)
- ¿Qué no hay? (What is not there?)
- ¿Dónde está exactamente tu casa? (Where exactly is your home?)
- ¿Cómo se puede llegar a tu casa o piso? (How can one get to your place?)

Me llamo…

6. LECTURA Y COMPRENSIÓN. READING COMPREHENSION.

6a. Lee los siguientes enunciados e identifica en el plano de abajo los lugares.
Estás en la parada del metro. Read the following statements and identify the location of the different places. You are in the subway.

1. Sigue todo recto al final de la calle está **la universidad**.
2. Sigue todo recto gira la primera calle a la izquierda. A mano izquierda está **la iglesia**.
3. Sigue todo recto gira la primera calle a la derecha. A mano derecha está **el banco**.
4. Toma la primera calle gira a la izquierda y a mano derecha está **el parque**.
5. En la segunda calle gira a la derecha y a mano derecha está **el hotel**.
6. Toma la segunda calle a la derecha. A mano izquierda está **la oficina de turismo**.
7. En la tercera calle gira a la izquierda. A mano izquierda está **el teatro**.
8. Todo recto hasta el final de la calle. Gira hacia la derecha y a mano izquierda está **la piscina**.
9. Todo recto hasta el final de la calle. Gira a la derecha y a mano derecha está **el museo**.
10. Todo recto hasta el final de la calle. Gira a la izquierda y a mano derecha está **la gasolinera** al lado de la universidad.

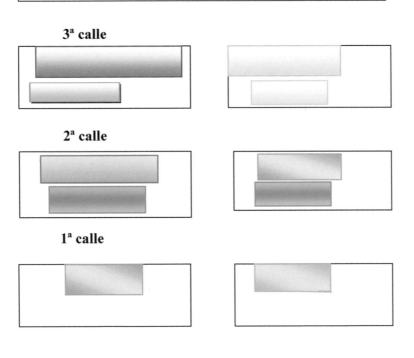

3ª calle

2ª calle

1ª calle

6b. Lee el siguiente anuncio de viviendas y contesta en español a las siguientes preguntas sobre el piso en venta. Read the following advert about housing and answer in Spanish the following questions on the flat for sale.

Piso en venta en calle Dolores Armengol, Nº 18, 3º Planta,
Vista Alegre, Carabanchel,
Madrid.
100.000 €

Se trata de una tercera planta en el barrio madrileño de Carabanchel. Piso moderno, cómodo y nuevo. Se compone de dos dormitorios, salón de 24 m², cocina y cuarto de baño. Para más información contacte con nosotros sin compromiso y concierte una cita en la que visitaremos la vivienda.

Datos básicos

Superficie: 69 m² construidos/55 m² útiles
Habitaciones: 2 habitaciones
Baños: 1 baño
Planta: 3ª
Antigüedad: Entre 30 y 50 años
Gastos de comunidad: entre 10 y 20 €

Armarios empotrados: 0
Aire acondicionado: frío y calor
Cocina equipada
Portero automático
Exteriores: Soleado

1. ¿Cuánto cuesta?
2. ¿Cuál es la dirección?
3. ¿Dónde está?
4. ¿Cuál es la superficie en m²?
5. ¿Qué hay?
6. ¿Cómo es?
7. ¿Cuánto hay que pagar por gastos de comunidad?

7. VAMOS A ESCRIBIR. LET'S WRITE.

Dibuja el plano del área donde vives y escribe una carta a tu amigo/a. Explica lo siguiente:
Draw a map of the area where you live and write a letter to your friend. Explain:

• **¿Cómo es tu casa/piso?**	• How does your house/flat look like?
• **¿Qué hay en tu casa/piso?**	• What's in your house/flat?
• **¿Dónde está exactamente?**	• Where is it exactly?
• **¿Cómo llegar?**	• How to get there?
• **¿Qué hay en tu barrio?**	• What's in your neighbourhood?

GRAMÁTICA

- **Artículo determinado + sustantivo + está(n).** Definite article + noun + to be (in a place).

  La iglesia está al lado del banco……..The church is next to the bank.
  El jardín está detrás de la cocina……The garden is behind the kitchen.

- **Hay + artículo indeterminado + sustantivo.** There is/are + indefinite article + noun.

  Hay una piscina…. There is a swimming pool.
  Hay un piso.………There is a flat/apartment.

- **Números ordinales:** Ordinal numbers.
  Like many other adjectives, the ordinal numbers have a masculine and a feminine form. Primero and tercero drop the -o in the masculine singular adjective form.

  1º primero/a (**primer).** El primer mes.
  3º tercero/a (**tercer).** El tercer libro.

- **Preposiciones de direcciones.** Prepositions of directions.

  a la derecha, a la izquierda, todo recto, al final de la calle

- **Verbos irregulares en el presente: ir, hacer.**
  Irregular verbs in present tense: to go and to do/to make.

Pronombres personales sujeto	ir	hacer
yo	voy	hago
tú	vas	haces
él/ella	va	hace
usted	va	hace
nosotros	vamos	hacemos
vosotros	vais	hacéis
ustedes	van	hacen
ellos/ellas	van	hacen

- **Tener que + infinitivo (ar/er/ir).**

  Tienes que estudiar. You have to study.

- **Verbos que se utilizan para dar direcciones.**
  Verbs used to give directions.

  gira ………………. turn
  toma/coje ………… take
  continúa …………. continue

- **Verbos en el presente con irregularidad vocálica: pensar, querer y preferir.**
  Present tense verbs with vowel irregularity: to think, to want and to prefer.

  e → ie

Pronombres personales sujeto	pensar	querer	preferir
yo	pienso	quiero	prefiero
tú	piensas	quieres	prefieres
él/ella	piensa	quiere	prefiere
usted	piensa	quiere	prefiere
nosotros/as	pensamos	queremos	preferimos
vosotros/as	pensáis	queréis	preferís
ustedes	piensan	quieren	prefieren
ellos/ellas	piensan	quieren	prefieren

> **Nota:**
> **La primera y segunda persona del plural (*nosotros/as y vosotros/as*) permanecen regulares.**
> The first and second person plural (*nosotros/as y vosotros/as*) remain regular.

EJERCICIOS

1. Lee el siguiente texto y contesta a las preguntas.
Read the following text and answer the questions.

Se vende Chalet. Precio 295.000€

Chalet impresionante, moderno y grande. Está a 10 minutos en coche de Barcelona. Al lado de la estación de autobuses y enfrente de un colegio. En la planta baja hay: hall, cocina, despensa, aseo, salón– comedor y garaje. En la planta alta hay: 3 dormitorios dobles, 2 baños y una terraza. Muebles de cocina y electrodomésticos están incluidos. Para más información llamar a: Tel 985 75 40 65/663 80 92 71.

a) ¿Cuánto cuesta?
b) ¿Dónde está?
c) ¿Qué hay en la planta baja?
d) ¿Hay balcón?
e) ¿Tiene muebles de cocina?

f) ¿Qué hay en la planta alta?
g) ¿Cómo es?
h) ¿Tiene garaje?
i) ¿Dónde llamar para más información?
j) ¿Están incluidos los electrodomésticos?

2. Escribe la palabra correcta para completar la frase.
Write the correct word to complete the sentence.

a. El dormitorio es _____ .

i. simpático
ii. indefinido
iii. grande

b. Las habitaciones son _____ .

i. bonitas
ii. enfrente del baño
iii. bonitos

c. El jardín es _____ .

i. moreno
ii. pequeño
iii. pequeña

d. El aseo está _____ .

i. al lado del dormitorio
ii. bastante grande.
iii. tiene ducha

3. Rellena los espacios vacíos con la forma verbal correspondiente: hay, ser o estar.
Fill in the blanks with the appropriate form of the verb: 'there is/are' (**hay**), 'to be' (**ser** or **estar**).

a) Los jardines _____ bonitos.
b) El baño _____ entre el dormitorio y el salón.
c) Los dormitorios _____ en la planta alta.
d) La casa _____ grande, vieja y blanca.
e) En nuestra casa _____ diez habitaciones.
f) El restaurante _____ cerca de mi casa.
g) En mi piso no _____ un garaje.
h) En el comedor _____ una ventana grande.
i) Los dormitorios de la casa _____ grandes.

4. Completa las frases con «es» o «está». Después escribe la pregunta que corresponde a cada frase: ¿Cómo es? / ¿Dónde está? Complete the sentences with 'it is' (es/está). Then write the question that corresponds to each sentence: What does it look like? /Where is it?
Ejemplo: El piso **es** bonito. ¿Cómo es el piso?

a) La casa _____ grande.   ¿_____?
b) La silla _____ al lado del sofá.   ¿_____?
c) La ducha _____ en el cuarto de baño.   ¿_____?
d) El armario _____ marrón.   ¿_____?

5. Escribe la forma correcta del verbo para cada frase.
Write the right form of the verb for each sentence.

a) Yo _____ (preferir) ir al cine.
b) Mi marido _____ (querer) estar en casa.
c) Nosotros _____ (pensar) ir de vacaciones.
d) Ustedes _____ (querer) comer en un restaurante.
e) ¿Tú qué _____ (preferir) tomar una cerveza o una gaseosa?
f) Vosotros _____ (pensar) ir de vacaciones el próximo año.
g) Tú _____ (querer) comprar un coche nuevo.

6. Escribe el número ordinal en los espacios vacíos. Write the ordinal number in the empty spaces.

1. Mi hijo está en _____ (4°) grado de primaria.
2. Yo soy la _____ (7ª) de mi familia.
3. Vivimos en el _____ (5°) piso.
4. Marta es la _____ (2ª) de la clase.

7. Escribe las siguientes frases en plural. Write the plural of the following sentences.

1. La cocina es pequeña y fea.   ....
2. El baño es grande.   ....
3. Tiene un dormitorio individual.   ....
4. Hay un jardín grande y bonito.   ....
5. El salón es muy pequeño.   ....
6. El parqueadero está detrás del piso. ....
7. El garaje es nuevo y moderno.   ....
8. En el piso hay un balcón muy grande. ....

8. Completa las siguientes frases con la forma verbal adecuada «ser» o «estar».
Complete the following sentences with the appropriate form of the verb 'to be' (**ser or estar**).

1. La casa _____ muy fea y vieja. _____ en el sur de la ciudad.
2. La cocina _____ vieja y grande. _____ al lado del salón- comedor.
3. Mi piso _____ pequeño y moderno y _____ muy cerca del centro.
4. El baño _____ blanco y pequeño. _____ al lado del dormitorio individual.
5. El piso de Pedro _____ pequeño y moderno. _____ enfrente de correos.
6. Mi piso _____ lejos de la universidad. _____ viejo y grande.
7. La casa de Rita no _____ lejos de aquí y _____ muy bonita.
8. El garaje _____ al lado de la casa. _____ feo pero es muy grande.

VOCABULARIO

1. ¿VIVES EN UN PISO O EN UNA CASA?
1. DO YOU LIVE IN A FLAT OR IN A HOUSE?

apartamento (m)	*apartment*
casa (f)	*house/home*
chalet adosado (m)	*terraced house*
castillo (m)	*castle*
feliz	*happy*
granja (f)	*farm*
habitación (f)	*room*
piso (m)	*flat (UK)/apartment (US)*
porque	*because*
qué	*what*
¿Por qué?	*Why?*
¡Qué suerte!	*How lucky!*
¡Qué pena!	*What a shame!*

2. ¿QUÉ HAY EN TU PISO/CASA?
2. WHAT'S IN YOUR FLAT/HOUSE?

aseo/servicio (m)	*toilet/WC*
balcón (m)	*balcony*
cocina (f)	*kitchen*
comedor (m)	*dining room*
cuarto de baño (m)	*bathroom*
despacho/estudio (m)	*office/study*
dormitorio (m)	*bedroom*
escaleras (fpl)	*stairs*
garaje (m)	*garage*
jardín (m)	*garden*
pasillo (m)	*corridor*
salón (m)	*living room*

3. ¿CUÁL ES TU DIRECCIÓN?
3. WHAT IS YOUR ADDRESS?

avenida (f)	*avenue*
ayuntamiento (m)	*town/city hall*
calle (f)	*street*
carretera (f)	*motorway (UK)/ highway (US)*
cerca	*near*
estación de trenes (f)	*train station*
lejos	*far, a long way*
paseo (m)	*street, stroll*

parque (m)	*park*
piscina (f)	*swimming pool*
plaza (f)	*square (in a town)*
plaza de toros (f)	*bull ring*
universidad (f)	*university*

4. ¿CÓMO LLEGO?
4. HOW DO I GET THERE?

academia (f)	*college*
al final de la calle	*at the end of the street*
banco (m)	*bank*
bar (m)	*pub*
centro comercial (m)	*shopping centre*
colegio (m)	*primary school and secondary school*
derecha (f)	*right*
estanco (m)	*newsagents/ tobacconist*
gasolinera (f)	*petrol (UK)/gas (US) station*
gira	*turn*
hospital (m)	*hospital*
idioma (m)	*language*
instituto (m)	*high school*
izquierda (f)	*left*
parqueadero (m)	*car park (UK)/ parking lot(US)*
restaurante (m)	*restaurant*
supermercado (m)	*supermarket*
todo recto	*straight ahead*
toma	*take, he/she drinks*
¿Cómo es tu casa/piso?	*What does your house/flat look like?*

VERBOS
VERBS

girar	*to turn*
pensar	*to think*
preferir	*to prefer*
querer	*to want*

10 DE COMPRAS

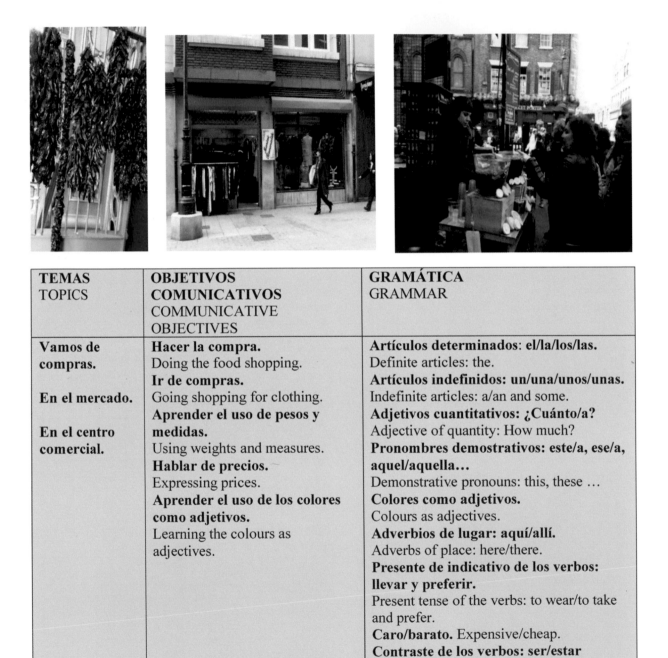

TEMAS TOPICS	OBJETIVOS COMUNICATIVOS COMMUNICATIVE OBJECTIVES	GRAMÁTICA GRAMMAR
Vamos de compras. **En el mercado.** **En el centro comercial.**	**Hacer la compra.** Doing the food shopping. **Ir de compras.** Going shopping for clothing. **Aprender el uso de pesos y medidas.** Using weights and measures. **Hablar de precios.** Expressing prices. **Aprender el uso de los colores como adjetivos.** Learning the colours as adjectives.	**Artículos determinados: el/la/los/las.** Definite articles: the. **Artículos indefinidos: un/una/unos/unas.** Indefinite articles: a/an and some. **Adjetivos cuantitativos: ¿Cuánto/a?** Adjective of quantity: How much? **Pronombres demostrativos: este/a, ese/a, aquel/aquella…** Demonstrative pronouns: this, these … **Colores como adjetivos.** Colours as adjectives. **Adverbios de lugar: aquí/allí.** Adverbs of place: here/there. **Presente de indicativo de los verbos: llevar y preferir.** Present tense of the verbs: to wear/to take and prefer. **Caro/barato.** Expensive/cheap. **Contraste de los verbos: ser/estar (compras).** The contrast between: ser/estar (shopping).

1. HACER LA COMPRA. DOING THE FOOD SHOPPING.

1a. Escucha la conversación entre Rosa y Luis, observa las fotos y marca dónde hace la compra Rosa y dónde la hace Luis. Listen to the conversation between Rosa and Luis and label the photos, according to the place where they do their shopping.

Luis	¡Hola! ¿Qué tal estás?
Rosa	Muy bien gracias. Acabo de moverme a este barrio y quiero hacer la compra de la semana. ¿Dónde haces tú la compra normalmente?
Luis	Normalmente hago la compra los sábados por la mañana en el supermercado que está enfrente de la plaza al lado de la farmacia. Pero cuando estoy muy cansado hago la compra por internet y llega ese mismo día por la tarde.
Rosa	Vale, pero a mí me gusta más hacer la compra en el mercado. ¿Dónde hay un mercado por aquí cerca?
Luis	El mercado está al final de la Avenida Colón cerca del banco. En ese mercado siempre hay verduras frescas y fruta muy buena.
Rosa	¿Hay carnicería y pescadería?
Luis	Sí claro y también hay panadería y una tienda donde venden zumos frescos.
Rosa	Me gusta ir al mercado, hago la compra casi todos los días para comprar comida fresca.
Luis	Adiós.
Rosa	Hasta luego.

1b. Marca verdadero o falso enfrente de cada texto. Tick true or false.

	V	F
1. Rosa es nueva en el barrio y quiere hacer la compra de la semana.		
2. Luis normalmente hace la compra los domingos por la mañana en el mercado.		
3. A Rosa le gusta más hacer la compra en el supermercado.		
4. El mercado está cerca del banco. Siempre hay verduras frescas y fruta muy buena.		

Audio 62

1c. Escucha y relaciona las palabras con las tiendas y practica el diálogo.
Listen and match the shops in the box below with the products shown in the photos and practise.

> **a** pescadería **b** carnicería **c** panadería **d** pastelería
> **e** charcutería **f** frutería **g** verdulería

1. fruta   2. verdura   3. pan   4. pescado   5.jamón   6. carne   7. pasteles

A: ¿Dónde se compra la **fruta**?
B: En la frutería.

Audio 63

1d. Escucha y escribe el nombre de cada producto al lado de la fotografía correspondiente.
Listen and look at the picture, then write the name of each product next to the picture.

a) un bote de mermelada	e) un kilo de tomates	i) una piña
b) una barra de chocolate	f) un cuarto de kilo de queso	j) una botella de agua
c) una lata de atún	g) dos kilos de arroz	k) una barra de pan
d) una botella de aceite	h) medio kilo de plátanos	l) un litro de leche

1		7	
2		8	
3	a) un bote de mermelada	9	
4		10	
5		11	
6		12	

1e. Practica con tu compañero/a diálogos similares al del ejemplo utlilizando los productos de los ejercicios 1c y 1d. Practise with your partner similar dialogues of the following example using the products of the exercises 1c and 1d.

Ejemplo:

A. ¿Qué hay en la tienda?	A. ¿Qué no hay en la tienda?
B. Hay leche.	B. No hay agua.

1f. Estás en una tienda. Practica con tu compañero/a el siguiente diálogo.
You are at the shop. Practise the following dialogue with your partner.

Empleado/a	**Buenos días. ¿Qué desea?**
Cliente	Buenos días. ¿Hay aceite?
Empleado/a	**Sí hay. ¿Cuántas botellas quiere?**
Cliente	Quiero una botella de litro.
Empleado/a	**Vale. ¿Algo más?**
Cliente	¿Hay queso?
Empleado/a	**Sí hay. ¿Cuántos gramos quiere?**
Cliente	Quiero 150 gramos.
Empleado/a	**¿Algo más?**
Cliente	¿Hay pan?
Empleado/a	**No, no hay. ¿Algo más?**
Cliente	Quiero una lata de atún y media docena de huevos.
Empleado/a	**Bien. ¿Algo más?**
Cliente	No gracias, la cuenta por favor.
Empleado/a	**Son 11,60 euros (once euros con sesenta céntimos).**
Cliente	Aquí tiene.
Empleado/a	**Adiós.**

GRAMÁTICA
Los demostrativos

este/esta	this
estos/estas	these
aquel/aquella	that
aquellos/aquellas	those

¡DESCUBRE!

un kilo de…
medio kilo de…
cuarto kilo de…
cien gramos de…
una docena de…
media docena de…
un litro de…
medio litro de…
un melón
una sandía
una lata de…

2. EN EL MERCADO. AT THE MARKET.

Audio 64

2a. Escucha la conversación y contesta a las preguntas.
Listen to the conversation and answer the questions.

1. ¿Qué compra el cliente?
2. ¿Cuánto compra?
3. ¿Cuánto vale el kilo de zanahorias?
4. ¿Cuánto es?

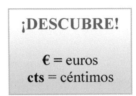

Dependiente	**Buenos días. ¿Qué quiere comprar?**
Cliente	Quiero un kilo de tomates, medio kilo de uvas y 150 gramos de jamón.
Dependiente	**¿Qué uvas, estas de aquí o aquellas de allí?**
Cliente	Prefiero aquellas de allí.
Dependiente	**¿Algo más?**
Cliente	Sí, quiero un litro de aceite, una lechuga y dos kilos de plátanos.
Dependiente	**¿Qué plátanos prefiere, estos de aquí o aquellos de allí?**
Cliente	Prefiero estos de aquí.
Dependiente	**¿Quiere algo más?**
Cliente	Sí ¿Cuánto vale el kilo de zanahorias?
Dependiente	**Un kilo de zanahorias vale 1,70 €.**
Cliente	Quiero dos kilos. ¿Cuánto es en total?
Dependiente	**Son 10 €.**

Audio 65

2b. Escucha los precios de los siguientes productos y escríbelos en el espacio correspondiente. Listen to the prices of the following products and write them in the appropriate spaces.

Producto	€	Producto	€	Producto	€
un kilo de aguacates		**una piña**	**1,00€**	una botella de vino tinto	
un kilo de limones		una lechuga		una botella de vino blanco	
un kilo de manzanas		una sandía		una botella de agua	
un kilo de naranjas	**1,90€**	una barra de chocolate		**una docena de huevos**	**1,80€**
un kilo de cebollas		una barra de pan		**100 gramos de jamón**	**2,80€**
un kilo de pimientos		**una lata de atún**	**1,95€**	300 gramos de queso	
un kilo de tomates		una caja de galletas		1kilo de carne roja	
un melón	**1,10€**	un litro de aceite		un pollo	
un bote de aceitunas		**un litro de leche**	**99cts**	**dos kilos de merluza**	**3,00€**

Practica con tu compañero/a el siguiente diálogo. Practise the next dialogue with your partner.

A: **¿Cuánto vale un kilo de** naranjas**?**
B: (Vale) un euro con noventa céntimos.

2c. Practicar en parejas. Practise in pairs.
   Hay que hacer la compra para el fin de semana. You need to do the shopping for the weekend.
   Estudiante A es el/la cliente (hace la compra). Estudiante B es el/la dependiente.
   Student A is the customer (is buying food). Student B is the shop assistant.

Estudiante A Cliente	Estudiante B Dependiente
- ¿Cuánto vale…? - quiero - un kilo de… - 100 gramos de… - una caja de… - un bote de… - prefiero - este/a… - aquél/aquella… - aquí/allí… - ¿Cuánto es?	- ¿Qué quiere comprar? - Buenos días/tardes - estas/estos - aquel/aquellas - aquí/allí - ¿Qué? - ¿Algo más? - El kilo de…. vale … - Son…….(euros/céntimos)

2d. Escoge el demostrativo adecuado. Choose the right demonstrative.

1. ¡Qué ricos los plátanos! Quiero *estas/aquellos/estos* de aquí.
2. Prefiero *aquellos/este/estas* pimientos verdes del fondo.
3. ¿Quiere *estos/aquellos* tomates de aquí o *este/aquellos* del fondo?
4. Me gusta *este/esta/aquel* melón de aquí.
5. Quiero *estas/esa/aquellas* uvas de allí, las que están al fondo.

2e. Escoge el artículo correcto: un, una, unos o unas. Choose from un, una, unos or unas.

un	una	unos	unas	
				sandías
				tomate
				plátanos
				lechuga
				limones
				cebolla
				galletas
				vinos

2f. Escribe la palabra correcta: Cuánto, Cuántos, Cuánta o Cuántas. Write the appropriate word.

1. ¿.............................. cuesta una piña?
2. ¿.............................. zapatos tienes?
3. ¿.............................. comida hay en la nevera?
4. ¿.............................. naranjas quieres?
5. ¿.............................. dinero tienes?

3. IR DE COMPRAS. GO SHOPPING FOR CLOTHES.

3a.Traduce al inglés o a tu primer idioma las siguientes prendas de vestir.
Translate the following items into English or into your native language.

a) la falda	b) la blusa	c) el vestido
d) el pantalón	e) el monedero	f) la camisa
g) las botas	h) la cartera	i) el traje
j) la chaqueta	k) los zapatos	l) el bolso
m) el cinturón	n) la corbata	o) los pantalones vaqueros

3b. Escribe en los espacios vacíos el artículo determinado correcto: el, la, los o las.
Fill in the blanks with the appropriate Spanish definite article: the.

1. _____ blusa roja y pequeña
2. _____ vestido negro
3. _____ zapatos marrones
4. _____ camisas grandes y azules
5. _____ corbata bonita
6. _____ botas moradas y feas
7. _____ cinturón muy grande
8. _____ monedero blanco

GRAMÁTICA

	Masculino	Femenino	
Singular	¿Cuánto?	¿Cuánta?	How much?
Plural	¿Cuántos?	¿Cuántas?	How many?

Nota: Los colores se encuentran en la sección de gramática y en la unidad 6.
Note: The colours are in the grammar section and unit 6.

3c. Completa las frases cambiando el género del adjetivo como en el ejemplo.
Complete the sentences with the corresponding adjective.

Ejemplo: El abrigo es **rojo**. .... La blusa **es roja.**

1. El vestido es [   ] . → La chaqueta es **azul.**
2. El pañuelo es **morado.** → La bufanda es [   ] .
3. El bolso es [   ] , → La mochila es **negra.**
4. El jersey es *blanco*. → La camiseta es [   ] .
5. El traje es [   ] → La camisa es rosa.
6. El pantalón es amarillo. → La corbata es [   ] .

3d. En parejas, describe qué ropa llevan tus compañeros/as de clase. Tu compañero/a tiene que adivinar quién es él/ella. In pairs, describe what clothes your classmates are wearing in class. Your partner must guess who it is.

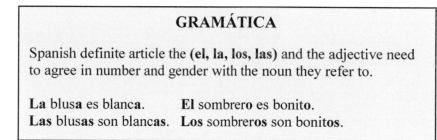

> ### GRAMÁTICA
>
> Spanish definite article the (**el, la, los, las**) and the adjective need to agree in number and gender with the noun they refer to.
>
> **La** blusa es blan**ca**. **El** sombrero es bonit**o**.
> **Las** blusas son blan**cas**. **Los** sombreros son bonit**os**.

Audio 66

3e. Lee y escucha la conversación. Escribe la información en el cuadro de abajo.
Read and listen to the conversation. Write the information in the box below.

Dependiente	**Buenas tardes. ¿Qué desea?**
Cliente	Quiero un traje.
Dependiente	**¿Cuál es su talla?**
Cliente	La 44.
Dependiente	**¿Qué color?**
Cliente	Negro.
Dependiente	**Aquí están todos los trajes. ¿Se los quiere probar?**
Cliente	Sí claro. ¿Dónde están los probadores?
Dependiente	**Allí al final del pasillo a la derecha.**
Cliente	Me gusta este traje. ¿Cuánto vale?
Dependiente	**Este traje negro vale 320 euros.**
Cliente	¡Es muy caro! Pero lo compro.
Dependiente	**¿Quiere algo más?**
Cliente	Sí quiero estos zapatos marrones.
Dependiente	**¿Qué número tiene usted?**
Cliente	El 48 por favor. ¿Cuánto cuestan?
Dependiente	**Estos zapatos marrones valen 20 euros.**
Cliente	Son muy baratos, los compro también.
Dependiente	**¿Cómo va a pagar en efectivo o con tarjeta de crédito?**
Cliente	Voy a pagar con tarjeta de crédito.

artículos	color	talla	precio	número	lo compra: sí o no

155

3f. Practica con tu compañero/a la conversación anterior utilizando el vocabulario del ejercicio 3a. Tienes que cambiar la información en negrita. Practise the previous conversation with your partner using the vocabulary from **3a**. You have to change the information in **bold**.

3g. Escoge el adjetivo del recuadro correcto. Choose the right adjective from the box.

barato   grande   pequeños   pequeñas   verde   caros

1. Las camisas......................son muy bonitas.
2. Estos zapatos son muy......................... No tengo dinero.
3. Este monedero me gusta es muy....................., solamente cuesta 2 euros.
4. Prefiero este vestido porque es de color............................
5. Mario prefiere aquel cinturón porque es........................ y bonito.

GRAMÁTICA

llevar   to wear
preferir to prefer

¡DESCUBRE!

caro/a   expensive
barato/a   cheap

---

4. LECTURA Y COMPRENSIÓN. READING COMPREHENSION.

4a. Lee el siguiente artículo y contesta a las preguntas en español.
Read the following article and answer the question in Spanish.

Pirámide alimentaria

La pirámide alimentaria o pirámide nutricional es un gráfico diseñado a fin de indicar en forma simple cuáles son los alimentos que son necesarios en la dieta, y en qué cantidad consumirlos, para lograr una dieta sana y balanceada. Esta pirámide incluye todos los grupos de alimentos, sin intentar restringir ninguno, sólo indica de manera sencilla cuánto consumir de cada uno de estos grupos a fin de mantener una buena salud. Aunque las primeras pirámides alimentarias fueron creadas a comienzos de la década de 1970, posiblemente la más conocida es la versión introducida por el Departamento de Agricultura de los Estados Unidos en 1992, En una nueva pirámide (basada en la Guía dietética para los estadounidenses publicada en 2004) se mantienen los 6 grupos de alimentos.

El propósito de la pirámide alimenticia es animar a las personas a consumir variedad dentro de cada grupo de alimentos o categoría, y seleccionar alimentos con alta densidad de nutrientes, y no alimentos con baja densidad de nutrientes o calorías vacías como el azúcar. A continuación definiremos las porciones mínimas/máximas de cada categoría de alimentos según la pirámide nutricional.

1. Pan, cereales y arros: consumir 6/11 porciones al día. 1 porción equivale a: 1 rebanada de pan, ½ taza de pasta o cereal cocidos, 28 gr de cereal listo para comer, ½ panecillo, 3-4 galletas tipo crackers pequeñas.

2. Verduras: consumir 3/5 porciones al día. 1 porción equivale a: ¾ taza de caldo de zumo de verduras, ½ taza de verduras cocidas, 1 taza de verduras crudas, ½ tazas de legumbres y guisantes cocidos.

3. Frutas: consumir 2/4 porciones al día. 1 porción equivale a: 1 unidad de tamaño mediano, 1 tajada de melón, ½ taza de fresas, 3/4 taza de zumo, ½ taza de fruta enlatada.

4. Lácteos: leche,yogur o quesos: consumir 2/3 porciones al día. 1 porción equivale a: 1 taza de Leche o yogur 60 gr de queso blando o 50 gr de queso.

5. Carne, aves, pescado, huevos, alubias secas y nueces: consumir 2/3 porciones al día. Una porción equivale a: 70 gr de carne a la plancha, aves o pescado (un total diario de 150-200 gr), 1 huevo ½ taza de legumbres cocidas, 30 gr de frutos secos.

6. Grasas, aceites y dulces consumir ocasionalmente. Son alimentos altos en grasas: margarina, mantequilla, mayonesa, natas, quesos cremosos.
   Se aconseja aumentar el consumo de aceite de oliva

Sacado y adaptado de:
- https://es.wikipedia.org/wiki/Pir%C3%A1mide_alimentaria
- http://www.zonadiet.com/nutricion/piramide.htm

4b. Marca verdadero o falso. Tick true or false.

	V	F
1. Grasas, aceites y dulces: consumir todos los días.		
2. Verduras: consumir 3/5 porciones al día.		
3. Pan, cereales, pasta y arroz: consumir ocasionalmente.		
4. Lácteos: leche, yogur o quesos nunca consumir.		
5. Carne, aves, pescado, huevos, alubias secas y nueces: consumir 2/3 porciones al día.		

4c. Escribe qué tipo de comida corresponde a las porciones indicadas.
Write what kind of food is appropriate to the indicated portions.

1. **2/4** porciones al día.　...
2. **2/3** porciones al día.　...
3. **6/11** porciones al día.　...
4. consumir **ocasionalmente.**　...
5. **3/5** porciones al día.　...
6. **2/3** porciones al día.　...

4d. Contesta a las siguientes preguntas en español. Answer the following questions in Spanish.

- **¿Cuál es el propósito general de la pirámide alimentaria?**
  What is the overall purpose of the food pyramid?

- **¿Qué es la pirámide alimentaria?**
  What is the food pyramid?

5. VAMOS A ESCRIBIR. LET'S WRITE.

Contesta a las siguientes preguntas y escribe un texto sobre tu ciudad/pueblo y las compras.
Answer the following questions and write an article about your city/town and shopping.

- ¿Dónde está exactamente tu ciudad/pueblo?
- ¿Cómo es?
- ¿Qué tiendas hay en tu ciudad/pueblo?
- ¿Qué horarios tienen las tiendas en tu ciudad/pueblo?
- ¿Dónde compras tú la comida y por qué?
- ¿Cuándo haces la compra?
- ¿Qué comida compras para la semana?
- ¿Dónde compras tú la ropa y por qué?
- ¿Qué otras cosas compras para ti, tu familia y para tu casa?

GRAMÁTICA

- **Adverbios de lugar.** Adverbs of place.
  -aquí…..here
  -allí……there

- **El artículo y el adjetivo concuerdan con el sustantivo en género y el número.**
  The article and the adjective need to agree in number and gender with the noun they refer to.

  -**La** camisa es blanca.   **El** vestido es bonito.
  -**Las** camisas son blancas. **Los** vestidos son bonitos.

- **Adjetivos de cantidad.** Adjectives of quantity.
  There are two words for 'how much' (one for masculine and one for feminine) and also two words for 'how many'

Masculino	Femenino	
¿Cuánto?	¿Cuánta?	How much?
¿Cuántos?	¿Cuántas?	How many?
¿Cuánto queso?		How much cheese?
	¿Cuánta carne?	How much meat?
¿Cuántos limones?		How many lemons?
	¿Cuántas uvas?	How many grapes?

- **Caro/barato.** Expensive/cheap.

Singular			Plural	
Masculino	Femenino		Masculino	Femenino
caro	cara		caros	caras
barato	barata		baratos	baratas

- **Colores como adjetivos.** Colours as adjectives.

Adjetivos	Singular		Adjetivos	Plural
Masculino	Femenino		Masculino	Femenino
blanco	*blanca*		*blancos*	*blancas*
negro	negra		negros	negras
amarillo	amarilla		amarillos	amarillas
rojo	roja		rojos	rojas
morado	morada		morados	moradas

Invariable singular		Invariable plural
verde		verdes
azul		azules
marrón		marrones

- **Hay colores que son nombres de flores y frutos que normalmente no cambian de género ni número.** There are colours that are names of flowers and fruits that normally do not change gender or number.

Singular		Plural	
Masculino	**Femenino**	**Masculino**	**Femenino**
el vestido es **rosa**	la blusa es **rosa**	los vestidos son **rosas**	las blusas son **rosas**
el traje es **naranja**	la camisa es **naranja**	los trajes son **naranjas**	las camisas son **naranjas**

(de color) **rosa**
(de color) **naranja**

- **Pronombres demostrativos.** Demonstrative pronouns.

Los Pronombres demostrativos son <u>pronombres</u> que denotan grados de proximidad en relación con el hablante y el oyente. Demonstrative pronouns are pronouns denoting degrees of proximity in relation to the speaker and the listener.

este/a, estos/as (denotan cercanía). .... this, these (denote proximity).
ese/a, esos/as (denotan distancia media). .... that, these (denote middle distance).
aquel/aquella, aquellos/as (denotan lejanía). ...... that, those (denote distance).

Masculino		Femenino	
Singular	**Plural**	**Singular**	**Plural**
este (this)	estos (these)	esta	estas
ese	Esos	esa	esas
aquel	Aquellos	aquella	aquellas

- **Verbos llevar y preferir.** The verbs to wear and to prefer.

Preposiciones	**llevar** (to wear)	**preferir** (to prefer)
(yo)	llevo	prefiero
(tu)	llevas	prefieres
(él/ella)/usted	lleva	prefiere
(nosotros/as)	llevamos	preferimos
(vosotros/as)	lleváis	preferís
ellos/ellas/ustedes	llevan	prefieren

- **Verbo ser/estar (de compras).** Verb to be (shopping).

La fruta **está** barata.	We normally use **estar** to talk about buying food because prices are constantly changing.
El vestido **es** caro.	We normally use **ser** to talk about buying clothes because prices tend to be static.

EJERCICIOS

1. Escribe el artículo indeterminado correspondiente: un o una. Write the appropriate indefinite article: a/an **(un/una).**

a) _____ cebolla
b) _____ bote
c) _____ lechuga
d) _____ docena de huevos
e) _____ bote de aceitunas
f) _____ kilo de naranjas
g) _____ barra de chocolate
h) _____ botella de vino

2. Corrige el orden de las palabras en las frases siguientes. Correct the order of the words in the following sentences.

a) aceite el vale euros tres
b) pantalones aquí los están
c) kilos valen tres dos de patatas euros
d) verduras muy caras las están
e) baratos plátanos muy hoy los están
f) de quiero una vino botella tinto
g) este vale cien euros vestido
h) muy aquellos tomates baratos están

3. Pon en el orden correcto el siguiente diálogo. Put the following dialogue in the correct order.

- ¿Cuánto vale esta camiseta gris?
- ¿Dónde están los probadores?
- ¿Cuál es su talla?
- ¿Tiene camisetas de color gris?
- Vale 90 euros.
- La cuarenta y dos.
- Están allí al final del pasillo a la derecha.
- Buenas tardes. ¿Qué desea?
- Sí, sí tenemos. Aquí están todas las camisetas.
- ¡Qué cara! No la compro.

4. Escribe en los espacios vacíos el demostrativo adecuado («este/a», «aquel/aquella», «estos/as» o «aquellos/as») correspondiente. Write the appropriate demonstrative in the empty spaces.

1. _____ camisa de aquí es grande.
2. _____ pantalones de aquí son pequeños.
3. _____ traje de allí es muy bonito.
4. _____ zapatos de aquí están muy baratos.
5. _____ sandía de allí es muy grande.
6. _____ melones de allí están muy caros.

5. Escribe los siguientes productos en la lista correspondiente del cuadro de abajo. List the products below under the correct headings.

Tomates sardinas pollo lechuga cordero fresas bacalao merluza calamares naranjas lomo cebollas melón salchichas mangos zanahorias cerdo pimiento ~~manzanas~~ sandía patatas(papas) pulpo pavo mariscos

frutas	carnes	verduras	pescados
manzanas			

VOCABULARIO

1. HACER LA COMPRA — 1. DOING THE FOOD SHOPPING.

acabo de llegar	*I just arrived*
aceite (m)	*oil*
agua (m)	*water*
arroz (m)	*rice*
atún (m)	*tuna*
barra (f)	*loaf/bar (bread/chocolate)*
bote (m)	*jar*
botella (f)	*bottle*
carnicería (f)	*butcher*
charcutería (f)	*delicatessen*
frutería (f)	*greengrocers*
huevo (m)	*egg*
lata (f)	*can*
leche (f)	*milk*
litro (m)	*litre (UK)/liter (US)*
mercado (m)	*market*
mermelada (f)	*jam*
panadería (f)	*bakery*
pastelería (f)	*pastry shop*
pescadería (f)	*fishmonger*
piña (f)	*pineapple*
plátano (m)	*banana*
queso (m)	*cheese*
supermercado (m)	*supermarket*
tomate (m)	*tomato*
verdulería (f)	*greengrocers (UK)/ produce shop (US)*
¿Algo más?	*Anything else?*
¿Cuánto cuesta/vale?	*How much is it?*
¿Cuánto es?	*How much is the total?*

2. EN EL MERCADO — 2. AT THE MARKET

aceituna/oliva (f)	*olive*
aguacate (m)	*avocado*
caja (f)	*box*
carne (f)	*meat*
carne roja (f)	*red meat*
cebolla (f)	*onion*
lechuga (f)	*lettuce*
limón (m)	*lemon*
manzana (f)	*apple*
melón (m)	*melon*
merluza (f)	*hake*
naranja (f)	*orange*
pimiento verde (m)	*green pepper*
producto (m)	*item*
sandía (f)	*watermelon*
vino (m)	*wine*
vino tinto/blanco	*red/white wine*

3. IR DE COMPRAS — 3. SHOPPING FOR CLOTHES.

artículo (m)	*article/item*
blusa (f)	*blouse*
bota (f)	*boots*
bolso (m)	*handbag*
camisa (f)	*shirt*
cartera (f)	*wallet*
chaqueta (f)	*jacket*
cinto (m)	*belt*
corbata (f)	*tie*
falda (f)	*skirt*
monedero (m)	*purse*
número de zapatos	*shoe size*
pantalones	*trousers (UK)/ pants(US)*
precio (m)	*price*
talla (f)	*size*
traje (m)	*suit*
vaqueros (mpl)	*jeans*
vestido (m)	*dress*
zapato (m)	*shoe*

11 LA RUTINA DIARIA

TEMAS TOPICS	OBJETIVOS COMUNICATIVOS COMMUNICATIVE OBJECTIVES	GRAMÁTICA GRAMMAR
El reloj. La rutina diaria. El calendario.	**Preguntar y decir la hora.** Asking and saying the time. **Hablar de tu rutina diaria.** Talking about your daily routine. **Aprender los días de la semana y los meses del año.** Learning the days of the week and months of the year. **Usar el calendario.** Using the calendar. **Invitar, aceptar/rechazar invitaciones.** Inviting, accepting/declining invitations. **Preguntar y responder: ¿Por qué? /porque.** Asking and saying: Why? /because	**La hora: Es la una, son las dos, son las tres y media…** Time: It's one, It's two, It's half-past three… **Preposición a + artículo (el/la).** The preposition a + article (the). **Presente de indicativo de algunos verbos regulares e irregulares.** Some regular and irregular verbs in the present tense. **Presente de indicativo de los verbos reflexivos: levantarse, ducharse y acostarse…** The Reflexive verbs in the present tense: to get (oneself) up, to shower (oneself) and to go to bed… **Verbos irregulares con cambio vocálico.** Irregular radical changing verbs. **Tengo que + verbo en infinitivo (ar/er/ir).** I have to + verb in infinitive.

1. ¿QUÉ HORA ES? WHAT TIME IS IT?

Audio 67

1a. Escucha cómo se dice la hora en español. Listen to the time in Spanish.

¿Qué hora es? What time is it?

Son las doce y cuarto.   **Son** las diez y veinte.   **Es** la una y veinte.

Son las cinco y media.   **Son** las doce **menos** veintisiete.   **Son** las siete **menos** veinticinco.

GRAMÁTICA

Es la una
Son las dos/tres…
Es mediodía
Es medianoche

¡DESCUBRE!

Son las 7:00 **de la mañana**
Son las 12:00 **de la tarde**
Son las 8:00 **de la noche**

Audio 68

1b. Escucha y lee.

Son las doce en punto.

menos cinco

menos diez

menos quince/cuarto

menos veinte

menos veinticinco

y cinco

y diez

y quince/cuarto

y veinte

y veinticinco

y treinta/media

1c. Practica con tu compañero/a.
A: ¿Qué hora es?
B: Son las ocho (de la mañana)

1. 05:00 am
2. 06:15 am
3. 09:10 pm
4. 11:45 pm
5. 12:00 pm
6. 08:35 pm
7. 01:20 pm
8. 03:15 am

1d. Dibuja cuatro relojes con sus horas y practica con tu compañero/a.
Draw four watches with their time and practise with your partner.

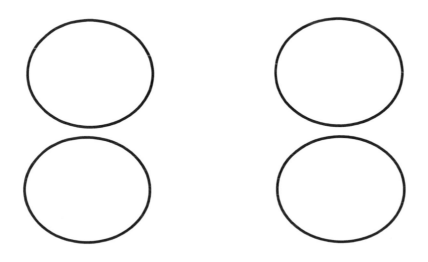

2. MI RUTINA DIARIA. MY DAILY ROUTINE.

Audio 69

La rutina diaria de Rosa

2a. Escucha y escribe debajo de cada fotografía el verbo que le corresponde. Listen and write under each photograph the appropriate verb.

me despierto

me levanto

me ducho

me peino

desayuno

me lavo los dientes

salgo de casa

tomo el autobús

llego la universidad

estudio

como con mis amigo

vuelvo a casa

tomo un cafe

mando

veo la televisión

como

leo un libro

me lavo

me acuesto

me duermo

Después de escuchar el audio 69, comprueba tus respuestas con el siguiente cuadro. After listening to audio 69, verify your answers with the following box.

> **1 me** despierto **2 me** levanto **3 me** ducho **4 me** peino **5** desayuno **6 me** lavo los dientes
> **7** salgo de casa **8** tomo el autobús **9** llego a la universidad **10** estudio
> **11** como con mis amigas **12** vuelvo a casa **13** tomo un café **14** mando mensajes por el móvil
> **15** veo la televisión **16** ceno **17** leo un libro **18 me** lavo **19 me** acuesto **20 me** duermo.

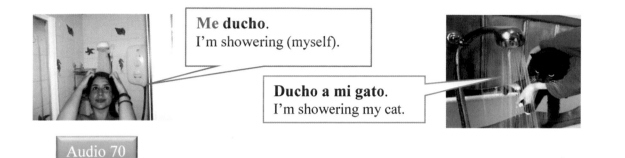

Me ducho.
I'm showering (myself).

Ducho a mi gato.
I'm showering my cat.

Audio 70

2b. Escucha la entrevista a Pedro sobre su rutina diaria y completa las respuestas.
Listen to the interview with Pedro about his daily routine and complete the answers.

1. **¿A qué hora te despiertas?**	**Me despierto a las 6:30 de la mañana.**
2. ¿A qué hora te levantas?	Me levanto a las …………………..........
3. ¿A qué hora te duchas?	Me ducho a las ………………………….
4. ¿A qué hora desayunas?	Desayuno a las ……………………………
5. ¿A qué hora sales de casa?	Salgo de casa a las………………….......
6. ¿A qué hora comes?	Como a la ………………………………
7. ¿A qué hora vuelves a casa?	Vuelvo a casa a las……………………..
8. ¿A qué hora cenas?	Ceno a las ……………………………...
9. ¿A qué hora te acuestas?	Me acuesto a las………………………..
10. ¿A qué hora te duermes?	Me duermo sobre las…………………..

2c. Completa los espacios vacíos con el verbo correcto, utiliza la 1ª persona del singular.
Fill in the blanks with the appropriate form of the verb, using the 1st person singular.

A las 6:00 de la mañana _____ _____ (**1. despertarse**) y _____
(**2. ver**) la televisión. Luego a las 7:00 ____ _____ (**3. levantarse**) pero no
_____ (**4. desayunar**) solamente _____ (**5. tomar**) café. Salgo de casa
y camino a la parada de autobuses. A las 8:00 _____ (**6. tomar**) el autobús y a las
8:45 _____ (**7. llegar**) a la universidad y _____
(**8. desayunar**). Durante la mañana _____ (**9. estudiar**) y _____
(**10. ir**) a clases. _____ (**11. comer**) sobre la una._____ (**12. salir**) de
clases a las 6:00 y _____ (**13. caminar**) a la academia de idiomas._____
(**14. estudiar**) inglés de 7:00 a 8:00 de la noche. _____ (**15. volver**) a casa sobre
las 9:00 y _____ (**16. cenar**). Después _____
(**17. leer**) un libro o _____ (**18. ver**) las noticias. Antes de ir a la cama siempre
____ _____ (**19. lavarse**) los dientes y ____ _____ (**20. acostarse**) sobre
las 11:00.

GRAMÁTICA

Pronombres personales	Pronombres reflexivos	levantarse to get up	ducharse to have a shower	bañarse to have a bath
yo	me	levanto	ducho	baño
tú (informal)	te	levantas	duchas	bañas
él/ella/usted	se	levanta	ducha	baña

Audio 71

2d. Escucha y escribe la acción correspondiente. Listen and write the correct form of the verb.

1. A las seis de la mañana _____ _____ y _____ la televisión.
2. A las siete _____ _____ pero no _____, solamente _____ café.
3. A las ocho _____ el autobús y a las ocho y media _____ a la universidad y desayuno.
4. _____ y _____ a clases.
5. _____ sobre la una.
6. _____ de clases a las seis y _____ a la academia de idiomas.
7. _____ inglés de siete a ocho de la noche.
8. _____ a casa sobre las nueve y _____.
9. _____ un libro o _____ las noticias.
10. _____ _____ sobre las doce.

2e. Lee y rellena la tabla con la información que falta. Utiliza la 3ª persona del singular.
Read and write in the box the information using the 3rd person singular as an example.

¡Hola! me llamo Mario y esta es mi rutina diaria. A las seis y media de la mañana me despierto. A las siete me levanto, me ducho y a las siete y media desayuno. Salgo de casa a las ocho. Voy a mi trabajo en coche, normalmente llego a las ocho y media. Trabajo de nueve a una. Como en la cafetería del trabajo entre la una y las tres. A las tres vuelvo a mi trabajo. Salgo del trabajo a las siete y voy al gimnasio. Llego a casa sobre las 9:00 y ceno con mi familia. Después sobre las diez navego en el ordenador, mando mensajes, miro las noticias o un programa interesante en la televisión, tomo una copa de vino y me acuesto sobre las once.

Hora	La rutina diaria de Mario.
a) 6:30am	Se despierta
b) 7:00am	Se levanta
c) 7:30am	Se ducha
d) 8:00am	Sale
e) 8:30am	llega
f) 9:00am -1:00 pm	
g) 1:00 - 300pm	
h) 3:00pm	
i) 7:00pm	
j) 9:00pm	
k) 10:00pm	
l) 11:00pm	

2f. El fin de semana.

Lee, subraya los verbos y escribe un texto similar sobre ti mismo.

Read, underline the verbs and write a similar paragraph about yourself.

> ¡Hola! Soy Luis. Normalmente los sábados me levanto tarde y almuerzo con mi compañero de piso. Voy a hacer la compra. Por la tarde salgo con mis amigos, vamos a un bar y charlamos, tomamos algunas copas y después vamos al cine o al fútbol. Cenamos en un restaurante o en un bar. Los domingos me levanto tarde y visito a mi familia. Comemos todos juntos y salimos a pasear por el campo, volvemos a casa y cenamos. Me gustan mis fines de semana.

3. EL CALENDARIO. THE CALENDAR.

EL CALENDARIO

Audio 72

GRAMÁTICA

In Spanish, the days of the week and the months of the year are written with lower case letters.

3a. Escucha, lee y repite.

Los días de la semana	Los meses del año	
lunes	enero	julio
martes	febrero	agosto
miércoles	marzo	septiembre
jueves	abril	octubre
viernes	mayo	noviembre
sábado	junio	diciembre
domingo		

¡DESCUBRE!

día	day
semana	week
mes	month
año	year
mañana	tomorrow/morning
ayer	yesterday
es	it is
fue	it was
la fecha	the date
el uno de mayo	the first of May

martes 12 de enero de 2030

3b. Practica con tu compañero/a el siguiente dialogo.

A. Si hoy es viernes 5 de enero. ¿Qué día es **mañana**? B. **Mañana** es sábado 6 de enero.	A. Si hoy es lunes 7 de junio. ¿Qué día fue **ayer**? B. **Ayer** fue domingo 6 de junio.

3c. Escribe las siguientes fechas en español.
Write out the following dates in Spanish.

a) Monday 1st January 2030 _____
b) Tuesday 12th February 1983 _____
c) Friday 31st May 1999 _____
d) Sunday 25th December 1810 _____

3d. Contesta a las preguntas y practica con tus compañeros/as.

- ¿Cuál es la fecha de tu nacimiento?
- ¿Cuál es la fecha de tu cumpleaños?
- ¿Cuál es la fecha de tu graduación?

4. INVITACIONES. INVITATIONS.

Audio 73

4a. Escucha y repite.

¿Quieres venir al cine (conmigo)? Do you want to come to the cinema (with me)?
¿Quieres ir al cine (conmigo)? Do you want to go to the cinema (with me)?

al cine	**a la** biblioteca	**a** tomar un café
al teatro	**a la** cafetería	**a** beber unas copas
al partido de fútbol		**a** estudiar/bailar/cenar
al juego de baloncesto		

ACEPTAR
Sí, vale.............Yes, ok.
De acuerdo........Ok.
Claro...............Of course
¡Estupendo! ....Great!/Wonderful!

NEGAR
No lo siento...............No I'm sorry.
No puedo.................I can't.
No es posible.............It's not possible
No gracias................No thanks.

EXCUSAS

- Tengo que estudiar.
- Tengo mucho trabajo.
- Tengo dolor de muelas.

- Tengo dolor de cabeza.
- No me gusta el teatro.
- Mi madre está enferma.

4b. Empareja las frases. Match the sentences.

Español	English
a) Vale	1. Do you want to come to the cinema with me?
b) ¿A qué hora empieza la película?	2. Where shall we meet?
c) ¡Claro! ¿Qué ponen?	3. I'm going to invite another friend.
d) ¿Quieres venir al cine conmigo?	4. Do you want to go to the cinema with me?
e) ¿Por qué?	5. Because
f) Porque	6. Why?
g) No, lo siento.	7. Of course! What's on?
h) ¿Cuándo es?	8. What time does the movie start?
i) ¿Dónde quedamos?	9. Which cinema are we going to?
j) ¿A qué cine vamos a ir?	10. When is it?
k) ¿Quieres ir al cine conmigo?	11. No, sorry.
l) Voy a invitar a otro amigo.	12. OK

Audio 74

4c. Escucha las conversaciones.

Conversación 1. Aceptar

A -**¿Quieres ir al cine conmigo?**
B - Sí claro. ¿Cuándo?
A - **El viernes por la noche.**
B - Vale de acuerdo. ¿Qué película
    ponen?
A - **Drácula y los monstruos.**
B - Sí me gustan mucho las películas de
    monstruos. ¿A qué cine vamos?
A - **Al cine Doré.**
B – Vale. ¿A qué hora empieza la película?
A - **A las 8:00 de la noche.**
B - Estupendo. ¿Dónde quedamos?
A- **En el bar Pepe enfrente del cine.**
B – Vale. ¿A qué hora quedamos?
A- **A las 7:30.**
B -Vale. Quedamos enfrente del cine en el
    bar Pepe a las 7:30.
A- **Hasta el viernes. Adiós.**
B- Adiós.

Conversación 2. Negar

A -¿Quieres ir al teatro conmigo?
B - No, lo siento.
A - ¿Por qué?
B - Porque mi madre está enferma.
A - Vale, voy a invitar a otro amigo.
    Adiós.
B- Adiós.

¡DESCUBRE!	
conmigo	with me
contigo	with you
quedar	to meet
quedamos	agree to meet
¿Dónde	Where shall
quedamos?	we meet?
Tengo que…	I have to…

Contesta a las preguntas en español. Answer the questions in Spanish.

1. ¿A dónde van a ir?
2. ¿Cuándo?
3. ¿Qué película ponen?
4. ¿Dónde quedan?

5. ¿Por qué no quiere ir al teatro
   (Conversación 2)?
6. ¿A qué hora empieza la película?

5. LECTURA Y COMPRENSIÓN. READING COMPREHENSION.

Lee la rutina diaria de Alfonso y contesta a las preguntas en español.
Read the daily routine of Alfonso and answer the questions in Spanish.

Me despierto a las 6:30 todas las mañanas. Aprieto el botón del despertador cinco veces cada mañana y después me levanto a las 7:00. Primero tomo una taza de café para despertarme más rápido. Me ducho, me visto y desayuno a las 8:00. Siempre me lavo los dientes después del desayuno. Como tengo el pelo corto entonces me peino muy rápido. Salgo de casa a las 8:30 cada mañana. A menudo voy al gimnasio después del trabajo, pero a veces voy antes. Todos los días conduzco a mi trabajo. Trabajo de 9:00 a 12:00 y de 3:00 a 8:00. Cuando estoy en mi escritorio generalmente trabajo en el ordenador. Lo primero que siempre hago es leer mis correos electrónicos, pero no siempre respondo inmediatamente. Normalmente como a la 1:00 con mis compañeros del trabajo y por lo regular hablamos un poco mientras comemos. Cuando trabajo, tengo que hacer muchas llamadas telefónicas. Si algo importante pasa organizo una reunión. Una vez al mes tengo reunión con mi jefe. Normalmente escribo un reporte antes de la reunión para que mi jefe pueda leerlo antes.

Después de terminar el trabajo, vuelvo a la casa y ayudo a los hijos con sus deberes del colegio. En casa normalmente cenamos todos juntos sobre las 9:00. Después de cenar saco la basura, ayudo a lavar los platos, leo el periódico o veo la televisión. Cuando veo televisión, generalmente veo las noticias. Luego me pongo el pijama. Lo último que hago es cerrar la puerta de la casa con llave, apagar todas las luces de la casa, pongo a cargar mi teléfono celular, activo la alarma para despertarme en la mañana y me acuesto sobre las 12:00.

a) ¿A qué hora se levanta?
b) ¿Qué hace antes del desayuno?
c) ¿A qué hora desayuna?
d) ¿Qué hace siempre después del desayuno?
e) ¿Por qué se peina rápido?
f) ¿A qué hora sale de casa?

g) ¿Conduce o camina a su trabajo?
h) ¿Qué hace en su trabajo?
i) ¿A qué hora come y con quién?
j) ¿Qué hace después de terminar su trabajo?
k) ¿Dónde cena normalmente y con quién?
l) ¿Qué hace después de cenar?
m) ¿Qué hace antes de acostarse?
n) ¿A qué hora se acuesta?

6. VAMOS A ESCRIBIR. LET'S WRITE.

6a. Escribe tu rutina diaria de un día normal y de un fin de semana.
Write your daily routine of a normal day and a weekend.

6b. Rellena el siguiente cuadro con tu rutina semanal utilizando diferentes verbos.
Fill in the following table with your weekly routine using different verbs.

	Por la mañana	Por la tarde	Por la noche
Lunes	me levanto a las 8:00	estudio	veo la tele
Martes			
Miércoles			
Jueves			
Viernes			
Sábado			
Domingo			

6c. Escribe la rutina diaria de un familiar/amigo. Utiliza la 3ª persona del singular.
Write the daily routine of a relative/friend, using the 3rd person singular.

GRAMÁTICA

- **La hora.** The time
  Es la una
  Son las dos/tres…

- **Preposición a + artículo «el» o «la»**
  a + el = al
  a + la = a la

- **Verbos reflexivos.**
  Reflexive verbs have the normal **–ar, -er,** or **ir** endings, but also have a reflexive pronoun to indicate that the person is doing something to, by or for himself/herself (the action reflects back on the subject). English reflexive verbs are easy to spot because they always involve a "self" word. Many verbs are reflexive in Spanish which are not in English.

  - **Regulares**

Verbos reflexivos
levantarse
ducharse
bañarse
peinarse
lavarse
afeitarse

Pronombres personales sujeto	Pronombres reflexivos	levantarse	to get up
yo	me	levanto	I get up
tú (informal)	te	levantas	you get up
usted (formal)	se	levanta	you get up
él/ella	se	levanta	he/she gets up
nosotros/as	nos	levantamos	we get up
vosotros/as (informal)	os	levantáis	you get up
ustedes (formal)	se	levantan	you get up
ellos/ellas	Se	levantan	they get up

  - **Irregulares con cambio vocálico excepto en la 1ª y 2ª persona del plural.**
    Irregulars (radical changing verbs) except in the 1st and 2nd person of the plural.

Pronombres personales sujeto	Pronombre reflexivo	despertarse	acostarse	dormirse
yo	me	despierto	acuesto	duermo
tú (informal)	te	despiertas	acuestas	duermes
usted (formal)	se	despierta	acuesta	duerme
él/ella	se	despierta	acuesta	duerme
nosotros/as	nos	despertamos	acostamos	dormimos
vosotros/as(informal)	os	despertáis	acostáis	dormís
ustedes(formal)	se	despiertan	acuestan	duermen
ellos/ellas	se	despiertan	acuestan	duermen

- **Verbo querer + infinitivo + sustantivo.** Verb to want + infinitive + noun.
  ¿Quieres venir/ir <u>al cine</u> (conmigo)? Do you want to come/go to the cinema with me?

EJERCICIOS

1. **Rellena los espacios vacíos con el verbo correspondiente.**
   Fill in the blanks with the appropriate form of the verb.

Pronombres personales sujeto	Pronombres reflexivos	levantarse	despertarse	peinarse	lavarse
yo	me	levanto		peino	
tú (informal)	te		despiertas		lavas
usted (formal)	se	levanta	despierta	peina	
él/ella	se	levanta			lava
nosotros/as	nos		despertamos		
vosotros/as(informal)	os	levantáis			
ustedes (formal)	se			peinan	lavan
ellos/ellas	se	levantan			

Pronombres personales sujeto	Pronombres reflexivos	ducharse	vestirse	afeitarse	dormirse
yo	me		visto		duermo
tú (informal)	te	duchas			
usted (formal)	se			afeita	
él/ella	se		viste		
nosotros/as	nos	duchamos			dormimos
vosotros/as (informal)	os				dormís
ustedes (formal)	se	duchan		afeitan	duermen
ellos/ellas	se		visten		

2. **Escribe el pronombre reflexivo adecuado en los espacios vacíos.**
   Write the appropriate reflexive pronoun in the empty spaces.

     a) Normalmente (yo) _____ ducho por las mañanas.
     b) Mario _____ lava los dientes todas las mañanas.
     c) Nosotros _____ levantamos a las siete todos los días.
     d) Rosa y Luis _____ bañan en el mar cuando van de vacaciones a la playa.
     e) Tú _____ despiertas temprano todos los días.
     f) La novia de Luis _____ peina muy bonito siempre.
     g) Vosotros _____ acostáis muy tarde los fines de semana.

3. **Escribe las siguientes fechas en español.** Write out the following dates in Spanish.

     a) Saturday 2nd March 1997._____
     b) Thursday 18th February 1959._____
     c) Wednesday 30th April 2016. _____
     d) Monday 1st July 1735._____

VOCABULARIO

1. ¿QUÉ HORA ES?	1. WHAT TIME IS IT?
de la mañana	in the morning
de la noche	at night
de la tarde	in the afternoon
Es la una en punto	It's one o'clock
la una	one o'clock
las cuatro	four o'clock
las siete menos cuarto	a quarter to seven
las siete y media	half past seven
mañana (f)	tomorrow, morning
media/o	half
menos	less
noche (f)	night
Son las cinco	It's five
Son las seis de la mañana	It's six in the morning
tarde (f)	afternoon
y media	half-past/(time)
¿Qué hora es?	What time is it?

2. MI RUTINA DIARIA.	2. MY DAILY ROUTINE.
a las (siete)	at (seven)
autobús (m)	bus
diente (m)	teeth
mensaje (m)	message
televisión (f)	television

3. EL CALENDARIO.	3. THE CALENDAR.
abril (m)	April
agosto (m)	August
año (m)	year
ayer	yesterday
cumpleaños (m)	birthday
día (m)	day
diciembre (m)	December
domingo (m)	Sunday
enero (m)	January
febrero (m)	February
fecha (f)	date
fue	it was
graduación (f)	graduation
jueves (m)	Thursday
junio (m)	June
julio (m)	July
lunes (m)	Monday

los días de la semana	the days of the week
los meses del año	the months of the year
martes (m)	Tuesday
marzo (m)	March
mayo (m)	May
mes (m)	month
miércoles (m)	Wednesday
nacimiento (m)	birth
noviembre (m)	November
octubre (m)	October
sábado (m)	Saturday
septiembre (m)	September
viernes (m)	Friday
¿Cuál es la fecha de…?	What is the date of…?

4. INVITACIONES	4. INVITATIONS
aceptar	accept
claro	of course
conmigo	with me
contigo	with you
de acuerdo	ok
dolor (m)	pain
enfermo/a	ill
estupendo	great/wonderful
excusa	excuse
lo siento	sorry
muela (f)	tooth (molar)
negar	refuse/deny
no	no
no es posible	it's not possible
no puedo	I can't
quedamos	we meet
sí	yes
tengo que	I have to
vale	okay

VERBOS	VERBS
afeitarse	to shave oneself
acostarse	to go to bed
bañarse	to have a bath
despertarse	to wake up
dormirse	to go to sleep
ducharse	to have a shower
lavarse	to wash oneself
levantarse	to get up
peinarse	to comb oneself

12 GUSTOS Y PASATIEMPOS

TEMAS TOPICS	OBJETIVOS COMUNICATIVOS COMMUNICATIVE OBJECTIVES	GRAMÁTICA GRAMMAR
Gustos. Tiempo libre/ Pasatiempos. Me gusta mi ciudad/pueblo.	Expresar y preguntar sobre qué te gusta/qué no te gusta. Talking about likes/dislikes. Hablar del tiempo libre/pasatiempos. Talking about leisure activities/ hobbies. Usar: también/tampoco. Using: too/also and neither/nor. Opinar de lo que te gusta o no te gusta de tu ciudad/pueblo. Talking about your hometown likes/dislikes.	Verbos: gustar/encantar. Verbs: (to like/to please)/to love it. Verbos en plural del presente de indicativo. Present tense of the verbs in plural. «A» personal. The personal 'a'. Pronombres de objeto indirecto: me/te/le/nos/os/les. Pronombres preposicionales: a mí, a ti, a él/ella/usted… Adverbios: también y tampoco. Adverbs: too/also and neither/nor. Cuantificadores: mucho, bastante… Quantifiers: a lot/very much, quite…

1. TIEMPO LIBRE. FREE TIME.

1a. Escucha la conversación entre María y Javier y rellena el cuadro de abajo con la información correspondiente. Listen to the conversation between Maria and Javier and fill in the table below with the appropriate details.

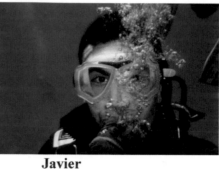

María   Javier

María	**¡Hola Javier! ¿Cómo estás?**
Javier	¿Qué tal María? Estoy muy bien.
María	**¿Qué te gusta hacer en tu tiempo libre?**
Javier	En mi tiempo libre me gusta mucho bucear, nadar, hacer puenting y hacer deporte. ¿Y tú? ¿Qué haces en tu tiempo libre?
María	**Me gusta nadar también y caminar por la playa. Me gusta estar con la familia. Me gusta ir al cine. ¿Te gusta ir al cine?**
Javier	No, no me gusta ir al cine, prefiero ir a ver un partido de fútbol o de baloncesto, me gusta ir a los bares con los amigos. ¿Te gusta el fútbol?
María	**No, no me gusta el fútbol, no me gusta cocinar ni hacer puenting pero me gusta bailar, cantar, escuchar música y ver la televisión.**
Javier	A mí también me gusta el baile y la música pero no me gusta trabajar ni estudiar.
María	**Vale, tengo que ir a estudiar. Adiós.**
Javier	Yo tengo que ir a trabajar. Hasta luego.

	Javier	María
me gusta 😊		
no me gusta ☹		

¡DESCUBRE!
tiempo libre….free time   **también**….too/also   **ni**….neither

1b. Marca verdadero (V) o falso (F). Tick true or false.

	V	F
Me gusta ver la tele.		
Me gusta salir con los amigos.		
No me gusta cantar.		
Me gusta hacer yoga.		
No me gusta estudiar.		
Me gusta el fútbol.		
Me gusta navegar en el ordenador.		
Me gusta mandar mensajes por teléfono.		
No me gusta el vino.		
Me gusta hacer deporte.		
No me gusta levantarme por las mañanas.		

¡DESCUBRE!

When you want to say you don't like something, the indirect object in a statement is preceded by:
"no" (no me gusta…)

1c. Pon en orden las siguientes frases. Put the following sentences into the correct order.

a) gusta me teatro el
b) me estudiar no gusta
c) gusta te a piscina la ir
d) a me ir gusta playa la
e) escuchar no te música gusta
f) ir gimnasio me gusta al
g) gusta ir te camping de

1d. Elige el pronombre adecuado para cada persona: Me o Te.
Choose the right pronoun for each person (**Me or Te**).

a) yo   **Me** gusta tomar el sol en la playa.
b) tú   _____ gusta hacer snowboarding.
c) yo   _____ encanta ir de compras.
d) yo   _____ gusta hacer deporte.
e) tú   _____ encanta esquiar en las montañas.
f) tú   _____ gustan los deportes.
g) yo   _____ gusta estudiar español.

GRAMÁTICA

me	gusta	I like
te	gusta	you like

*The verb 'gustar' literally means "to please" but idiomatically, it means, 'to like'.

Audio 76

1e. Escucha, lee y repite. Listen, read and repeat.

1. leer   **2.** montar en bicicleta   **3.** bailar   **4.** tomar el sol   **5.** cantar   **6.** tocar la guitarra
7. visitar museos   **8.** dormir   **9.** trabajar en el ordenador   **10.** hacer puenting   **11.** conducir
12. ir al parque   **13.** escuchar música   **14.** hacer snowboarding   **15.** jugar fútbol

1f. Relaciona las fotografías con la/s palabra/s correspondiente/s del recuadro de arriba y comprueba tus respuestas con el profesor.
Match the pictures with the expressions in the box and verify your answers with your teacher.

1g. Contesta a las siguientes preguntas y después practica con tu compañero/a.
Answer the following questions then practise with your partner.

¿Qué te gusta hacer en tu tiempo libre?
What do you like doing in your free time?

¿Qué no te gusta hacer en tu tiempo libre?
What don't you like doing in your free time?

Audio 77

2. ME GUSTA/N/NO ME GUSTA/N. LIKES AND DISLIKES.

2a. Escucha y lee.
Me gusta/No me gusta. Likes/dislikes.

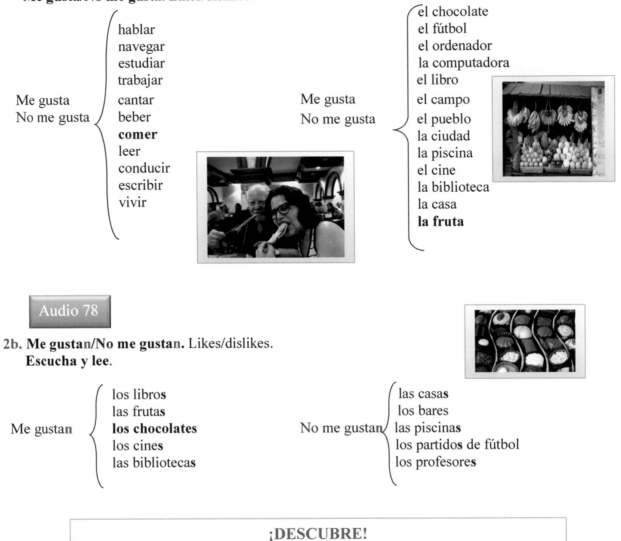

Me gusta
No me gusta
- hablar
- navegar
- estudiar
- trabajar
- cantar
- beber
- **comer**
- leer
- conducir
- escribir
- vivir

Me gusta
No me gusta
- el chocolate
- el fútbol
- el ordenador
- la computadora
- el libro
- el campo
- el pueblo
- la ciudad
- la piscina
- el cine
- la biblioteca
- la casa
- **la fruta**

Audio 78

2b. Me gustan/No me gustan. Likes/dislikes.
Escucha y lee.

Me gustan
- los libros
- las frutas
- **los chocolates**
- los cines
- las bibliotecas

No me gustan
- las casas
- los bares
- las piscinas
- los partidos de fútbol
- los profesores

¡DESCUBRE!

Me gusta **bailar**……………………….……...I like dancing.
Me gusta **el baile**…………………………….I like the dance.
Me gusta**n** los bailes modernos………..…….I like the modern dances.
Me gusta **ir** al teatro………………………I like going to the theatre.
Me gusta **el teatro**……………….................I like the theatre.
No me gusta**n** los teatros en mi ciudad…….I do not like the theatres in my city.

2c. Haz frases y practica con tu compañero/a. Compose sentences and practise with your partner.

Me gusta
Me gusta**n**
- el chocolate.
- leer libros.
- ir al teatro/ir a las fiestas.
- bañarme en el mar.
- los animales domésticos.
- las películas de terror.
- comer en restaurantes.
- estudiar en la biblioteca.
- la piscina.
- ducharme por la mañanas.
- las fiestas.
- salir con mis amigos.
- los deportes peligrosos.
- los programas de televisión policiacos.

GRAMÁTICA

Singular
Me gusta + verbo en infinitivo **(ar/er/ir)**
No me gusta + verbo en infinitivo **(ar/er/ir)**
Me gusta + sustantivo en singular (noun)
No me gusta + sustantivo en singular (noun)

Plural
Me gusta**n** + sustantivo plural (plural noun)
No me gusta**n** + sustantivo plural (plural noun)

3. LOS DEPORTES. SPORTS.

el surfing
la natación

el atletismo
el esquí

Audio 79

3a. Escucha y escribe el nombre del deporte correspondiente debajo de cada dibujo/fotografía.
Listen and label the sports correctly, according to the definitions below.

el ciclismo   el fútbol   el baloncesto   el snowboard
la equitación   la natación   el baile   el esquí

1	2	3	4	5	6	7	8

3b. **Mira los dibujos y las fotografías una vez más y ordénalos según tus gustos del 1 al 6 utilizando las expresiones del recuadro de abajo.** Look at the illustrations again and re-order them (1- 6) according to your preferences, using expressions from the box below.

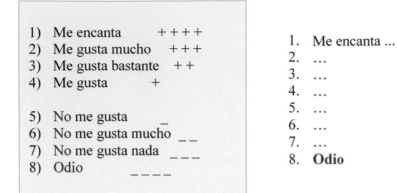

1) Me encanta	+ + + +	1. Me encanta ...
2) Me gusta mucho	+ + +	2. …
3) Me gusta bastante	+ +	3. …
4) Me gusta	+	4. …
		5. …
5) No me gusta	_	6. …
6) No me gusta mucho	_ _	7. …
7) No me gusta nada	_ _ _	8. **Odio**
8) Odio	_ _ _ _	

3c. **Practica con tu compañero/a como en el ejemplo.**
Practise with your partner following the example below.

Ejemplo:
A   **¿Te gusta el ciclismo?**
B   Sí, me gusta mucho.
A   **¿Te gusta el puenting?**
B   No me gusta nada.

GRAMÁTICA

me	gusta	*I like*
te	gusta	*you like*
le	gusta	*he/she likes*
nos	gusta	*we like*
os	gusta	*you like*
les	gusta	*they like*

¡DESCUBRE!

me encanta …. I love it.
(lo) odio……... I hate (it).

3d. Marca (√) lo que te gusta/n o no te gusta/n en cada cuadro y después practica con tu compañero/a. Tick (√) your likes and dislikes in each square and then practise with your partner.

	Me encanta	+ + +	+ +	+	-	- -	- - -	lo odio
dormir		√						
comer								
pasear								
pescar								
mandar mensajes en mi móvil								
tomar agua								
beber cerveza								
cocinar								
conducir								
jugar fútbol								
escribir correos electrónicos								
las arañas								
estudiar								
bañarme en el mar								
ducharme por las mañanas								
ver la tele								
ir al cine								
las películas de terror								
los ratones								
comprar zapatos								
los zumos naturales								
salir con los amigos								
escuchar música								
navegar en el ordenador								

GRAMÁTICA

*(A) mí me gusta/me gusta = I like it
*(A) ti te gusta/te gusta = you (singular) like it
 A él/ella le gusta = he/she likes
 A nosotros nos gusta = we like it
 A vosotros os gusta = you (plural) like it
 A ellos/ellas les gusta = they like it

*These expressions mean the same thing, except that the a + mí/ti provide emphasis.
A = preposition to

RECUERDA

¿Por qué?........Why?
porque.........because
es ....it's/it is
son.............. they are

3e. Mira el cuadro de abajo y completa las frases siguientes con los pronombres preposicionales apropiados. Look at the table below and complete the following sentences with the appropriate **prepositional pronouns**.

a) (A _____) nos gusta estudiar.

b) (A _____) les gusta ir a comer.

c) (A _____) me encanta cantar.

d) (A _____) te gusta bastante salir con los amigos.

e) (A _____) le gusta navegar en el ordenador.

f) (A _____) os gusta mandar mensajes por teléfono.

	Pronombres preposicionales Prepositional pronouns	Pronombres objeto indirecto Indirect objet pronouns	Gustar To like
A	mí	me	
A	ti	te	
A	él/ella/usted/ello	le	gusta/gustan
A	nosotros/as	nos	
A	vosotros/as	os	
A	ellos/ellas/ustedes	les	

3f. Completa las frases con el pronombre de objeto indirecto correspondiente.
Complete the sentences with the appropriate **indirect object pronouns**.

1. (A ti) _____ gusta beber.
2. (A mí) no _____ gusta estudiar.
3. (A Carlos) _____ gusta escuchar música.
4. (A María) no _____ gusta el golf.
5. (A nosotras) _____ gusta salir juntas.

6. (A vosotros) _____ gusta nadar.
7. (A ustedes) _____ gusta ir a la piscina.
8. (A ellos) _____ gusta el deporte.
9. (A usted) _____ gusta ir al teatro.
10. (A mí) _____ gusta estar en casa.

Audio 80

3g. Escucha y escribe. ¿Qué le gusta/les gustan?
Listen and write. What does he/she like/What do they like?

a) A Juan _____

b) A la Señora López _____

c) A ti _____

d) A nosotros _____

e) A vosotros _____

f) A Rosa y a Marcela _____

g) A mí _____

h) A mi marido _____

A Rita le gusta mandar mensajes en su móvil.

3h. Practica con tu compañero/a como en el ejemplo. Practise with your partner.

¿Cómo te llamas?	¿Qué te gusta?	¿Qué no te gusta?
Fernando	Me gusta ir al cine	No me gusta bailar

Practica con otros estudiantes tus respuestas. Relate the information you have gathered to other students. **Ejemplo: A Fernando le gusta ir al cine pero no le gusta bailar.**

4. TAMBIÉN - TAMPOCO. TOO/ALSO - NEITHER/NOR.

4a. Practica con tu compañero/a como en el ejemplo.
Practise with your partner, following the example below.

A. Me gusta el vino. ¿Y a ti?   A. No me gusta trabajar. ¿Y a ti?
B. A mí también/A mí no.   B. A mí **tampoco**/A mí sí.

4b. Practica con tu compañero/a.

A Me gusta [_____]. ¿Y a ti?   A No me gusta [_____]. ¿Y a ti?

B. A mí **también**/A mí no.   B. A mí **tampoco**/A mí sí.

Audio 81

4c. Escucha, lee y repite.

1. divertido/a   5. bueno/a   9. cruel
2. aburrido/a   6. malo/a   10. emocionante
3. relajante   7. sano/a   11. interesante
4. estresante   8. violento/a   12. peligroso/a

¡DESCUBRE!	
A mí también	Me too
A mí tampoco	Me neither
A mí sí	Yes, I do
A mí no	I don't/ I do not

Traduce al inglés o a tu idioma natal los siguientes adjetivos anteriores.
Translate the above adjectives into English or into your native language.

Practica con tu compañero/a. Practise with your partner.

A. ¿Te gusta la fruta?	A. ¿Te gustan las películas de terror?
B. Sí me gusta la fruta.	B. No, no me gustan nada.
A. ¿Por qué?	A. ¿Por qué?
B. Porque es sana.	B. Porque son estresantes.

Audio 82

4d. Escucha lo que le gusta y no le gusta a Sergio y escríbelo en el siguiente recuadro.
Listen to Sergio talking about his likes/dislikes and fill in the table below accordingly.

A Sergio le gusta/n	A Sergio no le gusta/n

4e. ¿Qué tipo de películas te gustan? What kind of films do you like?

Películas	Pintores	Escritores	Programas de televisión
Románticas De ciencia ficción Policiacas Del oeste	Pablo Picasso Salvador Dalí Fernando Botero Frida Kahlo	Gabriel García Márquez Isabel Allende Pablo Neruda Federico García Lorca	Culebrones Noticieros De concurso Deportivos

5. ¿QUÉ TE GUSTA DE TU CIUDAD/PUEBLO?
WHAT DO YOU LIKE ABOUT YOUR HOME TOWN?

5a. Escucha a Claudia de Madrid y a María de Higueras, hablar de sus lugares de nacimiento y escribe en el recuadro de abajo lo que les gusta y no les gusta. Listen to Claudia and María talking about their hometown and write in the box below what they like and dislike.

	Madrid	Higueras
Me gusta		
No me gusta		

5b. Escribe un texto sobre lo que te gusta y no te gusta de tu ciudad/pueblo y habla con tu compañero/a de lo que has escrito. Write a paragraph about what you like and dislike about your hometown then practise with your partner.

De mi ciudad/pueblo me gusta/no me gusta...

6. LECTURA Y COMPRENSIÓN. READING COMPREHENSION.

Lee el siguiente artículo y contesta a las siguientes preguntas en español.
Read the following article and answer the questions in Spanish.

¡Hola! Me llamo Isabel. A toda mi familia le gusta ir de vacaciones juntos. En invierno nos gusta ir a la montaña y jugar con la nieve. A mi marido Mario le gusta esquiar y a mi hija Verónica le gusta esquiar también. A mi otra hija María junto con mi hija mayor Laura y su marido Jaime también les gusta hacer snowboard. Pero a mí me gusta hacer trineo. No me gusta esquiar ni hacer snowboard. Al final del día a todos nos gusta ir a una cafetería juntos y hablar de nuestras aventuras y experiencias, tomando una bebida caliente.

En el verano nos gusta ir a la montaña o a la playa y quedarnos por unos días en una cabaña o en un apartamento al lado del mar. A mi marido le gusta montar en bicicleta, a mis hijas les gusta ir a nadar, a mi yerno le gusta leer y montar a caballo. A mí me gusta sacar fotos y bañarme en el mar, me encanta tomar el sol y leer un libro. A todos nos gusta hacer esnórquel, caminar y comer en restaurantes.

También hay cosas que no nos gustan. A mi marido no le gusta tomar el sol, prefiere leer un libro dentro de un restaurante con aire acondicionado. A mí no me gustan los insectos, odio las arañas. A mis hijas les gusta ir a bailar pero a mí no, no me gusta el ruido. Prefiero ir a un bar o a un restaurante y escuchar música tomando algunas copas.

a) ¿Qué les gusta hacer a todos juntos durante las vacaciones?
b) ¿Qué le gusta hacer a Mario?
c) ¿Qué no le gusta hacer a Mario?
d) ¿Qué le gusta hacer a la hija mayor Laura?
e) ¿Qué le gusta hacer a María?
f) ¿Qué le gusta hacer a Verónica?
g) ¿Qué le gusta hacer a Jaime?
h) ¿Qué le gusta hacer a Isabel?
i) ¿Qué no le gusta hacer a Isabel?
j) ¿Qué les gusta hacer a las hijas?

7. VAMOS A ESCRIBIR. LET'S WRITE.

Escribe un texto similar de lo que te gusta hacer a ti y a tu familia durante las vacaciones.
Following the example write about what you and your family like doing during the holidays.

EJERCICIOS

1. Completa las frases con Me gusta/n o No me gusta/n. Complete the phrases with likes and dislikes.

a) _____ las frutas.
b) _____ ir al fútbol.
c) _____ las películas de comedia.
d) _____ estudiar español.

e) No _____ los cucarachos.
f) _____ la playa del pueblo.
g) _____ comer en restaurantes.
h) No _____ ir de compras.

2. Elige el pronombre de objeto indirecto adecuado para cada persona.
Choose the right **indirect object pronouns** for each person.

Pronombres personales sujeto	Frases con pronombre de objeto indirecto
a. ella	**Le** gusta el vino tinto.
b. nosotros	_____ gustan las fiestas.
c. él	_____ gusta nadar.
d. yo	_____ encanta ir al cine.
e. vosotros	_____ gustan los animales.
f. ustedes	_____ gusta el café.
g. ellos	_____ gusta hacer deporte.
h. tú	_____ encanta bailar en las discotecas.
i. ellos	_____ gustan los chocolates.
j. vosotras	_____ gusta estudiar juntas.

3. Completa las frases siguientes con los pronombres preposicionales apropiados.
Complete the following sentences with the appropriate prepositional pronouns.

a) A **nosotros/as** nos gusta mucho esquiar.
b) A _____ les gusta ir a bailar.
c) A _____ me encanta correr.
d) A _____ te gusta bastante caminar.
e) A _____ le gusta nadar todos los fines de semana.
f) A _____ os gusta tomar el sol en la playa.

4. Completa las frases siguientes con los pronombres de objeto directo y los pronombres reflexivos. Complete the following sentences with the indirect object pronouns and reflexive pronouns.

Pronombres personales sujeto Subject pronouns	Pronombres objeto indirecto Indirect object pronouns	Pronombres reflexivos Reflexive pronouns
yo (I)	_____ gusta estudiar	levant**o**
tú (you) informal	_____ gusta estudiar	levant**as**
usted (you) formal	_____ gusta estudiar	levant**a**
él/ella (he/she)	_____ gusta estudiar	levant**a**
nosotros/as (we)	_____ gusta estudiar	levant**amos**
vosotros/as (you) informal	_____ gusta estudiar	levant**áis**
ustedes (you) formal	_____ gusta estudiar	levant**an**
ellos/ellas (they)	_____ gusta estudiar	levant**an**

GRAMÁTICA

- **Gustar**

  El verbo gustar significa literalmente 'to please' pero idomáticamente significa 'to like'. The verb '**gustar**' literally means 'to please' but idiomatically it means 'to like' so the literal meaning of Me gusta la casa (I like the house) is 'The house pleases me'.

  o **Gustar + verbo en infinitivo (ar/er/ir)**

  Me gusta
  {
  habl**ar** español.
  com**er** en casa.
  sal**ir** con los amigos.
  }

  o **Gustar + sustantivo (singular/plural)**

  - **Me gusta el libro**…………I like the book/The book pleases me (singular).
  - **Me gustan los libros**…….. I like the books/The books please me (plural).

- **Pronombre de objeto indirecto.** Indirect object pronoun.

  El verbo «gustar» siempre requiere un pronombre de objeto indirecto para indicar quién recibe el gusto; el sujeto del verbo es la persona o cosa que da gusto.
  The verb 'to like' always requires an indirect object pronoun to stand for the person who likes whatever it is they like. The subject of the verb is the person or thing which is liked (is 'pleasing to' the person).

me		I like
Te		you like
Le	**gusta/n**	he/she like**s**
Nos		we like
Os		you like
Les		they like

> **LOS NEGATIVOS**
> - No + gustar + infinitivo (ar/er/ir)
>   No me gusta estudiar.
>
> - No + gustar + sustantivo (singular/plural)
>   No me gusta la casa. (singular)
>   No me gusta**n** las casa**s**. (plural)

- **Pronombres de objeto indirecto + gustar (singular/plural).**

Pronombres personales sujeto Subject pronouns	Pronombres objeto indirecto Indirect objet pronouns	Gustar To like
yo (I)	me	
tú (you) informal.	te	
usted (you) formal	le	
él/ella (he/she)	le	gusta/gustan
nosotros/as (we)	nos	
vosotros/as (you) informal	os	
ustedes (you) formal	les	
ellos/ellas (they)	les	

> **Note** Here the English subject pronouns (I, you, etc) becomes an indirect object pronoun in Spanish.

- «A» personal + pronombres tónicos (a mí, a ti, a él/ella/usted, a nosotros/as, a vosotros/as, a ellos/ella/ustedes) se usan para dar énfasis pero no es obligatorio usarlos. The personal 'a'+ prepositional pronouns are used to add emphasis but it is not required to use them.

  * **A mí me gusta/me gusta** = I like
  * **A ti te gusta/te gusta**   = you like
  *These expressions mean the same thing, except that the **a + mí/ti** provides emphasis.

A él/ella le gusta = he/she likes

A + Pronombres preposicionales Prepositional pronouns	Pronombres objeto indirecto Indirect objet pronouns	Gustar To like
A mí	me	
A ti	te	
A él/ella/usted	le	
A nosotros/as	nos	gusta/gustan
A vosotros/as	os	
A ellos/ellas/ustedes	les	

- **(A mí)** me gusta salir con mis amigos.
- **(A ti)** te gusta bailar.
- **(A usted)** le gusta trabajar.
- **(A él)** le gusta comer paella.
- **(A ella)** le gusta comprar ropa.
- **(A nosotros)** nos gusta ir de copas.
- **(A vosotros)** os gusta estudiar en la biblioteca.
- **(A ustedes)** les gusta caminar.

- **Adverbios**. Adverbs.

  - **También/tampoco**. Too/also and neither/nor

o **Me gusta el vino. ¿Y a ti?**	o **No me gusta trabajar. ¿Y a ti?**
o B. A mí **también.**	o B. A mí **tampoco.**

  - **Cuantificadores: muy y bastante**
  - Quantifiers: very and quite

VOCABULARIO

1. MI TIEMPO LIBRE	**1. *MY FREE TIME***
al (a+el)	*to the*
baile (m)	*dance*
baloncesto (m)	*basketball*
bar (m)	*pub*
bicicleta (f)	*bicycle*
ciclismo (m)	*cycling*
deporte (m)	*sport*
fútbol (m)	*football (UK)/ soccer (US)*
guitarra (f)	*guitar*
libro (m)	*book*
mensaje (m)	*messages*
música (f)	*music*
ni…ni	*neither…nor*
partido (m)	*match*
prefiero	*I prefer*
teléfono (m)	*phone*
televisión/tele (f)	*television*
también	*also*
tengo que	*I have to*
tenis (m)	*tennis*
tiempo libre (m)	*free time*
tomar el sol	*to sunbathe*
puenting (m)	*bungee-jumping*
snowboard (m)	*snowboarding*
¿Cómo estás?	*How are you?*
¿Qué te gusta hacer en tu tiempo libre?	*What do you like doing in your free time?*
¿Qué no te gusta hacer en tu tiempo libre?	*What don't you like doing in your free time?*
¿Qué le gusta hacer a él/ella en su tiempo libre?	*What does he/she like doing in his/her free time?*

2. ME GUSTA/ ME GUSTAN	**2. *I LIKE***
animal (m)	*animal*
campo (m)	*field*
chocolate (m)	*chocolate*
fruta (f)	*fruit*
juntos/as	*together*
película (m)	*movie*
teatro (m)	*theatre (UK)/theater (US)*
terror	*horror*

3. DEPORTES	**3. *SPORT***
compras (fpl)	*shopping*
equitación (f)	*horse riding*
esquí (m)	*skiing*
natación (f)	*swimming*

4.TAMBIÉN- TAMPOCO	**4.*TOO/ALSO- NEITHER/NOR***
aburrido/a	*boring*
araña (f)	*spider*
bueno/a	*good*
cruel (m/f)	*cruel*
divertido/a	*funny*
emocionante (m/f)	*exciting*
estresante (m/f)	*stressful*
interesante (m/f)	*interesting*
malo/a	*bad*
peligroso/a	*dangerous*
porque	*because*
ratón (m)	*mouse*
relajante (m/f)	*relaxing*
sano/a	*healthy*
violento/a	*violent*
¿Por qué?	*Why?*
¿Qué tipo de..?	*What kind of ..?*

VERBOS	**VERBS**
bailar	*to dance*
bucear	*to dive*
caminar	*to walk*
cantar	*to sing*
cocinar	*to cook*
comer	*to eat*
comprar	*to buy*
conducir	*to drive*
dormir	*to sleep*
escuchar	*to listen*
estudiar	*to study*
hablar	*to talk/to speak*
hacer	*to do/to make*
ir	*to go*
jugar	*to play*
leer	*to read*
mandar	*to send*
montar	*to ride*

13 GRAMÁTICA

El alfabeto español. The Spanish alphabet.

There are 27 letters in the Spanish alphabet. The letters are all feminine, so the definite article that precedes them is **la**. They are referred to as: <u>la</u> **A**, <u>la</u> **B**, <u>la</u> **C** and so on. Digraphs (a group of two letters representing one sound) are: **ch, gu, ll, rr** and **qu**.

Letra	Nombre de la letra	Pronunciación	Ejemplo
A, a	a	/a/	**A**rgentina
B, b	be	/b/	**B**olivia
C, c	ce	/k/, /θ/	**C**olombia/**C**euta
D, d	de	/d/	**D**inamarca
E, e	e	/e/	**E**uropa
F, f	efe	/f/	**F**rancia
G, g	ge	/g/, /x/	**G**uatemala/**G**ibraltar
H, h	hache	no se pronuncia	**H**onduras
I, i	i	/i/	**I**talia
J, j	jota	/x/	**J**amaica
K, k	ca	/k/	**K**uwait
L, l	ele	/l/	**L**ima
M, m	eme	/m/	**M**éxico
N, n	ene	/n/	**N**icaragua
Ñ, ñ	eñe	/ɲ/	Espa**ñ**a
O, o	o	/o/	**O**viedo
P, p	pe	/p/	**P**erú
Q, q	cu	/k/	**Q**uito
R, r	erre	/r̄/, /r/	**R**eino Unido
S, s	ese	/s/	**S**evilla
T, t	te	/t/	**T**oledo
U, u	u	/u/	**U**ruguay
V, v	uve	/b/	**V**enezuela
W, w	uve doble	/w/	**W**ashington
X, x	equis	/ks/, /s/	Lu**x**emburgo
Y, y	i griega o ye	/y/, /i/	**Y**ucatán
Z, z	zeta	/θ/	**Z**aragoza

- **Pronunciación.** Pronunciation.

  In Spanish there are only 5 vowels: **a, e, i, o, u**. They always have the same sound.
  - The letter **h** is silent in Spanish: (h)ola, (h)ora.
  - The letters **b** and **v** are pronounced in the same way: (**B**arcelona, **v**ino).
  - **r** is sounded as follows:
    - **rr** between vowels (burro, perro).
    - **rr** at the beginning of a word (Rosa, Roberto).

- The letters **c, z** and **q**:

Se escribe	Se pronuncia *
za	/θa/
ce	/θe/
ci	/θi/
zo	/θo/
zu	/θu/

Se escribe	Se pronuncia
ca	/ka/
que	/ke/
qui	/ki/
co	/ko/
cu	/ku

- Las letras **g y j**:

Se escribe	Se pronuncia
ga	/ga/
gue	/ge/
gui	/gi/
go	/go/
gu	/gu/
güe	/gue/
güi	/gui/

Se escribe	Se pronuncia
ja	/xa/
je, ge	/xe/
ji, gi	/xi/
jo	/xo/
ju	/xu/

*Note, the 'th'(θ) sound is used in Spain, and the 's' sound is used in Latinamerica and the Canary Islands.

Reglas de acentuación. Spanish accents rules.

a) **Rule 1**. Words ending in a **vowel**, «**n**», or «**s**» are stressed on the next to the last (penultimate) syllable. No accent is required, e.g.

joven	examen	zapatos	limonada	estudiante
jo - ven	e -**xa** - men	za - **pa** - tos	li - mo - **na** - da	es –tu- **dian** -te

b) **Rule 2**. Words ending in **any consonant** except **-n** or **-s** are stressed on the last syllable. No accent is required, e.g.

reloj	ciudad	feliz	doctor	comer
re - **loj**	ciu - **dad**	fe -**liz**	doc - **tor**	co - **mer**

c) When rules **1** and **2** above are not followed, **a written accent is required.** An accent is placed over the vowel which requires the stress, e.g.

adiós	inglés	avión	compró	estudió
a - **diós**	in - **glés**	a - **vión**	com - **pró**	es - tu - **dió**

d) Written accents are also used to differentiate between words which have the same spelling but different meanings:

el - the	**si** - if	**mi** - my	**tu** - your	**esta** - this
él - he	**sí** - yes	**mí** - me	**tú** - you	**está** – he/she is

e) The mark wich is sometimes found over an **n** is called a **tilde** and is used to change the sound to ny.

España	año	niño	señor	eñe

Adjetivos. Adjectives.

- **Adjetivos calificativos.** Adjectives.
  Adjectives normally come after the noun and agree in number and gender with the noun they qualify.

Singular		Plural	
Masculino	**Femenino**	**Masculino**	**Femenino**
caro	cara	car**os**	car**as**
barato	barata	barat**os**	barat**as**
bonito	bonita	bonit**os**	bonit**as**
feo	fea	fe**os**	fe**as**
viejo	vieja	viej**os**	viej**as**
grande		grande**s**	
interesante		interesante**s**	

- **Adjetivos de cantidad.** Adjectives of quantity.
  There are two words for 'how much' (one for masculine and one for feminine) and also two words for 'how many'

Masculino	Femenino	
¿Cuánto?	¿Cuánta?	How much?
¿Cuántos?	¿Cuántas?	How many?
¿Cuánto queso?		How much cheese?
	¿Cuánta carne?	How much meat?
¿Cuántos limones?		How many lemons?
	¿Cuántas uvas?	How many grapes?

195

- **Adjetivos posesivos sujeto.** Possessive adjectives.

		Singular		Plural		
		Masculino	Femenino	Masculino	Femenino	
Singular	1ª	mi		mis		my
	2ª	tu (informal singular)		tus (informal singular)		your
	2ª	su (formal singular)		sus (formal singular)		your
	3ª	su		sus		his/her/its
Plural	1ª	nuestro	nuestra	nuestros	nuestras	our
	2ª	vuestro (informal)	vuestra (informal)	vuestros (informal)	vuestras (informal)	your informal plural
	2ª	su		sus		your formal plural
	3ª	su		sus		their

Note: su can mean his, her, your (formal) or their. The exact meaning is usually clear from the context.

- **Adjetivos posesivos.** Possessive Adjectives.

Pronombres personales sujeto Subject personal pronouns	Adjetivos posesivos Possessive adjectives	
	Singular	Plural
yo I	**mi** my	**mis** my
tú you	**tu** your (informal)	**tus** your (informal)
usted you	**su** your (formal)	**sus** your (formal)
él/ella he/she	**su** his/her	**sus** his/her
nosotros/nosotras we	**nuestro/nuestra** our	**nuestros/nuestras** our
vosotros/vosotras you	**vuestro/vuestra** your (informal)	**vuestros/vuestras** your (informal)
ustedes you	**su** your (formal)	**sus** your (formal)
ellos/ellas they	**su** their	**sus** their

- **Adjetivos y pronombres demostrativos**. Demonstrative pronouns and adjectives.

	Masculino	Femenino
Singular	este (this)	esta (this)
Plural	estos (these)	estas (these)

- **Colores como adjetivos**. Colour adjectives.

Singular	
Masculino	**Femenino**
blanco	blanca
negro	**negra**
amarillo	**amarilla**
rojo	roja
morado	morada

Plural	
Masculino	**Femenino**
blancos	blancas
negros	**negras**
amarillos	**amarillas**
rojos	rojas
morados	moradas

Invariable
verde
azul
marrón
rosa
naranja

Note: Colours that are derived from the names of flowers and fruit are usually invariable (they don't change according to gender or number).

Singular	
Masculino	**Femenino**
El vestido es rosa.	La blusa es rosa.
El traje es **naranja**.	La camisa es **naranja**.

Plural	
Masculino	**Femenino**
Los vestidos son de color rosa.	Las blusas son de color rosa.
Los trajes son de color **naranja**.	Las camisas son de color **naranja**.

Adverbios. Adverbs.

- **De cantidad**. Of quantity.

muy	very	**La ciudad es muy grande.**	The city is very big.
mucho/a	a lot of	**Hay mucho tráfico.** **Hay mucha comida.**	There's a lot of traffic. There a lot of food.
muchos/as	many	**Hay muchos restaurantes.** **Hay muchas bicicletas.**	There are many restaurants. There are many bicycles.

- **De lugar** of place
  - **aquí**.....here
  - **allí**......there

- **También/tampoco**. Too/also and neither/nor

o **Me gusta el vino. ¿Y a ti?**	o **No me gusta trabajar. ¿Y a ti?**
o B. A mí **también.**	o B. A mí **tampoco**

- **Cuantificadores: muy y bastante.** Quantifiers: very and quite.

Artículos. Articles.

- **Artículos determinados.** Definite articles.

	Singular	Plural	
Masculino	el	los	the
Femenino	la	las	the

- **Artículos indefinidos.** Indefinite articles.

	Masculino	Femenino	
Singular	un	una	a (an)
Plural	unos	unas	some

Conjunción «y». The conjunction 'and'.

y/e... and inglés **y** español.... English and Spanish
y changes to **e** before **i** and **hi** español **e** inglés.... Spanish and English

Comparativos y superlativos. Comparatives and superlatives.

más.........que	La ciudad es **más** grande **que** el pueblo.
menos......que	El tren es **menos** rápido **que** el avión.
tan..........como	La casa es **tan** bonita **como** el piso.
el/la más........de	El libro de español es **el más** interesante **de** todos.

Formación de los plurales. Plurals.

- Add **s**: When the singular noun ends in a vowel (a, e, i, o and u) e.g.: casas, padres, bicis, libros.
- Add **es**: When the singular noun ends in a consonant e.g.: ustedes, profesores, escritores, leones, países.
- Add **es**: When the singular noun ends in z, the z needs to change to c e.g.: pez →peces, lápiz →lápices.
- Add **es**: When the singular noun ends in a vowel with an accent e.g.: maniquíes, colibríes.
- Words that end in a vowel (a, e, i, o and u) + s stay the same e.g.: lunes, martes, cumpleaños.
- There are nouns that only exist as plurals e.g.: gafas, pantalones, tijeras.

Género (masculino o femenino). Gender (masculine or feminine).

Spanish **nouns** are classified as either **masculine** or **feminine**. Nouns which end in 'o' are **usually** masculine and those which end in 'a' are **usually** feminine. When a masculine noun ends in a consonant, the letter 'a' is added to make it feminine. Nouns which end in 'e' and 'ista' are invariable (they don't change).

Masculino	**Femenino**
cartero	cartera
profesor	profesora
	cantante
	electricista

Gustar. To please/to like.

- **Gustar. El verbo gustar significa literalmente** 'to please' **pero idiomáticamente significa** 'to like'. The verb **'gustar'** literally means "to please" but idiomatically it means 'to like' so the literal meaning of **Me gusta la casa** (I like the house) is 'The house pleases me'.

  - **Gustar + verbo en infinitivo (ar/er/ir).**

    Me gusta
    - hablar español.
    - comer en casa.
    - salir con los amigos.

  - **Gustar + sustantivo (singular/plural)**
    - **Me gusta el libro**.............I like the book/The book pleases me (singular)
    - **Me gustan los libros**........ I like the books/The books please me (plural)

    > **LOS NEGATIVOS**
    > - No + gustar + infinitivo (ar/er/ir)
    >   No me gusta estudiar.
    >
    > - No + gustar + sustantivo (singular/plural)
    >   No me gusta la casa. (singular)
    >   No me gustan las casas. (plural)

- **El verbo «gustar» siempre requiere un pronombre de objeto indirecto para indicar quién recibe el gusto; el sujeto del verbo es la persona o cosa que da gusto.**
The verb 'to like' always requires an indirect object pronoun to stand for the person who likes whatever it is they like. The subject of the verb is the person or thing that is liked (is 'pleasing to' the person).

me		I like
te		you like
le		he/she likes
nos	gusta/n	we like
os		you like
les		they like

- **Pronombres de objeto indirecto + gustar (singular/plural)**

Pronombres personales sujeto Subject pronouns	Pronombres objeto indirecto Indirect object pronouns	Gustar To like
yo (I)	me	
tú (you) informal	te	
usted (you) formal	le	
él/ella (he/she)	le	gusta/gustan
nosotros/as (we)	nos	
vosotros/as (you) informal	os	
ustedes (you) formal	les	
ellos/ellas (they)	les	

Note Here the English subject pronouns (I, you, etc) becomes an indirect object pronoun in Spanish.

- **«A» personal + pronombres tónicos (a mí, a ti, a él/ella/usted, a nosotros/as, a vosotros/as, a ellos/ella/ustedes) se usan para dar énfasis pero no es obligatorio usarlos.**
The personal 'a'+ prepositional pronouns are used to add emphasis but they are not obligatory.

Ejemplo:
A mí me gusta/me gusta = I like
A ti te gusta/te gusta = you like

These expressions mean the same thing, except that the 'a' + 'mí'/'ti' provides emphasis.

A + Pronombres preposicionales Prepositional pronouns	Pronombres objeto indirecto Indirect object pronouns	Gustar To like
A mí	me	
A ti	te	
A usted	le	
A él/ella	le	gusta/gustan
A nosotros/as	nos	
A vosotros/as	os	
A ustedes	les	

Ejemplo:

(**A mí**) me gusta salir con mis amigos.
(**A ti**) te gusta bailar.
(**A usted**) le gusta trabajar.
(**A él**) le gusta comer paella.
(**A ella**) le gusta comprar ropa.
(**A nosotros**) nos gusta ir de copas.
(**A vosotros**) os gusta estudiar en la biblioteca.
(**A ustedes**) les gusta caminar.

Números. Numbers.

1. uno/a	11. once	30. treinta	200. doscientos/as
2. dos	12. doce	40. cuarenta	300. trescientos/as
3. tres	13. trece	50. cincuenta	400. cuatrocientos/as
4. cuatro	14. catorce	60. sesenta	500. quinientos/as
5. cinco	15. quince	70. setenta	600. seiscientos/as
6. seis	16. dieciséis	80. ochenta	700. setecientos/as
7. siete	17. diecisiete	90. noventa	800. ochocientos/as
8. ocho	18. dieciocho	100. cien	900. novecientos/as
9. nueve	19. diecinueve		1.000 mil
10. diez	20. veinte		2.000 dos mil
			1.000.000 un millón
			2.000.000 dos millones

- **uno** changes to **un** before masculine nouns: **un** hombre, **un** hermano/hijo.
- **uno** changes to **una** before feminine nouns: **una** mujer, **una** hermana/hija.
- «**y**» is only used between tens and units: treinta **y** dos, noventa **y** ocho, cincuenta **y** tres.

Numbers are masculine but some numbers become feminine before a feminine noun: this affects numbers ending in, '**un**': 1, 21, 31, 41, 51, 61, 71, 81 and 91 and numbers including the word, '**cientos**': 200, 300, 400, 500, 600, 700, 800 and 900. The following examples explain this rule:

•	1 chair – una silla	• 200 people – doscientas personas
•	21 weeks – veintiuna semanas	• 500 cities – quinientas ciudades
•	41 tables – cuarenta y una mesas	• 900 pounds – novecientas libras

Números ordinales: 1°- 10°. Ordinal numbers 1st – 10th

Números ordinales: Ordinal numbers.

- Like many other adjectives, the ordinal numbers have a masculine and a feminine form.
- **Primero** and **tercero** drop the -o in the masculine singular adjective form.
  - **El primer niño.**
  - **El tercer piso.**

- Here are the ordinal numbers first - tenth:

- 1° primero/1ª primera/primer	- 6° sexto/6ª sexta
- 2° segundo/segunda 2ª	- 7° séptimo/7ª séptima
- 3° tercero/tercera 3ª/tercer	- 8° octavo/8ª octava
- 4° cuarto/4ª cuarta	- 9° novena/9ª novena
- 5° quinto/5ª quinta	- 10° décimo/10ª décima

Preposiciones. **Prepositions.**

- **para, con, sin** to/for, with, without

- **de** from

- **indicando un lugar específico.** Prepositions indicating exact location.
  - **al lado de**.......... next to/beside
  - **debajo de** .... under
  - **delante de** ....in front of
  - **dentro de/en**...... inside
  - **detrás de**........... behind
  - **en la esquina** ......on/at the corner
  - **enfrente de**.........opposite
  - **entre** ....between
  - **en/sobre/encima de**....on

- **El uso de las preposiciones: de/a + artículo determinado.** Usage of the prepositions **de/a** + article.

  - **de + el = del** (but) **de la = de la**
    - **Ejemplo**: Está cerca **del** banco (el banco).   It's near the bank.
      Está cerca **de la** biblioteca.   It's near the library.

  - **a + el = al** (but)   **a la = a la**
    - **Ejemplo:** Vamos **al** parque (el parque)   We'll go to the park.
      - Vamos a la biblioteca.   We'll go to the library.

Pronombres personales sujeto. **Subject pronouns.**

Pronombres personales sujeto	Subject pronouns	Pronombres personales sujeto	Personal pronouns
Singular	Singular	**Plural**	Plural
yo	I	**nosotros/nosotras**	we
tú	you (informal)	**vosotros/vosotras**	you (informal)
usted	you (formal)	**ustedes**	you (formal)
él	he	**ellos**	they
ella	she	**ellas**	they

Note: Subject pronouns are normally omitted in Spanish.

Pronombres demostrativos. Demonstrative pronouns.

Los pronombres demostrativos son pronombres que denotan grados de proximidad en relación con el hablante y el oyente. Demonstrative pronouns are pronouns denoting degrees of proximity in relation to the speaker and the listener.

- **este, esta, esto, estos, estas (denotan cercanía)** this, these
- **ese, esa, eso, esos, esas (denotan distancia media)** that, those

- **aquel, aquella, aquello, aquellos, aquellas (denotan lejanía)** that, those (denote distance)

	Singular this	Plural these			Singular that	Plural those
Masculino	este	*estos		Masculino	ese	*esos
Femenino	esta	estas		Femenino	esa	esas
Neutro	esto	*estos		Neutro	eso	*esos

	Singular that	Plural these
Masculino	aquel	*aquellos
Femenino	aquella	aquellas
Neutro	aquello	*aquellos

Note: *masculine plural demonstrative pronouns are written as neutral demonstrative pronouns.

Pronombres reflexivos. Reflexive pronouns.

Pronombres personales sujeto Subject pronouns	Pronombres reflexivos Reflexive pronouns
yo	**me**
tú (informal)	**te**
usted (formal)	**se**
él/ella	**se**
nosotros/as	**nos**
vosotros/as (informal)	**os**
ustedes (formal)	**se**
ellos/ellas	**se**

Verbos. Verbs.

Presente de indicativo de los verbos regulares. Present tense of regular verbs.

- **Verbos terminados en ar.** Present tense of -ar verbs.

Pronombres personales sujeto	hablar to speak
yo	**hablo**
tú (informal)	**hablas**
usted (formal)	**habla**
él/ella	**habla**
nosotros/as	**hablamos**
vosotros/as	**habláis**
ustedes	**hablan**
ellos/ellas	**hablan**

More -**ar** verbs: trabajar, estudiar, cantar, cenar, escuchar, tomar, llevar, llegar, navegar, mandar…

- **Verbos terminados en er.** Conjugation of -er verbs.

Pronombres personales sujeto	aprender to learn
yo	**aprendo**
tú (informal)	**aprendes**
usted (formal)	**aprende**
él/ella	**aprende**
nosotros/as	**aprendemos**
vosotros/as	**aprendéis**
ustedes	**aprenden**
ellos/ellas	**aprenden**

More **er** verbs: leer, beber, comer, entender, correr, comprender…

- **Verbos terminados en ir.** Conjugation of -**ir** verbs.

Pronombres personales sujeto	vivir to live
yo	**vivo**
tú	**vives**
usted (formal)	**vive**
él/ella	**vive**
nosotros/as	**vivimos**
vosotros/as	**vivís**
ustedes (formal)	**viven**
ellos/ellas	**viven**

More ir verbs: escribir, abrir, subir, asistir…

Presente de indicativo de los verbos irregulares. Present tense of irregular verbs.

- **Ser/estar.** To be.

Pronombres personales sujeto	ser	estar	to be
yo	soy	estoy	I am
tú (informal)	eres	estás	you are
usted (formal)	es	está	you are
él/ella	es	está	he/she is
nosotros/as	somos	estamos	we are
vosotros/as (informal)	sois	estáis	you are
ustedes (formal)	son	están	you are
ellos/ellas	son	están	they are

- **Ser y estar** ('to be'). In Spanish there are two verbs meaning, 'to be': **ser and estar.**

  - **ser**: is used for names, nationalities, professions, descriptions and adjectives (permanent qualities).
    - **Soy** Luis, soy español de Barcelona, soy arquitecto. Soy alto moreno y guapo.
    - **Eres** María, eres italiana de Roma, eres actriz. Eres baja, guapa y simpática.
    - **Es** Pedro, es argentino de Buenos Aires, es ingeniero. Es alto, rubio y trabajador.
    - **¿Sois** vosotros Luis y Carolina, los estudiantes españoles?
    - **¿Qué hora es?**

  - **estar**: is used to say where something or someone is.
    - **Estoy** en la universidad.
    - No **estoy** en casa, estoy en el restaurante Pepe.
    - Madrid **está** en Europa.
    - **Estamos** en la clase de español.

      - **soy/estoy casado/a** → I'm married
      - **soy/estoy soltero/a** → I'm single
      - **soy/estoy separado/a** → I'm separated
      - **soy/estoy divorciado/a** → I'm divorced
      - **soy/estoy viudo/a** → I'm a widower/widow

    Nota: to indicate marital states, it is possible to use either: **ser** or **estar**

- **Verbos irregulares: tener, salir, hacer e ir.**

Pronombres personales sujeto	tener to have	hacer to do/to make	salir to go out	ir to go
yo	tengo	hago	salgo	voy
tú	tienes*	haces	sales	vas
usted (formal)	tiene*	hace	sale	va
él/ella	tiene*	hace	sale	va
nosotros/as	tenemos	hacemos	salimos	vamos
vosotros/as	tenéis	hacéis	salís	váis
ustedes (formal)	tienen*	hacen	salen	van
ellos/ellas	tienen*	hacen	salen	van

- **Verbos en el presente con irregularidad vocálica: pensar, querer, preferir, jugar, volver y tener(*).**
  Present tense irregulars verbs with vowel irregularity: to think, to want and to prefer.

e → ie
u → ue   o → ue

Pronombres personales sujeto	cerrar to close	pensar to think	querer to want	preferir to prefer	jugar to play	volver to return
yo	cierro	pienso	quiero	prefiero	juego	vuelvo
tú	cierras	piensas	quieres	prefieres	juegas	vuelves
usted (formal)	cierra	piensa	quiere	prefiere	juega	vuelve
él/ella	cierra	piensa	quiere	prefiere	juega	vuelve
nosotros/as	cerramos	pensamos	queremos	preferimos	jugamos	volvemos
vosotros/as	cerráis	pensáis	queréis	preferís	jugáis	volvéis
ustedes (formal)	cierran	piensan	quieren	prefieren	juegan	vuelven
ellos/ellas	cierran	piensan	quieren	prefieren	juegan	vuelven

Note: the first and second person plural forms of the verbs (nosotros/as y vosotros/as) remain regular.

- **Tener que + infinitivo (ar/er/ir).** You have + verb in infinitive.

  - **Tienes que estudiar.** You have to study.
  - **Tengo que comer.** I have to eat.
  - **María tiene que dormir.** Maria has to sleep.

- **Verbo haber.** To have/to be.

  - **Hay**   There is/there are
  - **¿Hay?**   What is/are there?
  - **¿Qué hay?**   Is/Are there?

Presente de indicativo de los verbos con pronombre reflexivo.
Present tense of verbs with reflexive pronoun.

Reflexive verbs have the normal **–ar,-er,** or **ir** endings, but also have a reflexive pronoun to indicate that the person is doing something to, by or for himself/herself (the action reflects back on the subject). English reflexive verbs are easy to spot because always involve a "self" word. Many verbs are reflexive in Spanish which are not in English.

- **Llamarse.** To be called.

Pronombres personales sujeto	llamarse	to be called
yo	**me** llamo	I am called/My name is
tú (informal)	**te** llamas	You are called/Your name is
usted (formal)	**se** llama	You are called/Your name is
él/ella	**se** llama	He/she is called/His/her name called
nosotros/as	**nos llamamos**	We are called/Our name is
vosotros/as (informal)	**os llamáis**	You are called/Your name is
ustedes (formal)	**se llaman**	You are called/Your name is
ellos/ellas	**se llaman**	They are called/Their name is

- **Levantarse.** To get up.

Pronombres personales sujeto	Pronombres reflexivos	levantarse	to get up
yo	**me**	levanto	I get up
tú (informal)	**te**	levantas	you get up
usted (formal)	**se**	levanta	you get up
él/ella	**se**	levanta	he/she gets up
nosotros/as	**nos**	levantamos	we get up
vosotros/as (informal)	**os**	levantáis	you get up
ustedes (formal)	**se**	levantan	you get up
ellos/ellas	**se**	levantan	they get up

More ar verbs: **despertarse, ducharse, bañarse, lavarse, llamarse**…

- **Irregulares con cambio vocálico excepto en la 1ª y 2ª persona del plural.**
  Irregulars (radical changing verbs) except in the 1st and 2nd person of the plural.

Pronombres personales sujeto	Pronombres reflexivos	despertarse	acostarse	dormirse
yo	me	despierto	acuesto	duermo
tú (informal)	te	despiertas	acuestas	duermes
usted (formal)	se	despierta	acuesta	duerme
él/ella	se	despierta	acuesta	duerme
nosotros/as	nos	despertamos	acostamos	dormimos
vosotros/as (informal)	os	despertáis	acostáis	dormís
Ustedes (formal)	se	despiertan	acuestan	duermen
ellos/ellas	se	despiertan	acuestan	duermen

Abreviaciones. Abbreviations.

adj	adjetivo
art	artículo
Avda.	Avenida
C/	Calle
cts	céntimo
con	conjunción
Ctra.	Carretera
f	femenino
fpl	femenino plural
inter	interjercción
m	masculino
m/f	masculino y femenino
mpl	masculino plural
prep	preposición
pro	pronombre
Q.E.P.D.	Que en paz descanse
Sr.	Señor
Sra.	Señora
Srta.	Señorita
P.º	Paseo
Pza.	Plaza
verb	verbo

14 VOCABULARIO

A

a *(prep) at, to*
abogado/a *lawyer*
abril *April*
abuela (f) *grandmother*
abuelo (m) *grandfather*
aburrido/a *(adj) boring*
acabo de llegar *I just arrived*
academia *(f) college*
aceite *(m) oil*
aceituna/oliva *(f) olive*
acostarse *(verb) to go to bed*
actor *(m) actor*
actriz *(f) actress*
adiós *(interj) goodbye*
adulto/a *(adj) adult*
afeitarse *(verb) to shave yourself*
agosto *August*
agua *(m) water*
agua mineral (con/sin gas) *mineral water (with/without gas)*
aguacate *(m) avocado*
ajo *(m) garlic*
antiguo/a *(adj) old*
al *(conj) to the*
al lado de *(prep) next to*
alemán/-ana *(adj) German*
alemán *(m), German (language)*
Alemania *(f) Germany*
algo *(pron) something, anything*
algo más *something/anything else*
alto/a *(adj) tall*
ama de casa *(f) housewife*
amigo/a *friend*
ancho/a *wide*
animal *(m) animal*
antipático/a *(adj) unfriendly*
año *(m) year*
apartamento (m) *apartment*
apellido *(m) surname*
aquí *(advervio) here*
araña *(f) spider*
arquitecto/a *architect*
arroba (f) *at*
arroz (m) *rice*
arroz con leche *(m) rice pudding*
asar *(verb) to grill*
asado/a (adj) *grilled*
aseo/servicio *(m) toilet/WC*
atún *(m) tuna*
avenida (f) *avenue*
ayuntamiento *(m) town hall*
azúcar *(m) sugar*

B

bacalao *(m) cod*
bailar *(verb) to dance*

baile *(m) dance*
bajo/a *(adj) small*
balcón *(m) balcony*
baloncesto *basketball*
banco *(m) bank*
bañarse *(verb) to have a bath*
bar *(m) pub*
barra *(f) loaf/bar*
bastante *(adj) quite*
bastante *(pro) enough*
bicicleta *(f) bicycle*
blanco/a *(adj) white*
blusa *(f) blouse*
bocadillo *(m) sandwich*
bolso *(m) handbag*
bota *(f) boot*
bombero/a *fire-fighter*
bonito/a *(adj) nice*
bote *(m)* jar, *boat*
botella *(f) bottle*
británico/a *British*
bucear *(verb) to dive*
bueno *(interj) well, ok*
bueno/a *(adj) good, nice*

C

café capuchino *(m) capuchino*
café con leche *(m) white coffee*
café latte *(m) latte coffee*
café solo *(m) black coffee*
charcutería *(f) delicatessen*
caja *(f) box*
calamar *(m) squid*
calle *(f) street*
caminar *(verb) to walk*
camarero/a *(m/f) waiter/waitress*
camisa *shirt*
campo *(m)field*
cantante *(m/f) singer*
cantar *(verb) to sing*
carne *(f) meat*
carnicería (f) *butcher shop*
carpintero/a *carpenter*
cartera *men wallet*
cartero/a *(m/f)postman/postwoman*
carretera *(l) motorway (UK)/ highway (US)*
casa (f) *house/home*
castillo *(m) castle*
cebolla *(f) onion*
centro comercial *(m) shopping centre/mall*
cerca *(adv) near, close*
cerveza *(f) beer*
chalet adosado *(m) terraced house*
chaqueta *jacket*

chocolate *(m) chocolate*
chorizo *(m) spicy sausage*
chuletas *(fpl) chops*
ciclismo *(m) cycling*
científico/a *scientist*
cinto *(m) belt*
ciudad *(m) city*
cliente *(m/f) customer, client*
cocina *(f) cooker; kitchen*
cocinar (verb) *to cook*
cocinero/a *(m/f)cook*
color *(m) colour (UK)/color (US)*
colegio *(m) primary school and high school*
comedor *(m) dining room*
como *(adv) like, as*
cómo *(interr) how*
compañía (f) *company*
comprar *(verb) to buy*
con *(prep) with*
contable (Esp) *accountant*
contador/-ora (AmL) *accountant*
copa (f) *wine glass*
comer *(verb) to eat*
comprar *(verb) to buy*
ir de compras *to go shopping*
conducir/manejar *(verb) to drive*
corbata *(f) tie*
cordero *(m) lamb*
correo electrónico *(m) email*
correos *(m) post office*
cruel *(adj) cruel*
cuál *(pron interr) what? which?*
cuánto/a *(interrg) how much?*
cuántos/as *(interrg) how many?*
¿Cuánto vale/cuesta? *How much is it?*
¿Cuánto es? *How much is the total?*
cuarto de baño *(m) bathroom*
cuñada *(f) sister-in-law*
cuñado *(m) brother-in-law*

D

de *(prep) of, from*
de nada *you're welcome*
debajo *(prep) under*
delante *(prep) in front of*
delgado/a *(adj), (m/f) slim*
dentista *(m/f) dentist*
dentro *(prep) in, inside*
dependiente *(m/f) shop assistant*
deporte *(m) sport*
derecha *(f) right*
desorganizado/a (adj) *disorganized*
despacho/estudio *(m) office/study*
despertarse *(verb) to wake up*

detrás *(prep) behind*
día *(m) day*
dinámico/a *(adj)(m/f) dynamic*
divertido/a (adj) *fun*
doctor/-ora *doctor*
domingo *(m) Sunday*
dormir *(verb) to sleep*
dónde *(interroga) where?*
dormitorio *(m) bedroom*
dormirse *(verb) to go to sleep*
ducharse *(verb) to have a shower*

E

e *(conj) and*
él *(prep) (m) he*
el *(art) (m) the*
edificio *(m) building*
emocionante *(adj) exciting*
empanadilla/empanada (f)
    pasty(UK)/empanada(US)
enero *January*
en *(prep) in/on*
encantado/a *(m/f) nice to meet you*
enfermero/a *nurse*
enfrente *(prep) in front*
entre *(prep) between*
ensalada(f) *salad*
electricista *(m/f) electrician*
equitación *horse riding*
escalera *(f) stairs*
escocés/-esa *(adj), Scottish*
Escocia (f) *Scotland*
escritor/-ora *writer*
escuchar *(verb) to listen*
España (f) *Spain*
español/-ola *(adj), Spanish*
español/-ola *(m) Spanish (language)*
esquiar *(verb) to ski; go skiing*
esquí *(m) skiing*
esquina (f) *corner*
estación de trenes (f) *train station*
Estados Unidos *(mpl) United*
    States
estadounidense *(m/f) American*
estanco *newsagents/tobacconist*
estar *(verb) to be*
estresante *(adj) stressful*
estudiar *to study*
este/a *(adj dem) this*
este *(m) east*
estos/as *(adj dem) these*
estrecho/a *(adj) narrow*
euro *(m) euro*
exportación *(f) export*
expreso *(m) espresso*

F

falda *(f) skirt*
famoso/a *(adj) famous*
febrero *February*
feliz *(adj) happy*

feo/a *(adj) ugly*
final *(m) end*
finlandés/-esa (m/f) *(adj), Finnish*
finlandés, *(m) Finnish (language)*
Finlandia *(f) Finland*
flan *(m) flan*
francés/-esa *(adj), French*
francés *(m) French (language)*
Francia (f) *France*
fresa (f) *strawberry*
frito/a *(adj) fried*
frontera *(f) border*
fruta *(f) fruit*
frutería *(f) greengrocer*
funcionario/a de gobierno
    government officer
fútbol/futbol *(m) football (UK)/*
    soccer (US)

G

galés/-esa *adj), Welsh*
galés *(m) Welsh (language)*
Gales *(m) Wales*
gambas *(mpl) prawns*
garaje *(f) garage*
gaseosa (f) *fizzy drink (UK)/*
    soda water (US)
gasolinera *(f) petrol (UK)/*
    gas (US) station
gato/a *(m/f) cat*
gazpacho *(m) gazpacho (cold*
    vegetable soup)
girar *(verb) to turn*
gira *(verb, you formal) turn*
gordo/a *(adj) fat*
gracias *thank you*
grande *(adj) big/large*
granja *(f) farm*
Grecia *(f) Greece*
griego/a *adj), Greek*
griego/a *(m) Greek (language)*
guapo/a *(adj) handsome*
guión *(m) dash*
guión bajo *(m) underscore*
guitarra *(f)guitar*

H

habitación (f) *room*
habitante *(m) inhabitant*
hablar *(verb) to speak*
hacer *(verb) to make, to do*
hay *(verb) there is/there are*
helado *(m) ice cream*
hermana *(f) sister*
hermanastra *(f) stepsister*
hermanastro *(m) stepbrother*
hermano *(m) brother*
hermoso/a *(adj) beautiful*
hielo *(m) ice*
hija (f) *daughter*
hijo *(m) son*

hijos *(m/fpl) children*
hola *(inter) hello, hi*
hora *(f) hour*
horrible *(adj) horrible*
hospital (m) *hospital*
huevo *(m) egg*

I

idioma *(m) language*
iglesia *(f) church*
independiente *(adj) (m/f)*
    independent
infusión *(f) infusion/green tea*
ingeniero/a *engineer*
Inglaterra *(m) England*
inglés/-esa *(adj), English*
inglés *(m) English (language)*
inteligente (adj) *(m/f) intelligent*
interesante *(adj) interesting*
instituto *(m) high school*
investigador/-ora *researcher*
ir *(verb) to go*
Irlanda *(f) Ireland*
irlandés/-esa *(adj), Irish*
isla *(f) island*
Italia (f) *Italy*
italiano/a *(m/f), (adj), Italian*
italiano/a *(m) Italian (language)*
izquierda *(f) left*

J

jamón *(m) ham*
jardín *(m) garden*
joven *(adj), (m/f) young*
jueves *(m) Thursday*
jugar *(verb) to play*
julio *July*
junio *June*
juntos *together*

K

kilómetro *(m) kilometre (UK)/*
    kilometre (US)

L

lata *(f) can*
lavarse *(verb) to wash oneself*
leche (f) *milk*
lechuga *(f) lettuce*
leer *(verb) to read*
lejos *(adv) far, a long way*
Letonia *(f) Latvia*
letón/-tona *(adj), Latvian*
levantarse *(verb) to get up*
libra *(f) pound*
libro *(m) book*
limón *(m) lemon*
litro *(m) litre*
lituano/a *Lithuanian*
Lituania *(f) Lithuania*
lugar (m) *place*

lunes *(m) Monday*

M

madre (f) *mother*
madrastra *(f) stepmother*
mandar *(verb) to send*
manzana(f) *apple*
manzanilla (f) *chamomile*
mañana *(f) morning, tomorrow*
malo/a *(adj) bad*
marido/esposo *(m) husband*
más *(pron) more*
martes *(m) Tuesday*
marzo *March*
matrimonio (m) *married couple*
mayo *May*
mayor *(adj), (m/f) older*
media hermana *(f) half-sister*
medio hermano *(m) half-brother*
medio/a *(m/f) half*
melón *(m) melon*
menor (adj), *(m/f) younger*
mensajes *(m) messages*
mercado *(m) market*
mermelada *(f) jam*
merluza *(f) hake*
mes *(m) month*
mi *(adj) my*
miércoles *(m) Wednesday*
mirar *(verb) to look*
monedero *(m) women wallet*
montar *(verb) to ride*
moderno/a *(adj) modern*
moreno *(adj) brunette*
mucho gusto *nice/pleased to meet you*
muchos/as *(pron) a lot of, many*
muerto/a (adj) *dead*
mujer/esposa (f) *wife*
música *(f) music*
muy *(adv) very*

N

nachos *(mpl) nachos*
nacionalidad (f) *nationality*
nadar *(verb) swim*
nada (pron) *nothing*
naranja *(f) orange*
natación *(f) swimming*
negro/a *(adj) black*
ni … ni *(conj) neither...nor*
nieto *(m) grandson*
nieta *(f) granddaughter*
no *(adv) no, not*
noche *(f) night*
nombre *(m) name*
Noruega (f) *Norway*
noruego/a *(adj), Norwegian*
noruego/a *(m) Norwegian (language)*
norte *(m) north*

novio/a *(m/f) boyfriend, girlfriend*
noviembre *November*
nuera (f) *daughter-in-law*
nuevo/a *(adj)(m/f) new*
número *(m) number*
número de zapato(m) *shoe size*

O

o *(conj) or*
octubre *October*
oeste *(m) west*
oliva/aceituna *(f) olive*
optimista *(adj), (m/f) optimist*
ordenador/computadora *(m/f) computer*
organizado/a *(adj) organized*
origen *(m) origin*
oscuro/a *(adj) dark*

P

padrastro (m) *stepfather*
padre(m) *father*
paella *(f) paella*
país *(m) country*
pan *(m) bread*
panadería *(f) bakery*
pantalones *(mpl) trousers (UK)/ pants (US)*
papa (AmL) (f) *potato*
para *(prep) for*
para mí *for me*
pareja *partner*
parque *(m) park*
parqueadero *(m) card park(UK)/ parking lot(US)*
partido(m) *match*
paseo *(m) street, stroll*
pasillo *(m) corridor/hall*
pastelería *(f) pastry shop*
patata (Esp) *(f) potatoes*
patatas bravas *(fpl) potatoes with hot sauce*
patatas fritas (fpl) *crisps, chips*
peinarse *(verb) to comb*
película *(f) movies*
peligroso/a *(adj) dangerous*
pelirrojo/a *(adj) redheaded/ ginger hair*
peluquero/a *(m/f) hairdresser*
pensar *(verb) to think*
pequeño/a *(adj) small/little*
perezoso/a *(adj)lazy*
periodista *(m/f) journalist*
pero *(conj) but*
perro/a *(m/f) dog*
pescadería *fish shop*
pesimista *(adj), (m/f) pessimist*
pimiento verde *(m) green pepper*
pintor/-ora *(m/f) artist, painter*
piña *(f) pineapple*
piscina *(f) swimming pool*

piso (m) *flat (UK)/appartment (US)*
plátano *(m) banana*
plaza *(f) city square (in a town)*
plaza de toros *(f) bull ring*
polaco/a *(m/f) (adj), Polish*
polaco/a *(m) Polish (language)*
político/a *(m/f) politician*
pollo *(m) chicken*
Polonia (f) *Poland*
por *(prep) for*
por favor *(interj) please*
por qué *(interroga) why?*
porque (prep) *because*
postre (m) *dessert*
población *(f) population*
precio *(m) price*
preferir *(verb)to prefer*
primer *(adj),(m) first*
primero/a *(adj),(m/f) first*
primer plato *(m) first course*
primo/a *cousin*
producto/artículo *(m) item*
profesión *(f) profession*
profesor/-ora *teacher*
pueblo *(m) town*
puenting *(m) bungee-jumping*
punto *(m) dot*
en punto *o'clock*

Q

qué *(interrg) what?*
¿Qué tipo de..? *What kind of ..?*
querer *(verb) to want*
queso *(m) cheese*
!Qué pena! *(inter) What a shame!*
¡Qué suerte! *(inter) How lucky!*

R

ración *(f) portion*
ratón *(m) mouse*
recepcionista *(m/f) receptionist*
refresco (m) *soft drink*
Reino Unido (m) *United Kingdom*
relajante *(adj) relaxing*
residencia *(f) residence*
restaurante *(m) restaurant*
río *(m) river*
rubio/a *(adj) blond*
rumano/a *(m/f) (adj) Romanian*
Rumanía (f) *Romania*
ruso/a *(m/f) (adj) Russian*
ruso/a *(m) Russian (language)*
Rusia (f) *Russia*

S

sábado *(m) Saturday*
sandía *(f) watermelon*
sano/a *(adj) healthy*
salchicha (f) *sausage*
salón *(m) living room*
segundo/a *(m/f) second*

segundo plato (m) *second course*
semana *(f) week*
septiembre *September*
ser *(verb) to be*
si *(conj) if*
sí *(adv) yes*
simpático/a *(adj), (m/f) nice/*
pleasant
siempre *(adv) always*
snowboard *(m) snowboarding*
sobre/encima de *(prep) on/above*
sobrina (f) *niece*
sobrino (m) *nephew*
sopa (f) *soup*
sueco/a *(adj) (m/f) Swedish*
sueco/a *(m/f) (adj) Swedish*
(language)
Suecia *(f) Sweden*
suizo/a *(adj) (m/f) Swiss*
Suiza (f) *Switzerland*
supermercado (*m*) *supermarket*
sur/sud (*m*) *south*

T
talla *(f) size*
también *(adv) also, as well*
tarde *(adv) late*
tarde *(f) afternoon, evening*
té *(m) tea*
teléfono *(m) phone*
teléfono móvil *(m) mobile(UK)/*
cell(US) phone
televisión/tele *(f) television*
tenista *(m/f) tennis player*
tenis *(m) tennis*
tener *(verb) to have*
tengo que *I have to*
tequila *(m) tequila*
tercero/a *(adj, pron) third*
terror *horror*
tiempo *(m) time*; *weather*
tiempo libre *free time*
tienda *(f) shop*
tocar *(verb) to touch*
tocar *(verb) to play (an instrument)*
todo recto *straight ahead*
tomar *(verb) to drink, to have,*
to take
tomar el sol *to sunbathe*
tomate (*m*) *tomato*
tonto/a *(adj) silly, stupid*
tortilla de patata (f) *Spanish*
omelette
trabajar *(verb) to work*
trabajo *(m) work, job*
trabajador/-ora *hard working*
person
trabajador/-ora social *social*
worker
traje *(m) suit*
transporte *(m) transport*

tren *(m) train*
tu *(prep) your*
tú *(pron personal informal) you*
tú mismo *yourself*
turismo *(m) tourism*
turista (m/f) *tourist*
turístico/a *(adj) touristy*

U
un/una *(art) a/an*
unos/as *(art) some*
universidad *(f) university*
usted *(pron personal formal) you*

V
vacaciones *(fpl) holiday*
vale *ok*
vaqueros *(m pl) jeans*
vendedor/a *(m/f) salesman/*
saleswoman
verduras (fpl) *vegetables*
verdulería *(f) greengrocery (UK)/*
produce shop (US)
vestido *(m) dress*
viejo/a *(adj) old*
viernes *(m) Friday*
vino *(m) wine*
vino tinto *red wine*
violento/a *(adj) violent*
vivir *(verb) to live*

W
wáter *(m) toilet*
whisky *(m) whiskey (UK)/*
whisky (US)

Y
y *(conj) and*
yo *(pron per) I*

Z
zumo (Esp)/jugo (AmL) (m) *juice*
zapato *(m) shoe*